TYPES OF ROSES

GRANDIFLORA

FLORIBUNDA

DWARF

CLIMBER
CLUSTER-FLOWERED

MINIATURE

RAMBLER

CLIMBER LARGE-FLOWERED

CLIMBING
HYBRID TEA

K.B.

THE ROCKWELLS'
COMPLETE
BOOK OF ROSES

THE ROCKWELLS'

COMPLETE

BOOK

OF ROSES

by F. F. Rockwell and Esther C. Grayson

A PRACTICAL GUIDE TO THE USES,
SELECTION, PLANTING; CARE, EXHIBITION,
AND PROPAGATION OF ROSES OF ALL TYPES,
WITH ONE HUNDRED AND FORTY-SIX
PHOTOGRAPHS (FORTY-FOUR IN COLOR)
AND THIRTY LINE DRAWINGS

Revised and Lists Updated, 1966

AN AMERICAN GARDEN GUILD BOOK. DOUBLEDAY & COMPANY, INC.
GARDEN CITY, NEW YORK

ISBN: 0-385-06341-5
Library of Congress Catalog Card Number 58-11937
Copyright © 1958, 1966 by F. F. Rockwell and Esther C. Grayson
All Rights Reserved
Printed in the United States of America

9 8 7 6 5

To EUGENE BOERNER, whose friendship has been a bright spot in our lives and whose Rose creations have brought added beauty of form, color and fragrance to gardens throughout the world.

Foreword

It is a quarter century now since I wrote my first book about roses. I had been growing roses and making rose gardens for clients for a decade then, and I have grown roses every year since, sometimes but a few on a small plot, at others in sizable gardens; sometimes in heavy clay soil, at others in almost pure sand within a stone's throw of the ocean. Under all of these conditions it has been possible to produce an abundance of beautiful blooms.

Roses, of course, have always been popular in this country; and, for that matter, throughout the civilized world. But the increase of the number of persons in the United States who have taken up seriously the growing of roses to real perfection has been little short of amazing, as is attested by the growth of the American Rose Society, which now has a membership of over sixteen thousand, and throughout the length and breadth of the land sponsors shows devoted exclusively to the rose. And yet the actual membership of the Society represents but a very small percentage of our earnest and eager rose growers.

Nevertheless, not one home in hundreds, the country over, possesses the number of rosebushes that its occupants might well be enjoying. This is particularly true of roses of types other than those which are grown in rose gardens or in beds devoted to roses alone. The really tough and hardy climbers, and the many shrub and hedge roses, requiring no more care than the average flowering shrub, merit much more general use than they now enjoy. Unfortunately, they suffer in competition with the more colorful and glamorous "garden" roses, when it comes to the allotment of space and color plates in nursery catalogs and in general rose publicity. It is the hope of the authors that these pages may help inspire the homeowner with limited time for gardening to make greater use of these roses that demand little in the way of cultural attention.

vii

We would like here, too, to acknowledge the assistance we have had from many friends and organizations in preparing this book. Among them are *Flower Grower: The Home Garden Magazine,* and *Farm Journal,* for permission to use photographs that have first appeared in them; the authors of several articles in the *American Rose Society Annuals;* genial Gene Boerner and Charles H. Perkins of the Jackson & Perkins Company, for help and guidance in many ways; Florence Goldberg, of Nyack, New York, for the use of her extensive rose library, as well as for information gained in her lovely rose garden; and such good neighbors here on Cape Cod as Silas Clark, Mrs. E. Selwyn Kerfoot, and Eben Wood, for photographs taken in their gardens. And—as in several of our former books—we are indebted especially for the very patient co-operation of Katharine Burton in working out the end papers and line drawings that have helped to clarify the text in connection with many technical operations. Others whose assistance we thankfully acknowledge are Dr. M. A. Varzhabedian, Dr. G. E. Jorgenson, Dr. R. B. Streets of the University of Arizona, Dr. Cynthia Westcott (known as "The Plant Doctor"), Dr. P. P. Pirone of the Bronx Botanical Garden, New York City, Dr. Ray C. Allen, and Dr. L. M. Massey.

And perhaps this is as good a place as any to urge every reader of this book, even if he or she grows but a dozen or two rosebushes, to join the American Rose Society. You will enjoy being one of the organized rose enthusiasts in this country, and the news and information written by noted authorities in the Society's *Annuals* and in its *American Rose Magazine,* issued monthly, will keep you up to date on all matters concerning new roses, the latest advances in cultural practice, and the control of pests and diseases.

Let us here also give credit to the all-time "High Priest of Rosedom," Dean Hole, in his classic *A Book About Roses,* for the quotations which head the various chapters in this volume. It is a long, long time since they were written, but they are as pertinent today.

GrayRock on the Cape
Orleans, Mass.

Contents

PART II. CULTURE OF THE ROSE

Half-tone Illustrations

[PHOTOGRAPHS BY THE AUTHORS, EXCEPT AS NOTED]

Line Illustrations

[DRAWINGS BY KATHARINE BURTON]

Color Illustrations

[PHOTOGRAPHS BY THE AUTHORS, EXCEPT AS NOTED]

Introduction

What can be said that has not already been said in praise of the Rose, acknowledged down through the ages and over the entire globe as the "Queen" of all flowers?

Her reign began in the unrecorded past and has continued to the present day. The Chinese were her devotees centuries before such things as gardens existed among the barbarian hordes of Europe. Poets and lovers have acclaimed her as a symbol of all that is beautiful in the worlds of glamour and romance. Soldiers have followed her banners across the bloodstained fields of battle. Royal ladies have spent fortunes in their worship of her. Sappho, on lonely Lesbos, enshrined her in those song fragments which have come down to us.

But it is in the hearts of the people, not only of royalty and aristocracy but of common people everywhere—peasants, and farmers' wives, and shopkeepers, and even prisoners behind guarded walls —that her reign has continued, century after century, unabated and unchallenged.

And so, even into this completely mechanized and quite mad age, she continues to hold sway wherever there are those left who seek a symbol of beauty in its ultimate perfection of line, form, and color, and who desire some anodyne for the growing tensions of modern life.

Come with us, then, into the rose garden. Drop your bagful of daily cares and troubles at the gate; and in sun and wind, with hoe and pruning shears, pay homage to the "Queen" and let her work upon you that magic which has been her gift to man since the beginning of recorded time.

Part One

ROSES IN YOUR GARDEN

CHAPTER *1.* *The Rose—* *Whence and Whither?*

> *...her monarchy is the most absolute, and her throne the most ancient and the most secure of all, because founded in her people's heart. Her supremacy has been acknowledged, like Truth itself... always, everywhere, by all.*

Rosa, the favorite of all species of flowers pretty much the world over, was one of the very earliest to be brought under cultivation. *Rosa chinensis* and its close relative, *R. c. odorata,* which were brought to Europe from China late in the eighteenth and very early in the nineteenth centuries, were cultivated garden roses in their native country many centuries before Christ. Indeed the cultivation and improvement of the species is believed to have begun during the Shên Nung dynasty, about 2737–2697 B.C., and to have reached a high degree of perfection during the Han dynasties, 206 B.C. to A.D. 9.

Traveling westward, *Rosa centifolia* was described by Theophrastus in 300 B.C.; *Rosa damascena* was referred to by Virgil in 50 B.C., and *Rosa alba* was cultivated by the Romans; while the Rose of Miletus, referred to by Pliny in his *Natural History,* is thought to have been *Rosa gallica.* These ancient roses are believed by many authorities to be, in a truer sense, not species at all but hybrids of such antiquity that their ancestries can be deducted only from their characteristics.

Moreover, the natural distribution of wild roses just about covers the globe in the northern hemisphere. Hence it is to be expected that the ancestry of our modern roses should be complicated in the extreme.

The beginner with roses may well say: "So what? I'm interested only in roses I can buy and grow today. I don't give a tinker's tin teakettle where they came from, or how!"

Those modern growers who, on the other hand, have a romantic interest in the past, will be charmed and fascinated by the fabulous history of the rose, cherished in the East from the earliest times; carried westward by early explorers and soldiers; coaxed to rebloom by the Romans; cultivated in ancient monastery gardens in Europe, and hybridized in the gardens of Josephine de Beauharnais at Malmaison.

As a matter of fact, though you may care little about rose history, even a slight knowledge of the development of modern roses will enable you better to understand the characteristics, cultural requirements, and limitations of the different types you may be interested in growing. Moreover, some acquaintance, no matter how limited, with the ancestry of present-day groups, must inevitably give you more enjoyment as you grow them and learn to see the particular characteristics of this or that ancestor cropping out even in the newest of the modern roses you procure, and watch with increasing interest as they develop their first blooms.

Here then, in very brief and simplified form, we attempt to give the reader at least a scanty introduction to this fascinating field of study. For many it may fire the imagination and lead them on to months or even years of research, and to the delightful hobby of collecting Old Roses. Others will be more interested in what may lie ahead in rose development.

ANCESTRY OF OUR GARDEN ROSES

1789 *Rosa chinensis* (*R. indica*)	⎧ *c. semperflorens (Rosa semperflorens)* In England, 1789 Everblooming Chinese Rose *c. odorata (Rosa odorata)* In England, 1810 and 1824 Tea Rose
Hybrid Chinas	*R. chinensis* x *R. centifolia,* x *R. gallica*
1800 Bengal Roses	*R. chinensis semperflorens* x *R. gallica*
1817 Noisette Roses	*R. moschata* x *R. gallica* (Later crosses with *R. c. odorata* and others.)
Hybrid Noisettes	Hybrid Chinas x Noisettes

1822
Bourbon Roses   R. gallica x R. damascena bifera
                                (Autumn Damask)
Hybrid Bourbons   Hybrid Chinas x Bourbons

1837
Hybrid Perpetuals   R. c. odorata x Bourbons, x Hybrid Chinas,
(First variety   x R. damascena and others
   Princess Helene)

1867
Hybrid Teas   R. c. odorata x Hybrid Perpetuals
(First variety La France)

1875
Polyantha   R. chinensis (R. indica major) x R. multiflora
(First variety   and later by R. wichuraiana and others
   La Paquerette)

1900
Pernetianas   Hybrid Teas x R. foetida
(First variety Soleil d' Or)

1924
Floribundas   Hybrid Teas x Polyanthas
(First variety Gruss an Aachen)

1954
Grandifloras   Hybrid Teas x Floribundas
(First variety Buccaneer)

TYPES OF ROSES

In the preceding brief note on Rose history, the emphasis is on botanical variations. But roses differ in other ways, too, and may be grouped as certain "types" on the basis of their habits of growth and flowering, and their adaptability to different uses in and about the garden.

The most extensive use of roses today is, and for a long time past has been, in the rose garden, in beds especially designed for and devoted to roses alone, so we may designate our first type as:

Garden or Bush Roses. These are the roses to be planted by themselves to create beautiful one-flower gardens, for a space devoted

Even a moderate-sized bed of modern roses will provide blooms for display, and for cutting, from late spring until autumn frosts.

to roses alone is unique in that no other flowers are required to supplement them in order to provide that "constant succession of bloom" about which the landscape architects are always talking.

Until recently the three groups of roses most generally used for garden planting were the Hybrid Teas in moderate climates (Zones 6, 7, 8); the Hybrid Perpetuals in somewhat more severe climates (Zone 5); and for really frigid climates (Zones 3 and 4) the toughest of the old roses and some of the more modern species hybrids, such as those of the *Rugosas.* (See Zone Map on page 10–11.)

More recently, however, two other groups of increasing importance have come into the picture. These are the large-flowered Hybrid Polyanthas or Floribundas, somewhat hardier than the Hybrid Teas; and Sub-zero Hybrid Teas, hardiest of all the continuous-flowering garden roses. Within recent years the Floribundas have gained steadily in popularity and are now pushing the Hybrid Teas for first place. In the last popularity list of the

American Rose Society, of the fifty-one varieties scoring 8.0 or above (10 being the highest score) twenty-one were Floribundas.

These two groups are discussed in more detail in Part Three.

Climbing and Pillar Roses. Speaking literally, there are no *climbing* roses in the sense that we speak of a climbing vine, such as an ivy or a trumpet creeper. But roses which will grow erect to a height of eight feet or more, when they are provided with some suitable support, are called Climbers. Some of these, however, will not normally attain a height of more than eight to ten feet and these are often designated as Pillar Roses.

A distinction is made between Large-flowered Climbers and those having clusters of small flowers on one flower stem. Those with densely clustered heads of very small flowers are the Climbing Polyanthas. Another group—now but little used because of their susceptibility to mildew—are the hybrids known as Rambler Roses, after the first variety of this type, Crimson Rambler, which at the time of its introduction in 1893 was the sensation of the rose world. Some of the newer Ramblers, especially the splendid variety Chevy Chase, which has a rating of 8.9 in the American Rose Society's score book, give promise that this group may regain some of its lost popularity.

The Large-flowered Climbers are of two distinct types: those which are vigorous and hardy, such as New Dawn, Dr. Nicolas, Golden Climber, and Thor; and the climbing forms or sports of bush varieties, as exemplified by Climbing Heart's Desire, Climbing Peace, and Climbing Pinocchio.

These latter generally resemble, in hardiness, vigor of growth, amount and continuity of bloom, and resistance to or susceptibility to disease, the varieties from which they have sprung. As a group they are much less hardy than either the Ramblers or the Large-flowered Climbers which are not sports.

Creepers. These are not really a distinct group but include such of the Climbers as have thin, supple canes that readily spread or sprawl over the ground or over walls or banks to make a blossoming ground cover. The old Dorothy Perkins was ideally suited for this purpose, and it still graces many an unsightly railroad cut or embankment. Several of the Brownell Hardy Climbers such as Coral Creeper, Little Compton Creeper, and Creeping Everbloom, are excellent, as is also the Rugosa Hybrid Max Graf.

Shrub Roses, as the term implies, include species and varieties sufficiently vigorous, hardy, and self-supporting to be planted and grown in much the same way as other hardy shrubs, and without the constant care and meticulous attention which most garden roses require. They vary considerably in habit of growth and in height. Most of the older ones put on a real show only once during the summer. Among these may be mentioned Harison's Yellow and the more recently popularized Father Hugo's Rose (*Rosa hugonis*), and such old timers as Cardinal de Richelieu, Crested Moss, Maiden's Blush, and Maréchal Niel. The latter still maintains some degree of popularity in sections where it can be grown. Sarah Van Fleet and a number of others are of more recent introduction.

The term "park" or "dooryard" has been applied to some newer varieties suitable for growing as Shrub Roses, but of more compact and neater habit of growth than those mentioned above, and also possessing the added attraction of flowering more or less continuously until the end of the season. Examples of this type are Mabelle Stearns, Hon. Lady Lindsay, and The Fairy. Floribundas which make handsome specimen shrubs include the varieties Frensham, Lafter, and Masquerade.

Hedge Roses embrace the varieties which, because of exceptionally dense growth, lend themselves particularly well to use as informal, colorful, and more or less impenetrable hedges. The most widely known "hedge" rose is our old friend, the species *Multiflora,* so widely advertised in Sunday newspapers and by radio and sold by the millions to owners of small homes. It is a great rose for "suckers" in more senses than one, for in reality it is not a hedge rose in any sense of the word, but a thicket rose which will rapidly gain a height of six to eight feet or more and an equivalent spread; and of course it has but one flowering period—and a short one at that—during the year. The intentionally misleading, if not outright dishonest, statements made in advertisements such as those just referred to are a sad commentary on the low ethical level to which much horticultural advertising in our country has been allowed to fall.

Roses which are really suitable for the making of hedges are to be found among the Shrub Roses described above, some of which are excellent when employed as informal, colorful hedges. A few of the most popular for this purpose are such of the Floribundas

TEMPERATURE ZONE MAP
OF THE UNITED STATES

On the following page there is a map, marked off in zones extending from coast to coast. These different zones indicate the lowest winter temperatures that may normally be expected.

No zone map small enough to be reproduced in a book can begin to cover in any great detail the many temperature areas that exist. It would be impossible to indicate accurately those of even a single state. There are many conditions, quite aside from latitude, which affect temperatures: altitude, for instance. The proximity of large bodies of water; prevailing winds and their velocity; the general terrain; the presence or absence of neighboring forests, are others.

The gardener, therefore, can find in a zone map only a very general sort of reference chart. He must be guided by local conditions. These he learns from personal experience, which takes a long time; or from the experience of others in his vicinity—which, while it may be less accurate, is immediately available, and hence is invaluable to the beginner.

Then, too, one can do much in the way of *creating* micro-climates on his own grounds. He can utilize existing shelters; and he can make others with fences, hedges, and tree and shrub plantings. By adding pools and other water features he can increase humidity and lower high temperatures.

The grower of roses will find micro-climates of his own contriving especially helpful in protecting his plants from winter injury due to cold—*and drying*—winds from the north and west, and by providing air drainage to prevent the accumulation of pools of still air in low areas.

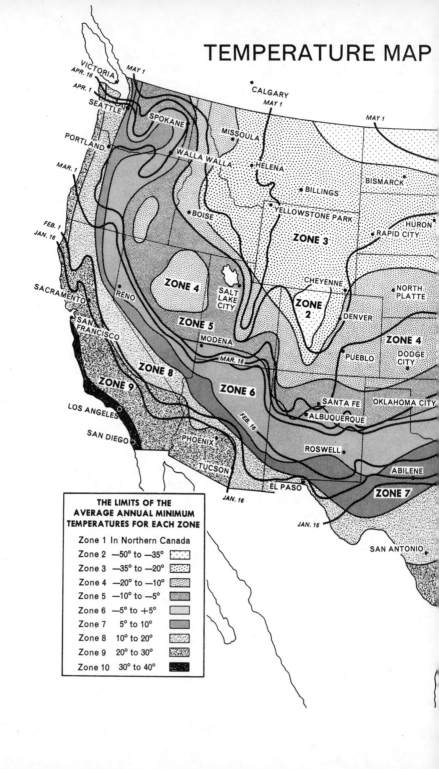

TEMPERATURE MAP

THE LIMITS OF THE
AVERAGE ANNUAL MINIMUM
TEMPERATURES FOR EACH ZONE

Zone 1 In Northern Canada
Zone 2 −50° to −35°
Zone 3 −35° to −20°
Zone 4 −20° to −10°
Zone 5 −10° to −5°
Zone 6 −5° to +5°
Zone 7 5° to 10°
Zone 8 10° to 20°
Zone 9 20° to 30°
Zone 10 30° to 40°

OF THE UNITED STATES

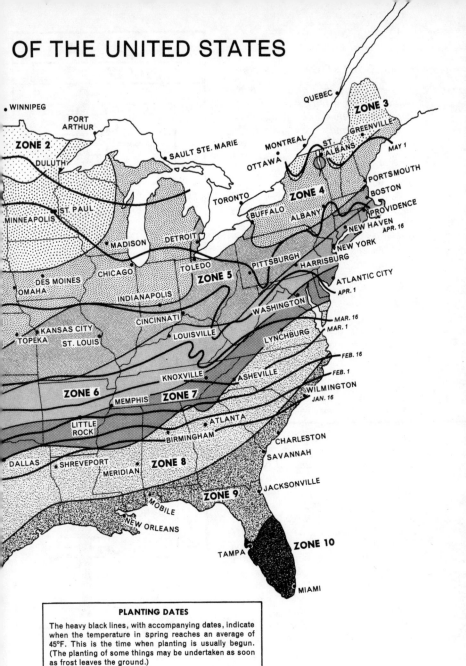

WINNIPEG

PORT ARTHUR

QUEBEC

ZONE 3

GREENVILLE

ZONE 2

DULUTH

SAULT STE. MARIE

MONTREAL

ST. ALBANS

MAY 1

OTTAWA

PORTSMOUTH

ST. PAUL

MINNEAPOLIS

MADISON

DETROIT

TORONTO

BUFFALO

ALBANY

ZONE 4

BOSTON

PROVIDENCE

NEW HAVEN

APR. 16

DES MOINES

CHICAGO

TOLEDO

ZONE 5

PITTSBURGH

HARRISBURG

NEW YORK

OMAHA

INDIANAPOLIS

WASHINGTON

ATLANTIC CITY

APR. 1

KANSAS CITY

CINCINNATI

LOUISVILLE

LYNCHBURG

MAR. 16

MAR. 1

TOPEKA

ST. LOUIS

KNOXVILLE

ZONE 7

ASHEVILLE

FEB. 16

FEB. 1

ZONE 6

MEMPHIS

WILMINGTON

JAN. 16

LITTLE ROCK

ATLANTA

BIRMINGHAM

CHARLESTON

DALLAS

SHREVEPORT

MERIDIAN

ZONE 8

SAVANNAH

MOBILE

ZONE 9

JACKSONVILLE

NEW ORLEANS

TAMPA

ZONE 10

MIAMI

PLANTING DATES

The heavy black lines, with accompanying dates, indicate when the temperature in spring reaches an average of 45°F. This is the time when planting is usually begun. (The planting of some things may be undertaken as soon as frost leaves the ground.)

12

THE QUESTION OF LIME

In growing plants of all kinds the matter of soil acidity is to be taken into consideration. Some plants thrive best in acid soils, some in alkaline (nonacid) soils. The great majority may be grown satisfactorily in soils that range from slightly acid to slightly alkaline.

To designate the degree of acidity or alkalinity, a chart known as the pH Scale is employed. This is arranged something like the scale of a thermometer; but the "zero" point, instead of being a zero, is pH 7, indicating soil that is neither acid nor alkaline, but neutral. The figures below pH 7 (6.9 to 4) indicate the degree of acidity; those above the neutral point (7.1 to 9) indicate the degree of alkalinity.

Tests of various types indicate the degree of acidity. The simplest of these is the litmus paper test. To decrease *acidity one point (say from pH 5 to pH 6) apply 75 pounds of agricultural lime per 1,000 square feet; or, on heavy clay soils, up to double that amount. To* increase *the acidity one point (as from 7 to 6) apply 50 pounds of aluminum sulfate, or 20 pounds of sulfur.*

In comparing figures on the acidity scale, it must be kept in mind that each full step indicates a multiple of ten. In other words, a reading of pH 5 is ten times as acid as a reading of pH 6. A reading of pH 4 indicates soil 100 (not 20) times the degree of acidity as compared with a reading of 6. And of course the same applies to the upper part of the scale.

Roses are quite tolerant as to soil acidity or the lack of it. Dr. J. H. Nicolas, a famous rosarian, in an extensive survey found plants thriving equally well in some of the great European rose gardens where tests showed a pH of 7.93, and in other soils that were decidedly acid. Both the physical character of the soil and the amount of humus *it contains affect the influence of acidity on plant growth.*

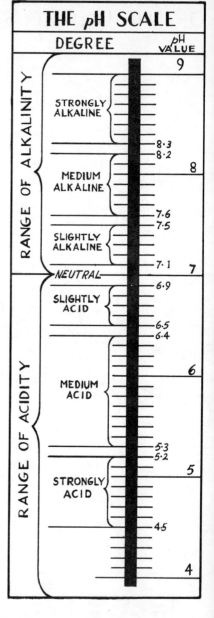

THE pH SCALE

DEGREE — pH VALUE

RANGE OF ALKALINITY

STRONGLY ALKALINE
8·3
8·2 — 8
MEDIUM ALKALINE
7·6
7·5
SLIGHTLY ALKALINE
7·1 — 7
NEUTRAL
6·9

RANGE OF ACIDITY

SLIGHTLY ACID
6·5
6·4
6
MEDIUM ACID
5·3
5·2 — 5
STRONGLY ACID
4·5
4

9

PLATE 1

Modern Large-flowered Climbing Roses provide a show of beautiful bloom throughout the season. Here one of the authors—on a five-foot stepladder—gathers a few choice specimens of Climbing Peace, a sport of the world's most acclaimed bush rose.

PLATE 2

Roses of the near future will bring us exciting new colors, such as that of Sterling Silver—shown in color in PLATE 29 *between pages 268–69. Here are several of the selected seedlings we found "on trial" in the garden of Gene Boerner, internationally famous rose hybridizer. (See also* PLATE 13 *between pages 44–45.)*

PLATE 3

PLATE 4

Roses at GrayRock, former home of the authors in Rockland County, N. Y. A gradual slope provides perfect drainage, even with a fairly heavy clay soil; and evergreens and shrubs afford protection from north and northwest winds.

PLATE 5

ABOVE: *The use of Climbing and Pillar Roses at rear of the garden gives a three-dimensional effect.* BELOW: *Roses for every place and purpose! Contrast this six-inch plant of the Miniature, Sweet Fairy, with Climbing Peace* (PLATE 1 *between pages 12–13*).

PLATE 6

as Betty Prior, Fashion, and Summer Snow. Varieties of course should be selected with the desired height for the prospective hedge in mind. (A list is presented on pages 277–78.)

Border Roses. These are roses for very low hedges or "borders" along walks, around flower beds and the like. Such plantings are becoming more and more popular for the many very small gardens being planted in development areas, where they are often employed with striking effect.

Such diminutive roses as the ranunculus-flowered Margo Koster and Carol Ann are well suited to this purpose; and undoubtedly the new Pygmy or Dwarf Floribundas, attaining a height of only eighteen to twenty-four inches or so, will prove immensely popular for this particular use.

Miniatures. These diminutive Fairy Roses form a distinct group botanically as well as in size and habit of growth, all parts of the plant being truly miniature—stems, leaves and flowers, the latter often not larger than a dime. Tough and wiry, they are excellent for edgings, and are in scale in small rock gardens. They are also becoming increasingly popular as pot plants for growing indoors.

ROSES TO COME

This summary of the great variety in types of roses available today might seem to indicate that little remains to be done in the way of getting improvement on what we already have; but the world's rose breeders, busy as a hive of bees gathering golden pollen, would by no means agree. They know that that mythical goal, the perfect rose, is many far horizons away, but their search for it continues unabated. Progress is being made, sometimes slowly, step by step; sometimes by leaps and bounds, as when a new variety such as Peace suddenly appears.

Among the many lines along which improvement is being accomplished are the following:

Disease Resistance. Undoubtedly the greatest boon which the breeders of roses could bestow upon those who grow roses would be varieties immune to the diseases which plague *Rosa,* particularly black spot and mildew. Possibly this goal will never be reached —it is like trying to find the safe and completely effective cure for the common cold! In the meantime however, progress is being made, especially with *yellow* roses, always susceptible to black spot because of the Noisette blood in their ancestry. Most of the Brownell Sub-zero introductions show a marked degree of resistance, even the pure yellow *V* for Victory seldom showing the slightest sign of infection in our garden when other yellows in the vicinity fell prey to it. Newer varieties, such as the Floribunda Gold Cup, with glossy, holly-like foliage, are also practically immune.

Rose breeders in general are more conscious than formerly of the fact that disease resistance has become a factor in the mind of the buying public, and are paying more attention to it.

More Vigorous Growth. Vigor in a rosebush does not imply size alone. There are plenty of varieties which are tall and broad-shouldered enough to suit anyone. Inherent vitality and strength in making strong canes and laterals producing flowering wood is even more essential, and many a present-day variety which has excellent individual blooms is lacking in this respect. This too is a problem which the breeders are working on with notable results.

Fragrance. One frequently hears the complaint that roses are not as fragrant as they used to be. It is doubtful that this is so. A recent carefully conducted survey indicated that the *percentage* of roses with marked fragrance is greater in modern roses than in those of the good old days half a century or more ago. We believe this to be true, although the senior member of this writing team must confess that he is no longer competent to judge as he is a tobacco addict and believes (to paraphrase Rudyard Kipling) that while a rose is only a rose a good pipeful is a smoke—and for 365 days in the year instead of only during the summer months. A rose that can tickle his olfactory nerve centers has to be *really* fragrant. Two of the most fragrant varieties in our garden for many years have been an old *centifolia* that we dug up near the ruins of an abandoned farm house (and the precise name of which we have never been able to get two experts on old roses to agree upon) and a comparative new-comer, Orange Everglow. When these are in bloom they really "stop traffic." Fragrance is to a rose what a good complexion is to a beautiful woman. Unfortunately the only odor possessed by some roses described in glowing terms in catalogs is the scent of the printer's ink used in making the beautiful color illustrations accompanying the descriptions. Unfortunately, too, a rose that is delightfully sweet-scented to one sniffer may leave another absolutely cold. The only way to make sure of buying a rose that is fragrant *to you* is to smell its blooms in a rose garden or display bed.

The men who are doing the breeding, however, are not unconscious of the fact that real fragrance is an asset and one of the qualities worth working for when they make and remake their crosses; and undoubtedly we are going to have more and more varieties that will justify the use of this term in their descriptions.

More Continuous Bloom. More progress has been made in this respect during the last quarter century or so than along any other line—with the possible exception of that of creating new colors, which is really of less importance to the rose grower, if not to the nurserymen who introduce and sell new roses.

For many decades, in fact for several generations, in rose breeding one of the prime objectives was to develop varieties that would flower more or less continuously from June until frost. The Hybrid Perpetuals constituted a step in this direction but they were "perpetual," in the case of most varieties, only in that they gave a very scant scattering of flowers after the June display. In our modern Hybrid Teas and Floribundas the goal of actual perpetual flowering has been approached. Rosarians of a generation or two ago, could they see many modern rose gardens, would gaze upon them in skeptical unbelief. The end is not yet, but we have come a long way.

What we need most now is satisfactorily Large-flowered Climbers that are really everblooming. With the introduction many years ago of those two grand old Climbers, New Dawn and Dr. Nicolas, we seemed to be on our way; but then came a long hiatus. Some more recent varieties such as New Blaze, Gladiator, and Spectacular seem to show a happy combination of more continuous bloom, greater hardiness, and good flower form.

Resistance to cold, combined with continuous bloom and ideal flower form, is a goal not yet fully attained. The Brownell Climbers, and the introductions of Dr. Hansen of South Dakota, have provided greater winter hardiness; but the perfection of flower form and the range of colors are still behind those of many Hybrid Teas and Floribundas, which are doubtfully hardy, even with ordinary winter protection, in our colder climates.

New Colors. Here indeed almost unbelievable progress has been made during the last decade or two and the end is not yet. The color Plate 2 between pages 12–13 gives some idea of what has been attained in this direction, but no reproduction in printer's ink can give any full realization of the wide scale of hues, with their delicate nuances, that are today available to the rose enthusiast.

Thornlessness. Would you want a thornless rose? Many gardeners say they would not, but others would welcome them; and with the price of leather gloves and the life expectancy of nylon stockings being what they are, this is understandable. The thornless rose is by no means an impossibility. Already thornless stocks on which to bud roses are available, and the almost satin-smooth stems with no prickles attached are indeed pleasant to handle. There is no reason why this quality cannot be bred into garden varieties, and a thornless Climber unquestionably would be a much easier proposition to manage, when it came to pruning or "laying down" for the winter, than those of the present day.

However, while we are waiting for the rose-breeding experts to give us some or all of these possible improvements, we have available many hundreds of excellent varieties, some very old and some as new as tomorrow, with which to decorate our gardens and make colorful and joyous our rooms indoors.

So now let us take a look around the garden to see where this wealth of loveliness can best be used to enhance our surroundings.

in the Home Landscape

Enter, then, the Rose-garden when the first sunshine sparkles in the dew, and enjoy with thankful happiness one of the loveliest scenes on earth. What a diversity, yet what a harmony of color . . . what a diversity, and yet what harmony of outline! Dwarf Roses and Climbing Roses, Roses closely carpeting the ground, Roses that droop in snowy foam like fountains, and roses that stretch out their branches upward as though they would kiss the sun. . . . Roses in clusters, and Roses blooming singly. . . . And over all this perfect unity, what a freshness, fragrance, purity. . . .

More and more the homeowners of America are coming to appreciate the fact that decoration of the space out-of-doors around their homes plays quite as important a part in gracious living as does the decoration of the rooms indoors. As a nation we are spending an ever-increasing amount of time in extramural activities; and as week-end trips become more hazardous and less pleasurable—in direct proportion to the number of millions of cars rolling the highways and throughways—a bigger and bigger percentage of this time is spent at home.

Another factor in the growing importance of making the home grounds attractive is the fact that we are becoming a nation of people who live in glass houses. The coming of the transparent house wall, and of its near relative the king-size view window that takes one to two thirds of the total exterior wall space of a room, has practically brought the garden into the house, and has gone far to obliterate the former conception that we could have beautiful living rooms no matter what the grounds out-of-doors looked like. As a result, garden design is assuming an importance for every home—even the most modest—which it never before possessed.

17

Where, then, do roses fit into this picture? What role can the queen of flowers play in making every home in our land a pleasanter place in which to live?

The answer is that *Rosa,* among all flowering plants, is best endowed to take the lead.

To begin with, roses may be had in bloom over a longer period than any other flower, for they give graciously of their bounty, even in our northern states, from late May or early June until killing frost. Add to this the fact that there are so many different types of roses that, for almost any decorative purpose one can think of, a rose may be found to fill the bill to perfection, and you have an unbeatable combination.

Do you want a flower bed that is colorful not only week after week, but month after month? Would you like to have the most beautiful of all flowers for decorating your rooms indoors and to provide unsurpassed fragrance? Or perhaps there is a garage wall to be screened, or a trellis or an arbor to be covered? Or an unsightly fence or a problem bank to be clothed in beauty? Or some unbeautiful object to be screened from view? Or perchance a boundary line to be protected from unwanted trespassers or from animals? Or maybe an out-of-the-usual, flowering edging for a bed of taller perennials? Name almost any problem situation in the garden that you can think of, and among the score of distinctly different types of roses you will find one than can provide the answer to it!

And by and large roses are not difficult to grow. If you want the finest of modern, large-flowered garden roses, you will have to give them special care; but not more than many other first-line perennials, or even annuals, require. There are, however, many roses that come as near to being able to look out for themselves as almost any other flower you can mention, with the possible exception of the few rampant growers, such as day-lilies (*hemerocallis*), globe thistle (*echinops*), plume-poppy (*Macleaya cordata*) and *tradescantia,* which are likely to spread and become pests.

Who has not come across our native wild roses, such as *Rosa virginiana* and *Rosa carolina,* native to all states up and down the eastern coast; or the good old *Rosa rugosa,* with its leathery, crinkled foliage? What can you find that is tougher? Only last night, on a jolting beach buggy ride over sand dunes, fifteen miles

The rose garden should be fitted into the general landscape plan. Here long, narrow beds lead the eye to the formal pool which is the garden's focal point.

from nowhere, we ran across (quite literally) a spreading colony of rugosas, gay with bloom, in a desert-like wind-and-sand-blown stretch where its only companions were beach grasses and *Artemesia maritima.*

Having made this brief survey of the kinds of roses that can be used in gardens in the home landscape, let us take a somewhat closer look at the various ways of employing them.

THE ROSE GARDEN

The most satisfactory way to use roses is in a rose garden, a space devoted primarily to roses of the general type known as garden roses: the large-flowered, everblooming kinds that make the biggest show, over the longest season, and are ideal as cut flowers. (These are described in detail in Chapter 19.)

Roses of this type are not the easiest to grow: in fact they are the most difficult, and unless one is prepared to devote a reasonable amount of time to their care, at intervals between early spring and late fall, it may be more satisfactory in the end to depend for one's roses upon other, more self-sufficient types, such as Climbers and Shrub Roses. This point each individual must decide for himself. The real rose lover, however, is not likely to be satisfied with anything less than a real rose garden.

Such a garden may be of any size, and as formal or as informal

This semiformal rose garden (at the 1958 International Flower Show in New York) won two gold medals and a memorial award. Climbing Roses and Tree Roses are here combined with bush varieties, and—with the use of two levels for the rose beds—give the garden as a whole an unusual three-dimensional effect. It is an excellent example of what may be accomplished in a small space.

as desired. A space four by twelve feet will accommodate a dozen rose plants of average bush size and form, and will produce many scores of beautiful, long-stemmed blooms during the year. Caring for such a rose bed should not require an average of more than one hour a week during the growing season; but the care must be constant—and intelligent. Even if one possesses the space and the means for a rose garden of much greater size, it is advisable to start with a dozen or two plants for at least one season, for only experience can provide the judgment and the know-how which make a successful rose grower.

When a larger garden is attempted, considerable thought should be given to its planning. Quite aside from its location in connection with cultural requirements (discussed in the following chapter), it should be in keeping with the general atmosphere of the house and its surroundings; an elaborately formal, geometrical design, for instance, is entirely out of harmony with a simple country-type ranch or Cape Cod (so-called!) residence.

For convenience in caring for the rose plants—pruning, spraying, mulching, etc.—it is well to keep the beds narrow, not over five feet at most. For the sake of design, or to follow the slopes of the terrain, it may be desirable to have them take the form of curves or other shapes. And of course the rose garden should be an integral part of the over-all landscape design rather than an unrelated unit that looks out of place.

Another aspect to be kept in mind in planning the rose garden is the picture *as seen from the house.* If possible it should be kept well within range of a view window, and so arranged and planted as to be three dimensional—that is, with considerable height at the back, as well as length and breadth.

The surroundings of the rose garden will have quite as much to do with its aesthetic appeal as the garden itself; in other words, the picture needs a frame. For this purpose both evergreens and shrubs may be used. Evergreens help to keep the scene attractive even during the winter months. Spring-flowering shrubs, such as azaleas, especially Schlippenbachi, mucronulata, and Mollis; cytisus; cydonia; deutzia and others (see list on page 319) give color before the roses begin. Summer and autumn-flowering species are best omitted except for a few like *Vitex macrophylla,* the blue spikes of which, in August, make an excellent foil for roses. Shrubs with attractive foliage are also desirable. Among these are *Viburnum opulus,* the three-lobed leaves of which turn crimson in the fall and are set off by scarlet fruit; its close American relative *V. trilobum; V. setigerum* with clean, large green leaves and scarlet fruit; *Abelia grandiflora,* with its semi-evergreen, small glossy leaves and dainty,

Here a semiformal rose garden skillfully has been made part of a naturalistic setting, and is protected from ocean winds.

inconspicuous but fragrant pink flowers throughout the season; the cotoneasters, and evergreen *Euonymus patens.*

Borders or edgings in the rose garden are desirable in some ways and objectionable in others. Neatly trimmed borders of dwarf box are traditional with the geometrically designed beds—they go together like the horse and carriage of the popular song. But in this case you *can* have one without the other, and unless you are so fortunate as to have the services of a gardener available, you will do well to omit box, even in a climate where there is not danger of winter killback. In addition to the trouble of keeping any kind of a permanent border alive and in good condition, there is the further disadvantage that it will interfere considerably with the various cultural operations required by rosebushes. Substitutes for box which are less architectural in form, but which have the advantage of fragrance, are teucrium (germander) and rosemary. There is also the possibility, of course, of edging the rose beds with some of the new low-growing Pygmy Rose varieties.

Temporary borders of low-growing annuals are sometimes used.

We consider them on the whole preferable to permanent ones. Of the several things which may be employed for this purpose (see list on page 320) our preference is Sweet Alyssum Royal Carpet (purple) or Carpet of Snow (white). The started plants are not set in until after all spring work in the rose beds—pruning, fertilizing, renewing mulch, etc.—have been attended to; they stay neat and compact with little trimming; the green foliage and tiny purple or white flowers do not compete with the roses for attention; and they remain in bloom until long after early frosts. Pansies, or better, violas, ageratum, lobelia, forget-me-not or nierembergia have the advantage of contributing to the roses a desirable supplementary color—blue—which is delightful with pink, white, or yellow roses but a less happy combination with reds.

Tree Roses. Garden varieties grafted on stiff, upright stems are sometimes used in the rose garden. Where the design of the planting is formal, and on the grand scale, their presence may be justified. In an informal garden, and especially in one of modest size, they invariably look out-of-place. It is much better, if one desires to have them, to employ them as specimen plants somewhere in the general landscape scheme. This has a further practical advantage because, except in very moderate climates, they will require particular care in the matter of winter protection, which it is difficult to provide when they are grown among other roses. When used in a formal planting, standard heliotrope plants may be used in combination with them, the soft lavender color and delightful fragrance making them ideal companions for the stately roses.

Ground covers consisting of low-growing plants in the rose beds are sometimes used, and occasionally are enthusiastically recommended. We have tried many, and sometimes with very pleasing results. On the whole, however, we decidedly do not advocate them. They are more or less messy; they interfere with cultural operations; and they prevent the use of proper mulching.

The most satisfactory ground cover we have found is *Viola cornuta,* the Johnny-jump-ups of great-grandmother's day. Once established, they self-seed freely and form a mat of growth on the surface of the mulch, and if they become too rampant or straggly they can be clipped back severely, soon to be once more a mass of perky little flowers with serious monkey faces that somehow do not seem too out-of-place as a rose-bed carpet.

To anyone inclined to think that a rose bed ground cover might be desirable, we would suggest trying out a small area for a season before attempting an entire bed.

Roses as Shrubs. As we visit gardens in many different sections of the country we are repeatedly surprised at how infrequently roses are employed as shrubs. There are several types, and a great many varieties, which are quite ideal for such use. They are perfectly hardy; they require less care than many of the usual shrubs, and bloom over a much longer season, some of them, such as the more vigorous of the Floribundas, from June to killing frost.

Treated as shrubs they may be employed in many ways: as individual specimens; in groups of three or more for bold mass effects; for hedges—quite impenetrable if the right varieties are selected; and for screens. Here, too, the Tree Roses provide material for very striking effects.

In general the Shrub Roses are more overlooked than any other type. It is difficult to imagine a place where at least a few of them could not be planted to advantage. If this chapter gives you no other profitable suggestions, we hope that it will at least persuade you to try two or three Shrub Roses. A number of varieties are listed on page 267.

ROSES IN THE AIR

In former years the only climbing roses sufficiently hardy were the Ramblers, such as Crimson Rambler, introduced in 1893, and its dwarf hybrid, Mme. Norbert Levavasseur or Red Baby Rambler (1903); Dorothy Perkins, which is of a similar habit of growth though not related to Crimson Rambler (a variety imported from Japan); and American Pillar, derived, like Dorothy Perkins, from *R. Wichuraiana.* These were followed by a number of others such as Neige D'Avril (1908), white; Ghislaine de Féligonde (1916), yellow flushed with pink; and the more recent Chevy Chase, (1939), a deep rose red, not a true Rambler but so similar that Roy E. Shepherd in his *History of the Rose* says it might be classified as an improved Crimson Rambler. All of these varieties have three serious faults: they bloom but once (with the exception of Ghislaine de Feligonde which tends to repeat in autumn) and their one blossoming period is short; they are (with the exception of Chevy

Climbing Roses transform unsightly fences into walls of beauty.

Chase) subject to mildew which often makes repulsive gray masses of buds and flowers just as they are coming into bloom; and their bunched clusters of many small flowers are of little value for cutting. Except in a few sections of the country where climatic conditions discourage mildew, as on Nantucket and Cape Cod, they are little grown today in this country.

For years now, however, rose lovers in northern parts of the country have, through the development of hardy, large-flowered Climbers, been able to enjoy roses equal in beauty—and in some cases in fragrance—to the tender Climbers for which Southern gardens have so long been famous.

Today the gardener who lacks the space or the time for a real rose garden may still enjoy dozens, or even hundreds, of long-stemmed, full-sized roses, either in loose clusters or as single blooms on stems eight to eighteen inches long, grown well up in the air! They make possible both a breath-taking display in the garden (as demonstrated by the Climbing Peace shown in Plate 1 between pages 12–13) and a wealth of bloom for decoration indoors, not normally available with so little demand on the grower's time.

It should be stated here perhaps—as will be explained in more detail later on in Chapter 20—that the word "hardy" as applied to Climbers, and particularly to the climbing forms (sports) of favorite Hybrid Tea varieties, should not be taken too literally. While hardy well north of the Mason and Dixon's line, and corresponding climates further west, they may *not* prove hardy in the northern tier of states, especially at high altitudes or in exposed positions.

Notwithstanding these limitations, however, there are so many really hardy varieties that no garden need be without its supply of Climbers to provide dramatic beauty out-of-doors and cut flowers indoors.

The possible uses for climbing roses in the home landscape are so many that one scarcely knows where to begin making suggestions as to how they can be employed.

Climbers on trellises would seem to be the favorite use, and certainly there is no other which shows them off to greater advantage. It is not, however, the form of display that lends originality to home landscaping, for one sees climbing roses by the score framing doorways or ascending lattice ladders to the house eaves in every new development throughout the land.

This comment is not meant to imply that trellises should never be used. Very definitely they often should be. But do not overlook other methods and opportunities which Climbers offer for more original effects.

The most pleasing and satisfactory supports for free-standing Climbers which we have ever discovered are dead cedar trees of a height suited to the variety being grown. The pale gray wood lasts indefinitely, never requires attention, and the irregularly placed, upward-turning branches, cut back to suitable lengths, provide ideal support, allowing the plants—with little or no tying—to assume a graceful, natural habit of growth. One unit of this sort, covered with the vigorous-growing Orange Everglow and Buff King, which are similar in color, and bloom in close succession, has always been one of the plantings most admired and commented upon at the old GrayRock. We are using the same supports for climbers about our new home on Cape Cod.

Posts, frequently used to support climbing roses, especially Pillars, are objectionable in that they necessitate frequent tying up of the canes, and make it difficult to secure lateral growths, with abundant bloom. A decided improvement may be made by converting the post into a sort of artificial tree, as described in Chapter 11.

The post-and-chain method of support is suitable where a fairly large number of plants must be accommodated. As the canes are trained horizontally, they produce a maximum of flowering spurs; and as they are fairly close to the ground, any necessary tying, pruning, or spraying may be attended to conveniently.

Fences of all kinds provide ideal support for Climbing and Pillar Roses. They may be made as high or as low as desired, thus giving a dense hedgerow, three to five feet high, or a semiopen screen up to eight feet or more. Ordinary post-and-rail fence (preferably of the split-rail type, if it harmonizes with the house) shows off the blooms at eye level, permits free circulation of air about the plants, and reduces to the absolute minimum any work connected with good culture.

ROSES ON THE GROUND

Trailing or Creeping Roses are not often given a place in home landscapes. One thinks of them chiefly in terms of railroad banks, highway slopes, and other waste places where they could well be accommodated. Steep banks, old tumble-down stone walls, terraces too steep for lawns, and the edges of ponds or streams are ideal spots for carpets of Creeping Roses.

In selecting varieties to cover banks or walls, be careful, if you live where mildew is prevalent, to avoid those that are particularly subject to it, such as Dorothy Perkins and other Ramblers. A few, such as Creeping Everbloom and Dream Girl, which will creep if left untrained, flower throughout the season.

Dwarf Roses provide another type which may be utilized where close-to-the-ground bloom is wanted. The old *Rouletti,* hardy as a rock, and the few others similar to it, with the new Pygmy class, are good subjects for edging beds and walks. The latter group, of comparatively recent introduction (see page 307) undoubtedly will find favor in this field.

Species and varieties of roses especially suited to the many uses suggested above are given, under several classifications, in The Rose Grower's Rose Finder, pages 303–20.

CHAPTER *3.* *Environment;*

Laying Out the Rose Garden

The good gardener ... makes the most of his means. . . . He knows that this world is no longer Eden, and that only by sweat of brow and brain can he bring flower or fruit to perfection.

In attempting to grow roses, most beginners give far too little attention to the matter of environment, and indeed rose literature in general does not have too much to say about it.

If by environment we mean merely the existing climatic conditions, this attitude can readily be understood, for there is little one can do about "climate." If, however, we consider environment in a more definitive sense, and as including such things as exposure, sun and shade, air drainage, and protection from drying winds, there is a great deal that can be done; and failure to do it may well spell the difference between success and failure in rose growing. For the rose garden it is usually possible to create a "micro-climate."

A micro-climate, as the term implies, is a miniature or spot climate, a sort of oasis that, because of its immediate exposure or surroundings, differs to some degree, and often to a considerable degree, from the climate of the general vicinity in which it is located. The old-fashioned sunny barnyard, in which cattle could bask leisurely on bright winter days, thoroughly protected from north and west winds by a tall building and stone-walled embankments, is a case in point; as is also the more modern open breezeway, which provides a cool and shaded spot for many a development home set in a treeless area.

Among the factors affecting the climate, or the micro-climate, in which your roses will be growing, are protection from wind; sun and shade; humidity; and air drainage.

29

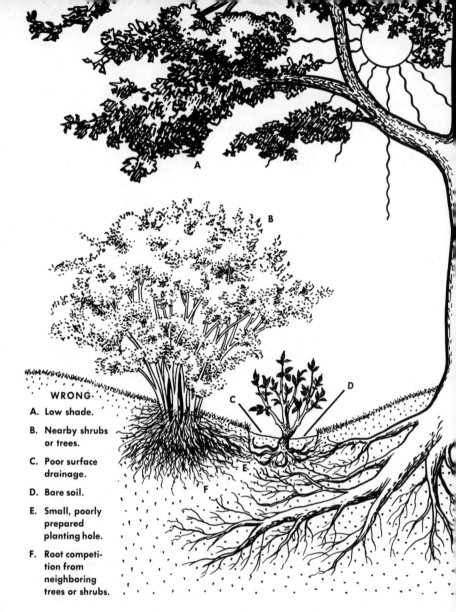

WRONG

A. Low shade.

B. Nearby shrubs or trees.

C. Poor surface drainage.

D. Bare soil.

E. Small, poorly prepared planting hole.

F. Root competition from neighboring trees or shrubs.

ENVIRONMENT—UNFAVORABLE *(left)*

(A) Low shade shuts out direct sunshine for most of the day. (B) Interference with free movement of air around plants. (C) Poor drainage—at surface, or below—keeps soil wet, with result that air cannot freely enter soil. (D) Exposed soil surface permits moisture to escape freely; gets too hot. (E) Small planting hole provides too little nourishment to roots; discourages expanding root system. (F) Roots of neighboring trees or shrubs compete with rose plant for nourishment and moisture.

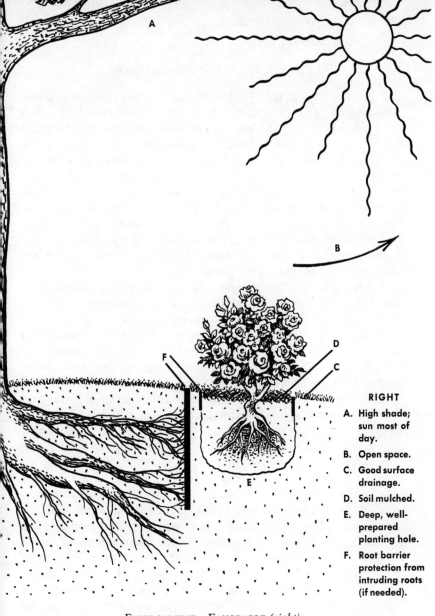

RIGHT

A. High shade; sun most of day.

B. Open space.

C. Good surface drainage.

D. Soil mulched.

E. Deep, well-prepared planting hole.

F. Root barrier protection from intruding roots (if needed).

ENVIRONMENT—FAVORABLE *(right)*

(A) High shade (or open sky) permits abundant direct sunshine during most of the day. (B) Open space around beds allows free circulation of air, and permits extremely cold air to drain away. (C) Surface drainage carries off surplus water; keeps soil open. (D) Mulched soil remains cooler in hot weather; keeps soil from packing hard; prevents most weed growth. (E) Adequate planting hole provides abundant plant food and moisture to sustain maximum growth. (F) Root barrier (of wood, metal, or concrete) keeps robber tree roots from stealing nourishment meant for roses.

CREATING A FAVORABLE MICRO-CLIMATE

It is quite true, as the rose books and the rose catalogs say, that roses can be grown practically anywhere in America. It does not follow, however, that any rose can be grown anywhere in America; nor does the statement take into account the fact that most roses, particularly those which we think of as garden roses, are quite decidedly affected, for better or for worse, by what might at first appear to be rather minor differences in their immediate surroundings.

Protection from winds, either the high, marrow-chilling and drying winds of midwinter and early spring, or the constant near-gale summer winds that so often are encountered along ocean shores or in certain inland locations, is most helpful in providing more favorable surroundings for a rose garden.

If there is not available a spot which is naturally protected from the slings and arrows of old Boreas, then a suitable fence or a sheltering band of shrubs and/or evergreens may be provided.

Protection from frost, that is, from early fall or early spring cold snaps, not from winter freezing, can be increased if the rose bed has good *air drainage.* Cool or cold air, though unseen, flows downgrade like water and builds up in the lowest depression available. Like water too, it can be dammed up, encouraged to pass along, or diverted in some other direction. Air in motion lessens the chance of injury from frost; held still, as in a valley or a small hollow, it increases the danger. A tight fence or a dense hedge so located that it will dam up the cold air, may result in serious frost injury. An example of this sort is shown in the photograph on page 33, where, in a garden well south of the Mason and Dixon's line, an unseasonable and prolonged cold spell killed all the roses near the foot of a slope bordered by a tight fence. Those part way up the slope, while injured, survived; and those nearest the top escaped without injury.

The free circulation of air within the rose garden itself is of equal importance. Rose beds closely surrounded by hedges, shrubbery, or walls are much more subject to diseases or insect pests than those through which air currents can freely pass. This is one of the reasons why it is so important to keep the individual rose plants pruned to open centers.

Sun and shade are other factors affecting the micro-climate with

Air drainage is extremely important. In this case a tight fence and a hedge at bottom of slope prevented cold air from draining off to the lower level. Result: plants at bottom of slope were killed outright (foreground); those halfway up were severely injured; while plants on highest ground escaped injury.

which we plan to provide our roses in order to have them do their best. High shade and shelter from trees on the north or west will help to ward off late frosts in spring when growth is just starting, and from early frosts in autumn when roses are still in full bloom. Such trees, of course, should not be so near that their roots will rob the rose beds of moisture. Under such conditions it is possible to resort to a "root barrier" (see line cut, page 31).

Some "high" shade in summer also is often helpful. While roses, under most conditions, will take full sun and like it, the scorching blaze of a midday summer's sun, especially if the plants are growing in a rather light soil, may prove to be too much of a good thing. Under such circumstances, high shade from three to five hours during midday, or during the afternoon, will prove helpful in prolonging the life of flowers on the plants and preventing or lessening the so-called "bluing" of many of the red varieties.

The other fundamentals for good growth—suitable soil, good drainage, and adequate moisture—are discussed in the chapters devoted to these subjects and therefore require no further comment here.

LAYING OUT THE ROSE GARDEN

The Rosarium must be both exposed and sheltered, a place both of sunshine and of shade. The center must be clear and open, around it the protecting screen. It must be a fold where the sun shines warmly on the sheep, and the wind is tempered to the shorn lamb. . . .

In selecting the spot where the rose garden is to be placed, there are two quite definite considerations to be kept in mind. The first is the selection of an area where the roses may be expected to *grow* best; and the second, the selection of an area where they will make the most effective *display,* both in the general garden scheme and in the outlook from view windows. The same considerations apply, of course, to the placing of Climbing Roses, Shrub Roses, and Rose hedges.

If a location can be found which will meet both of these objectives, there is no cause to seek further. If not, you will have to decide which consideration is to be given precedence. If you expect to be interested primarily in winning blue ribbons at rose shows or in having extra-choice blooms for cutting for decoration indoors, you will choose the first alternative; if not, the latter.

Once you have settled upon the location, the next step will be to decide how large a garden you are going to make, or how many individual plants—Garden, Climbing, and Shrub Roses—you wish to include in your landscape plan.

For the rose garden itself, whether it is to be formal or informal in general design, it is well to have beds that will be not over five feet in width. This permits most of the work in caring for them to be done from the adjoining turf or pathways without making it necessary to step into the beds themselves. Often beds are made as narrow as three feet to allow setting the plants in two rows about nine inches back from the edges, with eighteen inches between at the center, the plants being staggered to provide more room between them. This however is a bit crowded for normal growth of most varieties, and decidedly too little space for those that make vigorous growth. (In the lists of varieties given in Chapter 24, the

Plan for a small, semiformal rose garden.

average height of most varieties is indicated; and, in general, the tallest growers require the most lateral space.)

Unless you are planning a strictly formal rose garden, curving beds with correspondingly curving paths between them will provide the most pleasing effects and also add considerably to the apparent size of the garden.

If the bed is to be made on a fairly steep slope, it is well to follow contours as much as possible. This will help to prevent washing and runoff during heavy rains and, when artificial watering is required, assure an even penetration of the soil.

A rose garden built on sea sand soil. Rose in foreground is Gruss an Aachen, first of the modern Floribundas.

Before actually starting work on making the beds it is well to stake them out accurately so that the general effect can be viewed from entrance, walks, view windows, the terrace, or other vantage points from which the rose garden will be seen most frequently. The same holds true in locating the spots where Climbers or Shrub Roses are to go.

The sketch on page 35 and the photographs on pages 19 and 20 give examples of some attractive layouts for rose plantings.

Part Two

CULTURE OF THE ROSE

CHAPTER *4.* *The Soil*

and Its Preparation

How often has it been said to me: "Oh, what a garden is yours for Roses. We have a few nice flowers but . . . Old Mr. Drone, our gardener, tells us that he never saw such a soil as yours, nor so bad a soil as ours for Roses . . ." and herein is a fact in horticulture— Mr. Drone always has a bad soil. An inferior gardener . . . is always snarling at his soil. Only by superhuman efforts, they will assure you . . . can anything be induced to grow but weeds.

In going through the literature of the Rose it is interesting to note, in older books, what elaborate directions were given for the preparation of the soil, and in contrast how the importance of soil preparation, in most modern books and articles, is *de*-emphasized.

Perhaps the explanation of this contrast lies in the fact that in former times soil was much more of a mystery than it is today; and in the further fact that as a result of the influence of modern advertising on horticultural writing and editing, it is not considered good business to stress too strongly the amount of work involved in growing first quality roses in the home garden.

The truth about soil preparation for roses lies somewhere between these two extremes. On the one hand there is no formula— secret or otherwise—for soil preparation that will in itself assure you good roses. On the other hand you cannot expect really fine roses unless you are willing to make sure that the soil in which you plant them is such that they will find in it, in abundance, *and in readily available form,* the plant food elements they require.

Excellent roses may be grown on any reasonably good soil, and even on thin, sandy soil, although the latter requires more effort in the way of preparation.

"Good" soil? One of the clichés of the popular rose-advice garden writer has been that one can grow roses on any soil that will grow a good crop of corn or potatoes. That advice is not much help because not one person in a thousand these days has any idea of what kind of soil will grow a good crop of corn or potatoes. As a matter of fact it is much easier to produce a good crop of roses than to raise a good crop of potatoes—fortunately for those who love roses!

In contrast to this very skimpy modern advice on soil, in some of the older rose books one comes across the most elaborate directions for preparing rose beds.

To get down to the practical point of what the beginning rose grower should do in the way of soil preparation, let us disregard both the assumption that no particular attention need be paid to the soil, and the equally untenable theory that one cannot have excellent roses without double digging to a depth of two feet or so, bringing in clay soil unless you already happen to possess it, and procuring ample supplies of animal manure—preferably "old cow." Any soil which will grow vigorous shrubs and husky perennials is in condition satisfactorily to support rosebushes; and *almost* any soil can be put into condition to support good shrubs, perennials, *and* roses, even if it will not already do so, by application of a few basic principles of soil improvement.

The three most important characteristics which any soil must possess to be a "good" soil are:

> Drainage
> Humus
> Plant food (nutrients) in abundance and in available form.

Drainage. If the location where you plan to grow your roses is not naturally well-drained, then that will be your most serious problem. Poor drainage is indicated by standing puddles of water or wet, soggy areas remaining for a considerable time, often for days, after a heavy rain. This may be due to either or both of two causes: first, a heavy, dense clay which prevents the water from readily percolating down through it; and second, an impervious substratum of soil which does not have sufficient slope to let the underground water drain off to some lower point, but holds it as in a dish.

A simple test to determine whether good drainage exists is to

Where soil drainage is very poor, the only solution may be to employ tile drains. (Note the lateral drains branching to right and left.)

dig a hole eight to twelve inches in diameter and eighteen to twenty inches deep and fill it half full of water. If the water has not drained away in a day or two, steps should be taken to improve the drainage; or the beds may be raised somewhat above the soil level.

Heavy clay soils may be improved in any one of three ways: first, by the addition of coarse, gritty sand which tends to "cut" or break up the clay mass; second, by the addition of humus in the form of animal manures or of peatmoss or compost; and third, by the use of drain tile installed beneath the surface to help carry off the water when it has penetrated to a certain depth. Except in extreme cases and for areas much larger than the average rose garden, it should not be necessary to resort to tile drainage.

An impervious layer of hardpan or stone below the surface—

unless it is eighteen inches or more down—presents a much more serious problem. Sometimes it is possible to remedy the situation by excavating the bed and then loosening or cracking up the hard layer with a pickaxe or even with agricultural dynamite. Fortunately such a condition is seldom encountered.

Humus. By humus we mean any type of decaying vegetable matter in the soil. Please note that the adjective is used in the present tense—decay*ing*. Once it has completely decayed it ceases to exist. It must be in one way or another continually replaced—like adding wood to a burning fire.

Humus in the soil is a triple benefit: it absorbs and holds moisture which would otherwise drain off, releasing it slowly as plant roots require it; it encourages the growth of soil bacteria which are essential in making nutrients in the soil available to hungry roots; and it improves the mechanical condition of the soil so that water and air can readily penetrate it.

Much of the great stress placed by earlier writers on the use of generous quantities of manure in rose beds was due to the fact (the importance of which they did not recognize) that it provided humus as well as plant food. Indeed there is no doubt that, in many instances, the humus was of more importance than the very small amounts of actual nutrients. Animal manures today are as valuable as they ever were—if you can get them—but they are not essential.

Another advantage of maintaining an abundant amount of humus in the soil is that it serves as a reservoir for moisture. Peatmoss, for instance, will absorb and retain up to twenty-seven times its own weight of water. This fact makes it valuable as a substitute for manure. Maintaining moisture in the soil at all times is vitally important because plant roots can absorb or ingest their foods *only when they are in solution.* They drink, but they cannot "eat."

Plant Foods. It is not necessary here to make any extensive excursion into the subject of plant foods or nutrients. Almost any gardener these days, particularly anyone who has traveled far enough along the garden path to be taking up rose growing, knows that there are a dozen or more essential plant food elements; and that of these, those of foremost importance are nitrogen, phosphorus, potassium, and calcium. The others, usually referred to as "trace elements" are present in most soils in sufficient quantities to permit most plants to make normal growth. (In rose growing a deficiency of some of these may cause trouble in one respect or another, and such instances are discussed in the chapter on Rose Troubles, page 182.) Trace elements need not be considered in the general preparation of the rose bed.

In the growth of plants, the three important nutrients most likely to be present in insufficient quantities in any particular soil play different roles, so that a shortage of any one of them cannot be made up by a surplus of either, or even of both, of the other two.

Nitrogen stimulates vigorous vegetative growth, the production of new leaves and stems; and tends to delay maturity—in the case of roses, the production of flowers.

Phosphorus, on the contrary, hastens maturity, encourages the production of flowers, and tends to add strength to stems and branches.

Potassium is important in encouraging vigorous root growth; it serves as a balance wheel to counteract a surplus of either nitrogen or phosphorus; and there seems to be acceptable evidence that it increases the plant's resistance to disease.

Calcium (less likely to be deficient in most soils than the three elements mentioned above) not only serves as a plant food in itself, but is furthermore of great importance in converting the other plant foods, which may be present in the soil but in forms which cannot be absorbed by the plant's feeding roots, into forms that they can take up.

It is quite evident then, that if we expect to enjoy really first-class roses, we must provide them with a generous and a *well-balanced* larder.

Plant Food Materials. The sources of plant foods are many and varied. They are, to begin with, of two types: organic—such as animal manures, either raw or "processed," and bone meal; and nonorganic or chemical—such as nitrate of soda, potash salts, and phosphate rock. In both of these groups, most of the products readily available today have been processed so that they will be uniform in analysis and easy for the gardener to apply to his soil. These products vary greatly in the amount or percentage of actual plant food they contain, and in the availability of the food once it has been applied to the soil—that is, the rapidity with which the plant's roots can absorb it.

A "complete" plant food or fertilizer is one which contains at least three of the basic elements—nitrogen, phosphorus, and potassium. In most cases, however, the complete chemical fertilizers contain several of the trace elements also.

Complete plant foods vary in the relative amounts of the several nutrients they contain. These are expressed in terms of percentages. Thus a 5-10-5 mixture contains 5% of nitrogen, 10% of phosphorus and 5% of potassium.

Just what analysis in a complete plant food will be best in the original preparation of the rose bed will depend upon the type of soil you have to start with. If the bed is an extensive one it will definitely be worth while to procure a soil analysis in advance. You can make one yourself with a soil testing outfit, but more accurate results may be had by sending a sample or samples of the soil to your local county agricultural agent or to your state experiment station. (A list of these stations will be found on page 323.) However, thousands of small rose gardens are annually planted, and satisfactory results obtained, without benefit of a preliminary soil analysis.

Sources of Different Plant Foods. In the original preparation of the rose bed the important thing is to provide an abundance of plant food. The generous use of a complete fertilizer will assure this. If you do not know what analysis is usually considered best for soil in your section of the country, a telephone call to your local county agent will get you the information; or if you happen to be a member of a garden club, there is sure to be someone in it who will know. A 5-10-5 is standard in many parts of the country.

Special rose fertilizers are available and many of these are excellent, but in purchasing them you are apt to pay more per actual pound of plant food than if you use a standard analysis suitable for your type of soil. Keep in mind, however, that no fertilizer will in itself assure success. It is only one of many important factors contributing to the growth of your roses.

Special Plant Foods. After a season or two, when you have had a chance to compare the behavior of your plants with those in other rose gardens, you may conclude that something is lacking. You may, for instance, notice that in a heavy "slow" clay soil, growth does not start off as rapidly or as vigorously as it should in the spring. Some additional nitrogen, in quickly available form,

PLATE 7

PLATE 8

Fences and walls make ideal supports for Climbing and Rambler Roses. General effect is most artistic when fence is left partly revealed, as is the case in these two Cape Cod gardens. In one, a picket fence encloses a small dooryard garden; in the other a post-and-rail marks a boundary.

PLATE 9

These roses on a sandy hillside in Silas Clark's Cape Cod garden illustrate what can be done even under very adverse conditions. A moderate amount of terracing prevents rapid runoff of water, and native growth of trees affords protection from late afternoon sun.

Fourth-of-July piece: Rose Frensham, with white Madonna Lily and blue Delphinium.

PLATE 10

PLATE 11

Rose Day at New York Botanical Garden—an annual event which draws hundreds of rose lovers to evaluate new and old varieties, and to take part in the afternoon discussions on rose culture. Similar affairs are held the country over. Why not plan to attend one?

PLATE 12

The lovely semiformal rose garden on the estate of the Hill sisters (at Lynn-haven, Virginia), whose exhibits of outdoor-grown shrubs and flowers for many years have been a feature at New York's annual spring International Flower Show. BELOW: *For those who live in difficult northern climates, the Brownells' Sub-zero Roses offer a wide choice of colors in extra-hardy bush and climbing forms.*

PLATE 13

would help remedy this situation. Or weak stems and droopy flowers may indicate that more phosphorus is needed to make them stronger. Then the use of one or more of the materials mentioned in Chapter 7 may be advisable.

PREPARATION FOR PLANTING

After the rose garden or the rose bed has been laid out the next step is to prepare the soil to receive the plants you plan to put into it. *It is important that this soil preparation be done as far as possible in advance of the actual planting.*

If you expect to plant in the fall, try to get the beds made not later than August or early September. If for any reason you have to plant in the spring, get the beds ready the preceding fall. This gives the soil a chance to "mellow," the bed to settle down to its ultimate level, and the plant foods time to become thoroughly distributed through the soil and broken down into forms that the developing roots can assimilate.

Unless you are so fortunate as to have soil that is already in excellent condition, it will be well worth while to do a real job in making the beds. This will involve, as a first step, removing all of the surface soil to a depth of eight or ten inches. Piling this soil on a tarpaulin, heavy burlap bags, or heavy building paper spread out beside the bed will keep it from working down into the grass, and make a much easier as well as a neater job when you are ready to put it back into the bed.

The next step is to improve the texture and enrich the soil in the bottom of the bed. If this is heavy and hard it should be broken up by use of a spading fork, or if necessary, a pickaxe, going down to a depth of eight inches—about the length of a spade blade or the tines of a fork. If the soil is light and sandy however, it should be left undisturbed.

Next, add all the humus-making material you can possibly secure, whether the soil is heavy clay or light and sandy, but particularly in the latter case. If the soil is heavy, dig down into it and thoroughly mix the humus with the subsoil; if the soil is very sandy, the humus can be kept in a layer on top, and mixed with some of the soil which was previously removed.

In this same operation, apply and thoroughly mix in, at the rate

Where soil is very poor, soil should be excavated to a depth of 18 inches or more.

of 4 or 5 pounds for each 100 square feet of surface, a complete plant food such as has already been described (see page 42). If a very high analysis plant food is being used, of course less will be required.

The next, and final, step is to return the surface soil, mixing with it humus and fertilizer, as for the bottom layer. If the surface soil itself is very poor, consisting largely of coarse sand or light gravel

The removed soil is replaced by good topsoil to which manure, or peatmoss and/or fertilizer have been added.

which has not been supporting a fair amount of vegetation, it will be highly desirable to bring in the best loam that can be obtained from some other source. Fortunately, however, it is very seldom necessary to resort to this extreme.

Lime. Roses, with very few exceptions, do best in a slightly acid soil, that is, soil with a *p*H of 6 to nearly 7, which is the neutral line (see acidity scale on page 12). If your soil is too acid (*p*H 5 or lower), apply 7 to 8 pounds of raw, ground limestone (agricultural lime) per 100 square feet, or twice that amount if the soil is a very heavy clay. If the soil is not sufficiently acid, it may be made more so by applying 5 pounds of aluminum sulfate or 2 pounds of sulfur or ammonium sulfate per 100 square feet, which will bring it down from 7 pH to about 6.

In soils that are quite acid it may be necessary to repeat the liming for three or four seasons. A yearly test for acidity, which

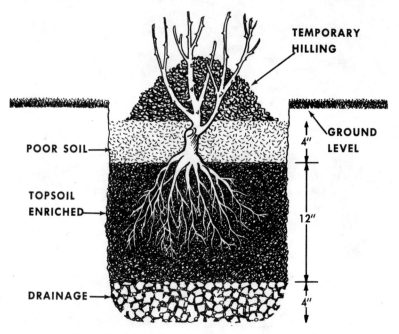

TEMPORARY
HILLING

POOR SOIL

GROUND
LEVEL
4"

TOPSOIL
ENRICHED

12"

DRAINAGE

4"

Pruned rosebush in properly prepared planting hole.

can be made in a few minutes, would be advisable. However, if your roses are growing with satisfactory vigor you will not need to worry on this score.

Personally, in preparing rose beds we like to use plenty of bone meal. This may be just an old-fashioned idea; in fact it is considered more or less open heresy by present-day agricultural chemists who point out that superphosphate as a source of phosphorus is both quicker-acting and less expensive. Undoubtedly it is true that

Preparing new soil for a rose bed (at Gray Rock). After soil has been dug to remove roots and stones, peatmoss and fertilizer are incorporated before the final working over, preparatory to planting.

superphosphate is preferable for farm crops, grown by the acre. However, the difference in cost is not a serious consideration in the making of a moderate-sized rose garden. As to the argument that bone meal is slower-acting, we consider this an advantage rather than a disadvantage in the preparation of soil that will not again be disturbed, to any great depth, for many years. And the growth that a rose plant makes during the first two or three seasons

Renewing soil in the famous display gardens of Jackson & Perkins at Newark, New York. Every three years the old soil is removed bodily and new soil put in. Subirrigation pipes, at a depth of two feet, water the beds.

has a considerable influence on how it will continue to thrive thereafter.

It should be emphasized—a point that is seldom mentioned in literature on the subject—that there are several types of bone meal with quite different characteristics. The kind which we like to use in the original preparation of a rose bed, and in making ready the planting holes for receiving Climbing Roses and Shrub or Bush Roses to be individually planted, is known as coarse, raw ground bone. This is the nearest one can get to the original "bag of bones," which for so long was used in Europe, being placed under a tree or a grapevine to contribute to its vigorous growth for several years. Steamed bone meal, often ground as fine as flour, is quite a different product and is not nearly so suitable for use in the rose bed.

The coarse, raw ground bone we use in preparing the lower layer of soil in a new rose bed (at the rate of 3 to 6 pounds per 100 square feet), and in individual planting holes (1 to 2 quarts per hole, dug in very deeply). It disintegrates very slowly, and remains effective for several years.

Edgings. There are several advantages in providing your rose beds with a permanent edging of some sort. If the beds are graded so that the surfaces are slightly below the level of the paths or grass turf around or between the beds, they will not interfere with mowing and no time-consuming clipping will be required. Also it will keep the grass from growing into the beds, giving them an untidy appearance.

Where rose beds have to be planted in the vicinity of trees or large shrubs, a fairly deep vertical edging will form a barrier sufficient to keep out spreading near-the-surface roots which of course have a heyday when they can penetrate into the rich soil of the rose bed. Such edgings also hold in place any mulches which may be applied, keeping these from spreading out over the grass, and to some extent preventing their blowing off.

In some cases, too, it is desirable to have the surface of the soil in the rose bed either several inches below the ground level, or well above it; the former, in locations where the soil is dry and must be watered very frequently; the latter, in areas where drainage is very poor. Having the rose bed a few inches higher than the surrounding surface will help greatly in combating this problem.

CHAPTER *5.*   *The Rose Plant*

> *. . . to the true Rose-grower must the Rose-tree be always a thing of beauty. To others, when its flowers have faded, it may be worthless as a hedge-row thorn; to him, in every phase, it is precious.*

The Rose Plant, botanically speaking, is a shrub: that is, made up of a low-growing, woody, multibranched, persistent top above ground, supported by a permanent root system below ground. The root, like the top of the plant, branches freely and vigorously; in fact, if one could follow the root system to its tips, one would often find it larger than the growth above ground.

As numerous references will be made throughout these pages to different parts of the rose plant, we will take time here to describe and illustrate them. Even a cursory study of the rose anatomy will give the grower an idea of the mechanism he is working with and help him to success.

DETAILS OF THE ROSE PLANT

The accompanying sketch (page 53) shows a typical garden rose plant and its several parts.

Starting underground, there is the root system (much abbreviated) with the main or trunk roots, fibrous branch roots, and threadlike root hairs.

Above ground there is the main stem or trunk, with its protuberant "knuckle"—a swelling resulting from the insertion of a bud (to provide the variety desired) in the stem of the seedling or stock on which it is to be grown (see page 205). Growths which develop

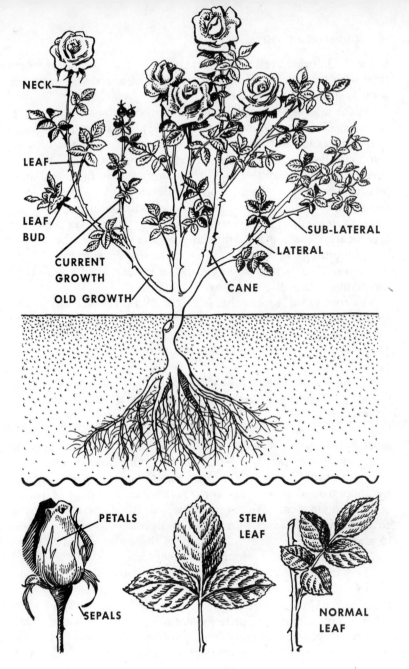

NECK

LEAF

LEAF
BUD

CURRENT
GROWTH

OLD GROWTH

SUB-LATERAL

LATERAL

CANE

PETALS

STEM
LEAF

SEPALS

NORMAL
LEAF

Anatomy of the rose.

below the knuckle are called "suckers." These, of course, are identical with the root stock, and therefore unwanted and cut off as soon as noticed.

On the main stem are the side branches which persist from season to season (until removed by pruning). These form the frame of the plant, and from them grow the new shoots which in turn develop additional side branches and stems terminating in flowers.

At the base of each leaf that grows along a stem there is a latent pointed swelling or "eye," ready to develop into a branch or a flower stem. Not all of these start into growth, but if the top of the stem is removed, by cutting a flower or by pruning, then the eye or eyes nearest the top are stimulated into growth. In the case of "everblooming" varieties, many of these will develop into flowering stems. Those which do not, grow on to form the framework of the plant for the following year.

The rose plant, too, is characterized by thorns—as anyone attempting to grow one soon realizes! The thorns vary greatly in size and shape, according to the ancestry of any particular variety. They have their uses—one of which is to discourage the too ardent pruner!

Not all kinds of roses follow this pattern of growth. Almost all the wild or species roses flower but once in a season, and for a rather short period, and hence develop plant structures differing from those of our present-day garden varieties. The same is true of most horticultural varieties of Shrub Roses; and—until very recently as Rose history goes—of most Climbing Roses. Many of the wild and Shrub Roses, such as *Rosa rugosa* and its varieties, spread by underground suckers and form many-stemmed clumps instead of single main stems. We have just been clearing a patch of ground covered with wild roses—for we grow vegetables as well as flowers to grace the dining table—and many of the underground *Rosa virginiana* runners were more than five feet long!

The parts of the rose *flower* are described and illustrated in detail in Chapter 15, page 210, so we will not take them up here. It is suggested, however, that the reader refer to this section so that he may have a more complete picture of the rose plant as a whole.

Roses in general are considered hardy shrubs although the several species, and especially horticultural types (which include most of the roses now grown in gardens) vary greatly in their ability to

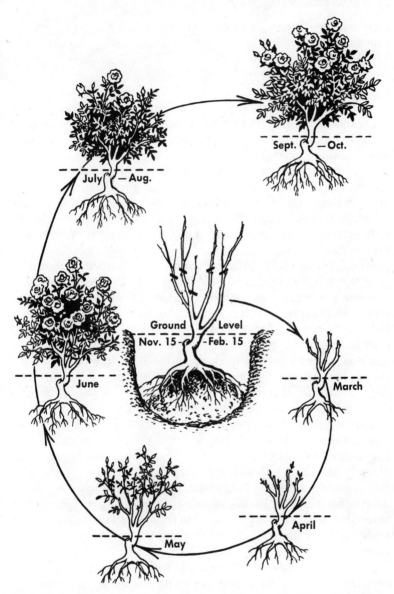

Typical growth cycle of rosebush in moderate climates. Further north the season of active growth is shorter; in mild climates, as in the South, it may continue practically around the year.

withstand low temperatures without being killed back to the ground, if not outright.

GROWTH CYCLE

Like other plants, the rose has a definite growth cycle, and this cycle determines to a great extent the whens, whats, and hows of its cultural requirements. The growth cycle of course varies somewhat with the type of rose and the climate in which it is being grown; but if we take as a typical example the Hybrid Tea, growing in a moderate-temperature climate (such as that in Zone 6 on the map on page 10), it will serve to illustrate the seasonal changes in the growth of the plant, and the ways in which they determine the treatment which should be accorded it. So let us follow such a plant—assuming it is already growing in the garden—around the year, through the eight important stages of its cycle of growth.

Roses are among the very first plants in the garden to begin growth in the spring. In fact a moderately prolonged warm spell in February or early March is likely to crack winter dormancy and start leaf buds into growth. If a severe cold spell follows, this may result in severe injury, not alone to the new growth, but to the entire plant. Obviously, then, the careful gardener will want to delay the buds from starting until it is safe for them to do so. (See Chapter 10.)

1. Normally the new growth will not start until March or early April, when the average daytime temperature is increasing with lengthening days. The growth at first is gradual, and becomes sufficiently hardened to withstand normal night temperatures below freezing without injury. It is at this point that the rose grower can determine which branches of his rosebushes have come safely through the winter, or just how far they have been killed back if there has been injury. This information is essential to his doing a proper job of pruning. (See page 110.)

2. During late March and early April growth continues at a more or less hesitant pace, depending upon the season and also upon the immediate surroundings. In a warm, sunny, sheltered spot it may be a week or ten days ahead of growth on the same variety in an exposed or shaded location. This is no advantage, for the faster this

first early growth develops, the greater the chance of its being killed—with subsequent injury to the plant—by a late cold snap.

With lengthening days and the coming of warm spring rains, new growth develops rapidly. Almost as though a magician's wand had been waved over them, the collection of bare brown sticks that has been the rose garden becomes clothed with sprays of delicate foliage, in shades that range from pale green to various tints of red, according to the ancestry which flows through the stems of the different varieties. Where *rubrifolia*, for instance, has had a part in the life line, the garnet-red leaves are a worth-while show in themselves.

3. Late April and May mark the season of most vigorous growth, and the root system of the plant is hard put to it to take up and transmit to the rapidly developing branches and foliage above ground all the nourishment they require. Consequently it is at this point in the growth cycle that nutrients in readily available form *and* an abundance of moisture are most urgently needed. If the weather is warm and spring rains are plentiful, new growth may reach the stage of flowerbud formation in as short a time as seven to ten weeks.

4. Late May and June bring on the period of maximum flower production—the time when the rose garden puts on its most gorgeous show. This is the period when many types of roses, especially Species and many Shrub Roses, give their only flowers, and even the everblooming garden roses make a display that will not again be equaled for a whole year.

This too, is the season for indoor rose shows, the height of the year for the rose enthusiast whose greatest ambition is a collection of silver cups and blue ribbons. But of this *Rosa*, though she holds the center of the stage in such events, takes no heed in her daily existence. She has put on *her* big show, biologically speaking, for the sole purpose of attracting bees and other insects, with waving colors and permeating fragrance, to transfer the golden, life-transmitting pollen from anther to stigma. With that accomplished, she is ready to take a rest. And this—despite all that the Meillands and Boerners and Lamberts of this and innumerable former generations have done to try to change her habits—she now proceeds to do.

5. So, in July and August, we come to the fifth stage of the cycle —one of the least exciting but in many ways one of the most important.

In a sense this midsummer rest period, when both branch growth and flower production are conspicuously slowed up, can be looked upon as a sort of second pre-spring, when the plant is pausing to gather and conserve its energies for another burst of vigorous growth during autumn. In nature this period is devoted to the creation of new branch growth and the development of the crop of fruit, the rose hips or "apples" which, in many species, make a display almost as attractive as the flowers which preceded them. And these, in turn, seem to carry out the plans of nature, for they serve to attract the birds that, in return for the food they provide, will distribute them far and wide.

Our man-made garden roses, with few exceptions, set very few fruits unless they are seduced by the gentlemen with the camel's-hair brushes and the test tubes; but they do give us, in most instances, a fine repeat show of fall bloom. Moreover, their flowers, in a great many sections of the country, are produced under weather conditions which make them much finer individual specimens than even those of the June crop that, during a hot spell, frequently are unduly hurried from bud to fully open flower and may begin to wilt or wither in a day. To reach perfection, a rose should develop rather slowly *within the bud* until it is ready to unfold into its full potential beauty.

Midsummer blooms are often poor, sometimes with only a fraction of the number of petals they should have, decidedly off color, and, particularly in the case of red varieties, "bluing" or fading out until not even the most expert could safely identify the varieties he is looking at.

So it would seem that the sensible thing to do with our roses during midsummer—from early July to late August—is to let them take it easy, with no heavy feeding or overabundant watering to try to force them into continued flower production. And if they have, or can be provided with, some shade, especially at midday during this period, they will appreciate it, and the blooms they do produce will be very much better than they would be if left exposed to a blazing summer sun.

This should not be interpreted, however, as an excuse for neglecting them. Far from it, for this is the time when insect pests are most likely to get in their nefarious work, and the time for such diseases as black spot and mildew to wreck the chances for a fine crop of fall bloom. Also, if the soil is allowed to become excessively dry, the plants will pretty much cease growth altogether, while the weeds that love heat and do not require much moisture will thrive exuberantly.

So during this section of the growth cycle, the rose garden should be visited and watched just as closely as though a great show of bloom were anticipated, for the production of fine fall bloom depends directly upon keeping the plants and the foliage in first-class condition during this interim period.

6. The cooler weather and copious rains of late August and early September see growth renewed and the initiation of many flowering shoots, in preparation for the really big autumn show that is soon to follow.

The most important need of the plants during this time is an ample supply of water to maintain vigorous growth. Additional feeding will not be required if the plants are growing well. Nitrogen especially should be avoided since it stimulates soft new vegetative growth subject to injury from early freezes.

7. Late September and October find the garden roses again in their glory, with many varieties—particularly the reds and yellows —providing more perfect and much longer-lasting blooms than they did in June. Flowering usually is maintained until a hard freeze. Light frosts that finish off most of the annuals and perennials leave most roses unharmed. At West Nyack, New York, where temperatures normally go below zero during the winter, we frequently cut blooms the first week of November; and here (on Cape Cod) good December blooms are not uncommon.

8. With the coming of really hard frosts and lower temperatures, growth ceases, and the rose plant goes into its dormant winter period. If the encroachment of winter has been normal, the most recently developed shoots and branches harden or ripen off gradually, and thus become able to withstand normally low winter temperatures without injury. If, however, they are, like Hamlet's father, "cut off even in the blossoms," as the result of a sudden hard freeze after a comparatively warm fall, they may be severely damaged.

Root action, however, does not cease with the dormancy of the tops: in fact it continues during the dormancy of the tops as long as the soil remains unfrozen, as anyone who has ever set out a rose in late fall, and transplanted it again in early spring, will have ob-served. Experiments have shown that the roots continue to func-tion until soil temperature falls below 40°F.

During the dormant—or more accurately the *top dormancy*—period, then, we have two objectives to consider: first, to give such protection as we can to prevent winter injury to the parts of the plant above ground; and second, to prolong root activity below ground, thus building up reserve strength for the big burst of growth that will start with the first warm days of spring.

These two objectives, while quite distinct from each other, have consistently been confused in rose literature. They are discussed in full in the chapter dealing with Winter Protection.

OTHER GROWTH CYCLES

The growth cycle described above is, as we have explained, that of a modern garden rose (Hybrid Tea or Floribunda) in a moder-ately cold climate—the sorts mostly grown by most gardeners. But while we are on the subject, let us take a look at the cycles followed by other roses, or under other conditions.

Tea Roses, which are themselves hybrids with a very complicated ancestry, and not a distinct race or species, are much less hardy than the Hybrid Teas and Floribundas grown in northern gardens. In warm climates they do not follow the winter dormancy pattern of Hybrid Teas, but tend to be almost perpetual—that is, year-round—flowering, retaining their foliage, and producing new growth through the winter months. In growth they develop much more wiry stems, and are inclined to spread, or, if supported, to "climb." Their natural rest period is induced by lack of moisture rather than low temperatures.

Climbing Roses, as regards growth habit, are of two types, the Ramblers and the Large-flowered. The former (such as the old Dorothy Perkins, and Chevy Chase) send up from the base each year strong new canes which do not flower until the following year. To make room for these, the old canes are usually cut back to the ground as soon as flowers have faded. (See page 124.)

The Large-flowered Climbers, including climbing forms of many Hybrid Teas, flower on old wood, which is left until overcrowding may require its removal. (See page 126.)

Rugosas and many other Shrub Roses send out stolons from the base of the old plant and eventually establish almost impenetrable hedges or thickets that, for maximum flower production, must occasionally be thinned out.

THE ROSE PLANT YOU BUY

> *I exhort novice and nurseryman alike . . . to lay a deep and sure foundation. Let the one order robust varieties, and the other send vigorous plants.*

The beginner's success with roses will depend largely upon the plants which he obtains. This applies particularly to the results he will get the first season, and so it behooves him to acquire some knowledge as to how to tell a good rose plant from a poor one.

Rose plants sold to the public from commercial sources are of several types. With the increasing standardization of rose plant production, however, the type now most widely sold is that known as "two-year, field-grown, budded stock." What this means is a plant the *root* of which is three years old, and the top (above the knuckle) two years old.

In growing such roses the nurseryman sets out in rows, his understocks—one-year-old plants, usually grown from seed but sometimes from cuttings. On these the varieties he wishes to grow are budded. This operation consists of inserting a bud or eye in a slit in the bark of the understock. (See page 205.) This is allowed to grow for the balance of the season, and then the top of the understock, just above where the bud was inserted, is cut off and discarded. The new top, developing from the bud that was inserted, is then grown on through the following season, at the end of which it is dug and prepared for marketing.

Ideally, such plants should be allowed to complete their growth cycle undisturbed; in other words they should not be dug until the tops have gone into dormancy. With the production of rose plants now largely concentrated in long-season areas, this is not feasible, and various methods, such as mechanical defoliation and treatment with gas or chemicals, or a combination of these techniques, are used to get rid of the unwanted foliage. In northern nurseries

Top quality rose plants, as received from nursery. Moist packing and tight wrapping have kept them in perfect condition.

the plants can more nearly finish their normal growing season, but usually make smaller growth.

Preparation for market involves removing most of the weaker growth, cutting back the tops to a fairly uniform length—twelve to eighteen inches or so according to the vigor of the plant—and trimming back the roots.

There is still "great argument, about it and about" concerning which understocks are best for use in growing budded roses. Some do best in certain sections, others in other sections; some are compatible with certain varieties, while other varieties seem to produce better results with other understocks. Multiflora (*R. multiflora Japonica*), an East Asian species, is the most widely used. Many California growers prefer Ragged Robin, apparently a local name for a very old Bengal Rose. For roses to be grown under glass Manetti is a favorite.

The buyer of rose plants, however, generally has little choice as to what understocks his plants are grown on unless he can purchase from some local nurseryman who grows his own plants, and such sources have become fewer and fewer.

What he can do, is to make fairly sure that he is getting good, strong plants: first by buying only from a reliable source; and second—if he has ordered by mail—by examining his plants immediately upon arrival and refusing to accept any which seem of doubtful quality. Most nurserymen will replace without question any plants promptly returned to them as being unsatisfactory.

A first-class plant should have several stout, undamaged and unshriveled roots, and at least two good canes. These canes should be fresh, plump, and green, with no indication of withering or drying out, and no decayed or diseased spots showing on the stems.

Fortunately for rose lovers, present-day methods of packing have done much to assure the arrival of plants in first-class condition. There are sprays which check desiccation of the bark; and pliofilm wrappers, with a little moist sphagnum moss or other packing about the roots, provide sufficient moisture to keep plants in good condition for a long period. Often buds will have started, but while this is undesirable, it is not a serious drawback unless they have developed to a point where they will shrivel when the plant is set out.

Budded vs. Own-root Plants. There has been considerable controversy in rose literature as to whether budded plants, such as described above, or "own-root" plants are better. Such discussion is now pretty much academic, for today practically all garden roses —Teas, Hybrid Teas, and Floribundas—are budded. But there seems to be no doubt that a vigorous understock adds vigor to the top growth of a great many varieties. The understocks have "wild rose vitality," which many of the most beautiful garden varieties, bred through centuries of hybridizing to get bigger flowers and more continuous bloom, do not possess. That this is not merely theory is attested by the fact that in a long and carefully conducted trial with a number of garden varieties, those grown on their own

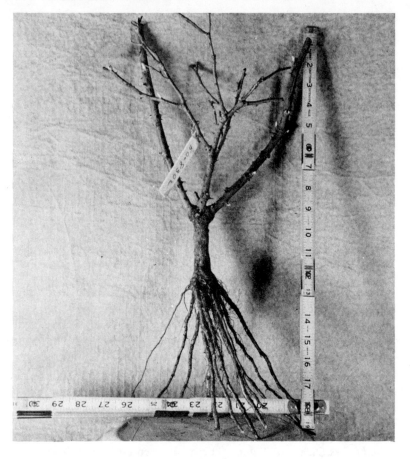

A good dormant rose plant for setting out in spring.

roots produced, during the first season, an average of ten flowers each; while the same kinds, budded on *Manetti* stock, produced nineteen flowers; and those on *Multiflora* produced twenty-seven flowers.

With every passing year more and more roses are sold as growing plants in pots, often late in the season, in bud and bloom. We prefer dormant plants, but have frequently had occasion to use plants in pots, especially in landscape work where a client wanted immediate results, and have found them satisfactory if properly

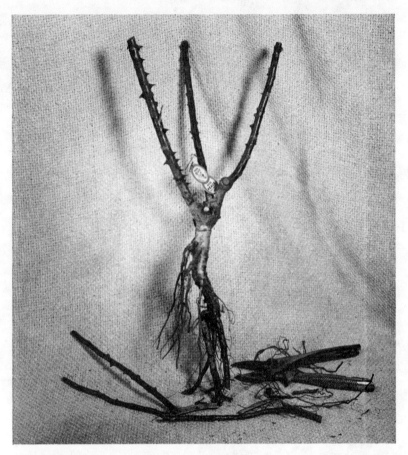

Any shriveled or broken canes are cut back to firm live wood; injured roots, and roots too long to be conveniently planted, also are cut back.

cared for after planting. One advantage of potted plants is that the purchaser can see exactly what he is getting, even to the flower itself if there is a bloom showing.

The potted plants referred to above are two-year, field-grown, in containers which hold about a gallon of soil. These are not to be confused with the small plants in small pots, raised from cuttings—and often little more than rooted cuttings when shipped out —sometimes sold by mail. Such plants, if well grown, have their

Roses started in pots make possible planting in spring, or even in early summer. However, the sooner they are set out the better.

place; in fact most Miniature or Fairy Roses are grown this way. But—*caveat emptor!*

The use of understocks applies to garden roses. Species, subspecies, and hardy Rambler roses all do well on their own roots.

Buying Rose Plants. Unfortunately a good price is not a guarantee of a good rose plant. It is also true that some concerns, because of lower production or operating costs can sell good plants at somewhat less than average prices.

In buying roses, as in buying most other things, the reputation of the concern selling them is one of the guideposts to satisfaction. Most companies these days guarantee "satisfaction or your money back." But *getting* it back is something else again, if you have ordered from an unreliable source. And anyway, getting your money back is poor compensation in place of a vigorous plant with a generous crop of blooms in your garden.

If you are a beginner with roses, it will pay you well to order at first from two or three different companies. Then you will have some basis for judging where your future purchases should be placed.

Current prices range from $2.50 to $3.50 each. Brand new varieties may occasionally be somewhat more, especially if they are patented—which means that the nurserymen cannot grow them without paying the holder of the patent a royalty on each plant produced. The patent does not guarantee a better rose; it merely means that it is sufficiently different from existing varieties to be entitled to a patent.

The first plant patent ever granted—under a law that was then new—was to the Climbing Rose New Dawn, a continuous-blooming sport of Dr. Van Fleet, in 1930. This rose is still one of the best Climbers in existence, but many which have since been granted patents have come and gone, some no longer to be found even in the catalogs of those who introduced them.

"Rose Bargains"—Beware! Occasionally unbelievable bargains in roses are offered, especially in radio and big-space newspaper advertising. Usually nothing definite is stated about the size or grade of the plants. Sometimes they will not even be true to name.

One of the sources for bargain roses is plants being discarded by commercial greenhouse rose growers. These have been intensively forced for two years or more and, if not sold to a "distributor" would be burned or go to the dump. In addition, they are likely to be varieties which, while good for greenhouse cut flowers, are not good as garden varieties.

Occasionally some plants from such a "bargain" collection of roses may be nursed back to good growth and eventually prove satisfactory in your garden. But buying them is a gamble that is not worth taking.

CHAPTER 6. *Planting*

> *. . . there is no royal road, no golden key to an excellent Rose-garden . . . but . . . a poor man . . . who* loves *the flower, may walk about in March with a Rose in his coat. . . .*

With the rose garden laid out, the soil within it prepared, and the plants that have been ordered finally received, we now face the exciting moment when they are actually to go into the ground —the culmination of the planning and the decisions that have gone before, and the beginning of the period of suspense when we wait for the great miracle: the unfolding of the first dewy petals that will make all the preceding work infinitely worth while.

WHEN TO PLANT

Before proceeding with the muddy details of just how to place a rose plant in the ground, however, let us stop to consider for a moment that much discussed question of *when* to plant. Some authorities are all for fall planting; others are equally insistent that they get better results with spring planting.

Now this is not altogether a matter of climatic conditions, as one might reasonably assume at first glance. There are other factors involved.

To begin with, the terms "fall planting" and "spring planting" are indefinite, if not actually misleading; and this has led to much of the confusion concerning discussions on the subject.

We quite agree with that noted and very widely experienced rose authority, Dr. J. H. Nicolas, that a better understanding of the whole matter would be achieved if we employed the terms "early

69

winter" and "late winter" instead of fall and spring. If we go by the book—or rather by the calendar—winter begins on December 21 and ends on March 20. In our experience, which extends from Massachusetts (inland as well as near the coast) to the Mason and Dixon's line, and the experience of many others both north and south of these latitudes, the nearer planting can be done to one of these two dates—and preferably the former—the better are the results likely to be.

There are sound reasons why this should be so. It is a well-established rule in horticulture that, when a plant is transplanted, the more root growth developed before top growth starts, the less injury to the plant. Transplanting is, at best, a major operation, even under the careful hands of the most skilled garden "surgeon," and anything which can be done to reduce the resultant shock increases the chances of ultimate success.

When a so-called "dormant" rose plant—dormant either from natural causes in its annual cycle of growth, or artificially dormant due to premature defoliation induced in the nursery where it was grown, before or after digging—is planted too early in the fall, there is still activity in the parts of the plant above ground, and a resulting effort to produce new growth buds (and in extreme cases new foliage) before real winter makes it completely dormant. With a well cut back root system practically devoid of all feeding roots, the result is that the plant goes into real winter in a highly debilitated condition and is extremely susceptible to winter injury.

On the other hand, spring planting—that is, anything later than March 21—is even worse. Here we have a plant that, after its long winter rest (which has not stopped physiological changes within the plant itself even though it may have spent the winter in a bin in a storage cellar) is literally bursting with energy ready to manifest itself in the creation of new top growth which quickly exhausts the food stored up in the root system. How often has the rose grower with any experience received rose plants in the spring which (even inside their cellophane wrappers) have already developed soft new shoots a half inch to two inches long!

The result of setting out such a plant in the spring—when longer days, more sunshine, and increasing temperatures are forcing the whole plant world into vigorous new growth—is that the root system, which has had no opportunity to develop new feeding roots, cannot keep up with the demands made upon it. The result, while it does not mean death to the plant, does mean curtailed growth both above ground and below.

Contrast these inevitable consequences of planting either too early in the fall or too late in the spring with what happens when your rose plant is set out either very late in the fall, or late in the winter—up to March 21 or as soon thereafter as possible.

As has already been noted, the root growth of roses continues long after the surface of the soil is frozen in autumn. It also begins in spring, *below* the frost line, before the top growth starts. Experiments have demonstrated that root growth is active at all times in temperatures of 40° or more. Under such conditions the tops remain dormant while the roots have an opportunity to make some new growth and re-establish the plant's system of root hairs, the minute organs through which the plant actually absorbs the nutrients essential to its continued growth. Until such time as growth buds start *above* ground, the resulting plant food is stored within the plant and is there ready, as a reservoir of energy, to be drawn upon by developing foliage, new growth, and later on by flower buds.

So there are the reasons why we feel so strongly that the advice given above—to plant as near as possible to the first day or the last day of winter—is sound.

Now let us consider for a moment the matter of planting. Obviously, if you live so far north or at so high an altitude that the ground is likely to be frozen solid long before the first of the above-mentioned dates, or to remain frozen long after the latter one, you will find it impossible to follow this advice. Or *will* you?

Why the question?

For the reason that by means of a very simple expedient planting *can* be done in cold sections several weeks later than is usually considered possible. This expedient consists merely in applying a really heavy mulch, one to two feet in depth, over the previously prepared bed before the ground begins to freeze. This mulch can be of any coarse material available, such as straw, bog hay, rough compost, leaves, pine needles. The mulch can be made even more effective if it is used with a sheet of heavy vinyl plastic, available at most hardware stores as "moisture barrier" or VisQueen. It can be applied directly over the prepared soil before the mulch is put on, or on top of the mulch. It prevents the soil of the bed from becoming soaked from late fall rains and also serves as a further barrier against the penetration of frost.

When plants are received, the mulch is removed, the plants are set in, and the mulch is returned to place; this time, of course, without the plastic covering because the plants will be benefited by any moisture which soaks through to them. Unless extremely low temperatures are encountered, the roots of the plants will be able to make some new growth before the ground freezes hard, and thus be in readiness to help support new *top* growth in the spring. The biggest trouble here, in our experience, is getting the plants shipped at the proper time for planting. One way of making sure that you will get them when you want them is to *order early*—not later than September first—giving the date when you would like to receive them. Then, as a further precaution, send a follow-up reminder on your order a couple of weeks before you want delivery.

If for any reason fall planting is not feasible, preparing the beds in the fall, mulching them heavily as suggested above to prevent deep penetration of frost, and then removing the mulch with the arrival of the first spring thaws, will be of great help in enabling you to get your planting done considerably *earlier* than you otherwise could—and remember that every day counts! Here too you should be careful to specify the date when you want plants delivered.

CARE OF PLANTS WHEN RECEIVED

Many rose plants are damaged, sometimes severely, between the time the gardener receives them and the time that he actually gets them into the ground. Examine them carefully, and if any of them seem to be unsatisfactory, make your complaint at once. You are much more likely to get a satisfactory adjustment than if you wait until later on in the season when they have failed to make good vigorous growth.

If either tops or roots seem to be at all dried out and shriveled, cover them at once with thoroughly damp peatmoss or sphagnum moss, both roots and tops, to plump them up. These days, with improved methods of packing and shipping, this will seldom be necessary.

If there is likely to be any considerable delay before you can begin planting, the best method is to bury plants completely. This can be done by digging a trench a foot or so in depth, placing the plants in it at a slight angle, and then burying them in moist soil. The next best thing (which requires somewhat less work) is to "heel them in": that is, dig a trench sufficiently deep to take the roots to slightly above the knuckle, cover them with moist soil, and throw compost or some other mulching material over the tops.

During these operations—and the later one of actual planting—do not leave tops or roots, even for a short period, exposed to drying winds or hot sun. Even though the plants are supposed to be dormant they cannot be treated like dry sticks. Needless to say, plants that are being held pending planting should be *kept cool;* slight freezing will not injure them, but a short period in dry atmosphere and a warm temperature, such as that existing in most present-day cellars, can be harmful.

THE PLANTING HOLE

Even when we have prepared our rose beds with the utmost care, we like to go one step further and provide something special in making ready the individual holes in which the plants are to be set. One knowledgeable rosarian once said (the remark has been credited to several different sources) that he would rather plant a ten-cent rose in a fifty-cent hole than a fifty-cent rose in a ten-cent hole. Of course the days of ten-cent, or even of fifty-cent, roses has long since passed, but the principle holds true; and when one is planting roses that cost from $1.50 to $2.50 each, it becomes even more important. Fortunately the cost of preparing the hole has not increased at the same ratio as the cost of plants!

It will save time and result in a more accurate job if, after the rose bed is prepared, small stakes are set to indicate exactly where each plant is to go.

With a transplanting spade, which has a slightly curved blade and is the handiest tool we have found for this purpose, we dig out a hole about twelve inches deep and twelve inches in diameter. The size will vary somewhat with the dimensions of the root system which is to be placed in it, but it should always be big enough to take the roots without crowding. So far as possible the roots should be allowed to remain in the same position in which they formerly grew.

Operation planting: locations have been marked and generous-sized holes dug.

Next, in the bottom of this hole we place three or four trowelfuls of a special mixture made up as follows:

½ peatmoss; ½ sifted compost or light, rich soil (by *bulk*) to which have been added dehydrated manure (sold under such names as Bovung and Driconure) at the rate of 4 quarts to a bushel, and bone meal at the rate of 2 quarts to a bushel.

We claim no miraculous power for this particular mixture but it is a well-known fact that peatmoss has a particular faculty for stimulating new root growth, and that bone meal and organic fertilizers are less likely than chemical fertilizers to injure any delicate new roots with which they may chance to come in contact. It is very little trouble to prepare such a mixture, and over the years we have

Peatmoss, dehydrated manure, and bone meal are well mixed with soil in the bottom of the hole.

found it of great value not only for roses but in planting most shrubs and perennials and even in setting out annuals.

OPERATION PLANTING

We are now ready to take the plants from their temporary storage and get them into the ground. The first step is to go over them carefully with pruning shears in hand, cutting back any damaged branches or roots to clean, firm wood. Small, twiggy branches are best cut out entirely, or at least cut back to one eye: since they will be of little future use to the plant, the nourishment they use up is largely wasted. Any roots giving evidence of having been torn or broken in the process of digging—a mechanical operation in the nursery fields where they were grown—are best clipped back so that the ends will present clean, fresh cuts that in the soil will callus properly and send out new rootlets. Some growers even brush the cut ends with Rootone, Semesan, or some similar root stimulant, but this refinement is hardly necessary even though each severed root is, in a sense, an underground cutting.

If your rose plants, when received, have rather long tops, harden your heart and cut them back to three to five eyes each, preferably just above an outward pointing bud. If planting must be done in the spring later than the date we have previously recommended, or if top growth has started, cut them back even more severely— to one or two eyes won't hurt—since it is very important to keep the top growth in check until the roots have had a chance to establish themselves. Hybrid Perpetuals and very vigorous Hybrid Teas may well be left somewhat longer.

If possible, avoid planting on a sunny or windy day, especially the latter. In any event the roots should be kept constantly moist. This is readily done by placing them in a pail of water or wrapping them up in a piece of burlap surrounded by moist peat or sphagnum. When a considerable number of plants are being handled, it is advisable to take only a dozen or two at a time from the place where they have been stored.

With planting holes ready and the plants properly trimmed back, we now proceed to the task of actually getting the plants into the ground. In much modern rose literature the planter, at this point, is instructed to build up a neat little cone of soil in the bottom of the hole and place the rose on top of it with the roots extending, "in the position in which they formerly grew," down the sides of the cone. This would be all very well if roses were manufactured and followed a uniform pattern. As a matter of fact they do anything else but! We have tried the cone system but have never found it to be worth while bothering with. Perhaps we had the wrong kind of roses and the wrong kind of soil, but to us it seems that this is

PLATE 14   PLATE 15

Remaking an old Shrub Rose. This Harison's Yellow, grown lanky and lop-sided, was badly in need of reshaping. After flowering, the top was bent over and tied down to induce new growth from near the base. BELOW: *Following spring the top was cut off; new canes produced some flowers. The succeeding year it was again in full bloom, with flowers clear to the ground.*

PLATE 16   PLATE 17

PLATE 18

A typical Pillar Rose. Growing to a height of eight to ten feet, this type—which includes varieties of many different species and hybrids—is often trained to a single post support; but it makes a more pleasing display on a trellis.

PLATE 19

Many Pillars, and even vigorous Climbers, make a most effective show when allowed to cascade in foamy sprays over rocks or down a bank, as we use them in our own garden. And the labor of pruning and spraying is reduced to a minimum! Varieties shown are Orange Everglow (above) and Polaris (below).

PLATE 20

The most important factor for success in the control of pests and diseases is dusting or spraying regularly from early spring until late fall. With "all-purpose" preparations, and equipment for applying them, twenty to thirty minutes a week is sufficient to care for a moderate-sized rose bed. An ordinary farm-size crank duster (shown above) applies an enveloping cloud of dust as rapidly as one can walk. Smaller-sized crank dusters are available. BELOW: *Black spot—most serious of rose diseases—in its initial stage (A); as it spreads and becomes noticeable (B); and in its final stage (C), when leaflets fall to the ground.*

Plants having been set, and soil worked in around roots, holes are filled with water to settle soil and thoroughly moisten peatmoss before balance of soil is filled in and rounded up about base of canes.

just another of those bright garden ideas which frequently get into print somewhere, and then are copied by garden writers the country over.

Our own method is simply to take the plant in one hand and lower it into the hole to a point where the knuckle (the swelling indicating where the rootstock and the top of the plant are joined together) is an inch or two below the general level of the bed; and then, with the other hand (ungloved!) to fill in soil around and between the roots, firming it with the fingers until the plant is self-supported in the desired position.

Next, with trowel or small planting spade, more soil is put in until the hole is one-half to two-thirds full. Then the soil is made really firm around the roots by being pressed with the feet—and don't be afraid to employ all your weight, not even if you are in need of a reduction diet. If the plant can be pulled out, even with a considerable tug, it is not in firm enough.

At this point the hole is filled with water up to the level of the soil, and we proceed with planting the next bush, following the same routine. If the soil is very dry and the water disappears quickly, the holes are filled a second or even a third time. The object is to get the spongy peatmoss or other humus at the bottom of the hole so thoroughly saturated that it will absorb no more, but will serve as a reservoir to supply moisture to the mass of new rootlets which will soon be developing.

Finally the holes are filled level full and this top layer of soil is firmed down lightly but not packed hard, the object being to leave it fairly open so that both water and air can penetrate readily to the roots below.

Hilling Up. The operation described above finishes the planting but there is one more very important step to be taken, whether the planting is being done in late fall or early spring. It consists of heaping up a mound of soil between and around the stems above ground—and the more nearly they can be completely buried the better. In spring planting, soil from the surface of the bed between the plants can be employed for this purpose because as yet it contains no roots. The purpose of this hilling up is to prevent the canes from drying out before growth starts, as may happen in very dry, windy weather. As soon as new growth definitely begins—and this should be watched for carefully—the heaped-up soil is returned to the surface of the bed.

In fall planting, soil for mounding up around the newly set plants should be brought in from some outside source rather than taken from the bed itself because in this case we want to keep the roots as deep as possible so that they will have unfrozen soil in which to develop. But here again the soil mounds are removed when growth starts in the spring. As a rule they can be worked into the surface soil of the beds.

Planting Individual Bushes. The suggestions above apply to the planting of garden-type roses in rose beds. Any lover of roses will want to have a few Climbing Roses, and possibly some Shrub Roses, and here we have a somewhat different problem.

As a rule most Climbing Roses and practically all of the Shrub Roses are considerably tougher than the garden varieties and are much more capable of taking care of themselves *once they have a good start.* This indeed is fortunate because they are very much more likely to be neglected.

However, the italics above are important. We have frequently seen Climbing Roses of the toughest varieties which, even after some years, made very scanty growth, and gave indication that they

(Left) When new growth is well established a surface application of a complete fertilizer is hoed or raked in. (Right) On poor or very light sandy soils this may well be followed with a second application as plants begin to bloom.

would never develop into the irrepressibly vigorous specimens that they should be. So don't take a chance with a Climber or a Shrub by merely hacking out a hole big enough to take the roots and sticking it in to shift for itself.

In planting any rose of this type we always dig out a generous-sized hole two feet or even more in diameter and fifteen to eighteen inches deep. Unless the soil is fairly good it is removed and discarded and the hole refilled with a wheelbarrow load or two of suitable soil. Two or three quarts of a general-purpose fertilizer and

Proof of the pudding. First season's first bloom on a plant treated as shown in preceding photographs.

coarse bone meal are mixed into the six inches or so of soil placed in the bottom of the hole, and after the rest is filled in, the plant is set with the same care and the same treatment that we give a Hybrid Tea in the rose garden. We have often had friends—and good rosarians too—marvel at the growth made by plants so treated, even during the first couple of years.

(Left) Transplanting. Sometimes it is desirable to transplant a rose growing in the garden. If possible secure a ball of soil with the roots. (Right) Tops should be pruned back two thirds or more. (In order to show branch and root structure most of the foliage was removed and soil was shaken from roots.)

In transplanting dormant roses in late fall or very early spring, secure maximum amount of roots; cut top back very severely.

TRANSPLANTING

Often for one reason or another it becomes necessary to transplant a rose bush. While this may be done at any season of the year, even when the plant is in flower, the best time is in late fall or very early spring. The most essential thing is to cut the plant back severely, removing one half to two thirds of the top growth if it is a Bush rose, and considerably more in the case of Shrub Roses and Climbers. This of course is done in order to give the roots a chance to re-establish themselves without having, at the same time, to support a full cargo of branches and foliage.

In addition to cutting back it will be of decided benefit to treat the top growth which is allowed to remain on the plant with Wiltpruf to decrease evaporation. Soil about the roots should be kept moist; and, if the weather is hot or windy, an occasional spraying of the tops during the first two or three weeks after transplanting will be a still further aid in helping the plant to re-establish itself quickly.

During the first season after transplanting it is important to provide particular care in the matter of protecting the tops from possible winter injury, as new growth is less likely to be as thoroughly hardened off as that on long-established plants.

LABELING

As roses should remain for many years—we have lost less than 10% of all varieties set out over a period of eighteen years—and as becoming well acquainted with all the different varieties is no little part of the fun of growing roses, it is well at the outset to provide substantial, long-enduring labels.

The principle desiderata in labels are: legibility, permanence, and inconspicuousness. Of the many types of labels we have tried, the one which seems best to combine these three qualities is that known as Permark. Numerous other types are available. Not all rose growers agree on labels any more than they do on the "best" roses, so trial and error will probably be the only method by which you can determine what label best suits you.

Whatever type of label you employ, put them in *when you plant.*

We say "in" rather than "on" because no label attached to part of the plant will long be satisfactory. Labels attached to the plants when they arrive should be removed as soon as the plants are put in the ground. Left attached, they frequently girdle rapidly growing canes to which they have been secured.

CHAPTER *7*. *Feeding*

Yes, here is the mine of gold and silver, gold medals and silver cups
for the grower of prize Roses; and to all who love them, the best
diet for their health and beauty, the most strengthening tonic for
their weakness, and the surest medicine for disease.

Once your roses have been safely planted, in beds or in
individual holes carefully prepared, you should have no need to
give further thought to the matter of supplying plant food for at least
a year.

There are however, two possible exceptions to this general rule.
The first is when planting has been done in extremely sandy soil
which will not retain all the necessary plant food elements—nitrogen, phosphorus and potassium—even for a single season, without
having losses through leaching. The second is the possibility—fortunately a rare one—that your particular soil is lacking in one of the
trace elements. If so, growth may be checked no matter how well
provisioned with all of the other required foods the rose larder may
be. The trace elements are discussed elsewhere (see pages 181 to 185,
Chapter 13, dealing with rose troubles) so we need not dwell on them
further at this point.

The rose is a shrub, and as with most shrubs, its roots are active
underground even when the top is dormant. For this reason, if you
wish to have not just roses, but the finest roses your soil and climate
can produce, you will need to keep your rose beds provided at all
times with an adequate supply of plant food.

In this connection it is important to remember that fertilizers are
only one factor among several that are essential to vigorous growth.
Maintaining the proper *structure* of the soil is quite as important
as maintaining the nutrients within it.

84

Humus is essential in the maintenance of good soil structure. Like nutrients, humus is in time used up, and must be replaced. Otherwise there will not be a constant reserve supply of moisture available to thirsty roots. Therefore replacing humus—and lime if needed—is the first step in maintaining fertility.

If the natural soil in your rose garden is either too acid or too alkaline (see page 12), it will tend to revert to the same condition and will in time require further applications of lime or of sulphur to maintain it at the required level of acidity. This is particularly true for the first two or three years after planting. The sandier the character of the soil, the more important it is to provide all the additional humus possible.

The method we use to maintain humus is to work into the soil early each spring the residue of the previous season's mulch, taking care to disturb roots as little as possible. This is done when the spring application of fertilizer is made, both humus and plant food being worked into the soil together.

WHEN TO FEED

As the annual growth cycle of the rose plant (page 55) indicates, there are two periods when growth is most active—early spring and early autumn. To make sure that plant foods are available in abundance at these periods, in our latitude, we apply a complete general-purpose fertilizer about March 15 and a second one about July 15. Further south, where the growing season is longer, the first application would be somewhat earlier and the second somewhat later. It is not advisable to apply fertilizer containing nitrogen late in the season because this element particularly stimulates succulent new growth which, if it has not had time gradually to harden off, will be very susceptible to winter injury.

Some rose growers apply fertilizer more frequently than twice during the season. Our experiments not only with roses but with many other plants indicate that "little and often" applications do give increased growth, particularly in sandy soils. Undoubtedly this is one reason why the new system of foliar feeding—discussed later in this chapter—has proved so effective. However, a twice-a-year program will be about all that the busy home gardener can fit into his schedule and it will provide him with excellent roses. Indeed

Time for spring feeding of established plants is immediately after first pruning and removal of winter mulch. Fertilizer is cultivated in and any overwintering weeds are removed, leaving clean, loose surface ready to receive new summer mulch.

many growers get very satisfactory results with the spring feeding alone. We feel, however, that a second application is well worth while, especially as there is ample evidence that continuous vigorous growth makes the plants less susceptible to diseases and more capable of withstanding attacks by insect pests.

WHAT TO FEED

There are all kinds of special rose fertilizers or rose foods on the market—and apparently there are all kinds of rosarians who buy them, for their sales continue year after year. Personally we have always obtained satisfactory results by using a general, all-purpose fertilizer, supplemented by extra nitrogen in the form of nitrate of soda when it seemed to be required; and extra potash in the form of wood ashes, when we have it. We have two fireplaces, and the accumulated residue from many pleasant winter evening fires is reserved for the rose beds and the onion patch, thus benefiting two crops which seem to like wood ashes particularly well. We certainly would not feel, however, that we could not grow roses—or for that matter good onions and leeks—without the benefit of ashes.

A good standard fertilizer for roses, according to many carefully conducted tests, is 6-10-4 (that is, 6% nitrogen, 10% phosphorus, and 4% potassium) for the spring feeding, and 5-10-5 for the summer application. If the formula for a standard all-purpose fertilizer in your vicinity is 5-10-5 or 4-12-4—the two formulas most widely available in different parts of the country—it is an easy matter to increase the nitrogen. The following table shows the amounts of several different materials, quite commonly available, that can be used to add 1% of nitrogen to 100 pounds of a fertilizer mixture.

	Pounds
Ammonium Nitrate (Nitrate of Soda)	6.6
Ammonium Sulfate (Sulfate of Ammonia)	5.
Urea	2.5
Milorganite (organic)	20.

While any of these materials may be mixed in with the fertilizer, often it is easier to apply them separately. To assure even distribution, it is advisable to combine them with at least twice, and preferably more than twice, their own bulk of sand, dry soil, sawdust, or some other "filler" material. The nitrogenous material and the filler of course should be very thoroughly mixed together before being spread.

The usual rate of application for either a 6-10-4 or a 5-10-5 mixture is 3 to 5 pounds per 100 square feet; or approximately 1 pint per 25 square feet or ½ level cupful per plant.

Application. In much rose literature one finds the advice that fertilizer should be applied in a narrow band forming a circle six or eight inches away from the stem. This hardly seems to make sense because once the rose plants have made any considerable amount of growth, the roots will have spread well out into the soil between the plants and in fact will have intermingled with the roots of their neighbors. Furthermore, the greatest quantity of *feeding roots* will be at a considerable distance from the main stem of the plant.

Our own practice is to distribute the fertilizer evenly over the entire surface, but allowing as little as possible of it to fall within six inches of the stem. (See illustration page 86.)

The mulch may be pulled up around the stems while the fertilizer is being put on and then redistributed after the fertilizer has been lightly raked in. Frequently, however, we apply the plant food to the surface of the mulch and depend upon a good thorough watering to carry it down into the soil.

Feeding Individual Plants. Too often individual plants such as Shrub Roses and Climbers, once they are planted, are left to take care of themselves. It is true that most of such roses, when they have become established, are quite capable of making good growth and producing hundreds or even thousands of flowers each season without any attention other than an annual pruning—and frequently not even that. It is equally true however that stronger growth and better blooms can be obtained if the plants are given, even once a year, an additional supply of plant food.

The time of the application, we have found, makes little difference. We aim to apply it any time within a month or two after the rose beds have been attended to. The plant food provides new growth and flowering sprays with some extra nitrogen at a period when they can make use of it, and a reserve for future growth during the summer. Many of the Climbers, particularly those which have any Rambler blood in their ancestry, do not take the usual midsummer rest characteristic of the garden roses but continue the vigorous growth of new shoots and side branches.

The quantity of fertilizer to use per plant will depend upon its size. After the first two or three seasons it may well be increased to a pint or more per plant. In the case of old plants which have reached almost tree-like proportions, it should be applied not just around the stems but in holes twelve inches or more in depth made with a crowbar in a circular area several feet in diameter. A vigorous Climber develops a root system of astounding proportions.

FOLIAR FEEDING

And now we come to one of the most interesting, most discussed, and most argued subjects in the whole field of rose culture—and for that matter, in the cultivation of garden plants in general. This is the practice of applying plant nutrients to the foliage rather than to the roots; and the still more recent idea of using antibiotics, such as streptomycin and Terramycin along with the plant nutrients.

Some of the results which have been achieved seem almost fantastic, but in many cases they have been substantiated by carefully kept records which leave no doubt as to their authenticity. Nevertheless when one recalls such "miracle" discoveries as Vitamin B_1, which was claimed to produce "daffodils as big as saucers," and the various soil conditioners heralded in newspaper advertisements as being the cure-all for soil problems, one hesitates to give this new technique unconditional endorsement.

The amateur rose grower who has done most to get his fellow rosarians interested in foliar feeding, and particularly in foliar feeding combined with antibiotics, is Dr. G. Ellington Jorgenson of Claremont, Iowa. Dr. Jorgenson began experimenting along this new trail in 1950. A brief summary of his experiments and the results he has obtained follows:

Dr. Jorgenson began his experiments with foliar feeding. He wished to use a plant food of high analysis and one containing hormones and vitamins (especially Vitamin B_1) as well as the three main elements and trace elements. He finally decided on the product Ra-Pid-Gro as a complete fertilizer which filled his requirements.

In the spring of 1950 he dipped the roots of two new roses in a solution of this product before planting them, using an untreated bush of the same variety as a check. The two treated bushes were fed every two weeks throughout the growing season with the same solution, foliar feeding only being applied. Their performance was so much ahead of the check plant and of his other roses that he was soon completely convinced of the merits of foliar feeding and extended its use to trees, shrubs, other flowers and to the vegetable garden, where it produced remarkable results.

The foliar-fed roses showed much heavier stems and branches; more new growth; heavier, darker, and cleaner foliage; and blooms which were larger, of better color, and more numerous than those of the other roses.

By 1953 he began applying the nutrient solution to the roots of established roses in early spring before growth had started. He also made root applications of an antibiotic in connection with regular foliar feeding, and was soon convinced that the two procedures were "inseparably linked," when the antibiotic was used together with a foliar nutrient containing Vitamin B_1.

In 1956 he had found that he could successfully add the antibiotic to the nutrient solution instead of applying it to the roots: that the addition of minute quantities of Terramycin, streptomycin (or a combination of both as in Agri-mycin) may produce a varying degree of growth stimulation when used as a supplement to foliar feeding. This variation ranges from the almost imperceptible to almost unbelievable growth patterns (as reported by various observers). There is no direct microbicidal effect from these minute traces of antibiotics, and any disease resistance observed must be regarded, in his opinion, as supplemental to or a part of the general ruggedness and vitality of the superbly well-nourished plants.

He is now working on the theory that pest- and mildew-control chemicals may be added to the foliar nutrient antibiotic solution.

Dr. Jorgenson's simple methods of procedure are as follows:

Dissolve 2 teaspoons of Ra-Pid-Gro (or other complete plant food containing Vitamin B_1, hormones, and other vitamins in addition to the three main elements and trace elements) in 2 gallons of water.

Add 4 milligrams of antibiotic. (Agri-mycin, Agristrep and Phytomycin for use on plants, now available, give specific directions for use.)

A sufficient quantity of this solution is applied to drench the leaves thoroughly, permitting the runoff to soak into the soil for subsequent absorption by the root system.

Dr. Jorgenson emphasizes the importance of (1) using a plant food containing an adequate quantity of Vitamin B_1; (2) applying enough of the *properly blended* plant food solution, to which has been added the *exact* minute quantity of antibiotic, to drench the leaves thoroughly. (Stronger concentrations of the antibiotic may cause temporary damage to the plants.)

The original field and laboratory research work of Dr. Jorgenson has recently been further strengthened by work carried out by Dr. H. B. Tukey of Michigan State College, and testified to by him before the Atomic Energy Commission.

Dr. Tukey used radioactive isotopes in his studies of foliar feeding, and in his testimony he made a number of interesting statements including: (1) that the leaf is ideally constituted to absorb properly concentrated plant nutrients in solution; (2) that such plant foods enter the circulation immediately, by night or by day, and once having entered the sap circulation, move in all directions at the rate of one inch every five minutes, reaching high into the apex and far into the roots. He stated that foliar feeding is an economical procedure since approximately 90% of soluble plant food applied to the leaves is promptly utilized, whereas only about 10% of material applied to the root system is absorbed. It was his belief that foliar feeding also is valuable because it may promptly correct a food deficiency in the plant at a critical period. He pointed out, for example, that when a seed is being formed there is a marked concentration of both magnesium and phosphorus in the area, and that if these substances are unavailable to the plant economy, serious deficiencies may develop to retard growth and yield. In this regard he stated that the various deficiencies may develop by reason of absence of the needed elements in the soil, or soil conditions militating against, and preventing absorption by, the root system. Either of these conditions may be circumvented by foliar feeding.

Our good friend and neighbor Silas Clark, whose roses are one of the main features of his famous Cape Cod garden, began foliar feeding soon after reading Dr. Jorgenson's first article in the 1951 *Rose Annual,* and since then has employed this method of fertilization exclusively. In our sandy soil, the "little and often" method of feeding is most effective. Not only does he give foliar feeding *once each week* throughout the growing season until late summer, but he places in the one solution Ra-Pid-Gro, antibiotic, pesticides, and fungicide. Half an hour spent in his garden will prove to the skeptic that this method has worked for him.

(Ra-Pid-Gro's own recommendation, however, is that foliar feeding with their product, combined with an antibiotic, be applied once every *two* weeks.)

Here is the combination which has proved so effective in Mr. Clark's rose garden:

To each gallon of water used add:

> 4 level teaspoons Ra-Pid-Gro
> ⅛ level teaspoon 15% streptomycin (Pfizer)
> 4 level teaspoons malathion
> 5 level teaspoons methoxychlor (Methocide)
> 5 level teaspoons captan (Orthocide)

This can be applied with a pressure sprayer. Mr. Clark uses a foliar-feeding jar-hose sprayer.*

GIBBERELLIC ACID

Another new material with which Dr. Jorgenson has experimented is gibberellic acid, that magic powder which is being advertised under various trade names as a wonder-growth stimulant.

Dr. Jorgenson found, in treating seventy rose plants throughout last summer, that when used alone it produced erratic, straggly growth of the main stems, which shot up out of all proportion to their neighbors; and produced blooms at unpredictable times.

When he combined the gibberellic acid with foliar-fed plant food, the new growth appeared more balanced and of more normal appearance, and "slightly above-normal numbers of blooms came early." On some plants, the size of the foliage was increased as much as 30% above normal.

Finding the evidence resulting from his experiments so indecisive, Dr. Jorgenson plans to make further tests, but in the meantime can only report results inconclusive, though no permanent injurious effects were noted.

With foliar feeding and the use of new materials such as gibberellic acid, as with other cultural practices like pruning and winter protection, the rose grower should feel his way with some caution before he goes "all out" for any one method. What works best under one set of conditions—climate, soil, temperature, rainfall, and the like—is not necessarily best for another. The rose plant in the color Plate 28 between pages 236–37 was foliar fed; the one in Plate 1 between pages 12–13, by conventional methods.

---

*Since the above was written, extensive tests made at one of the leading Experiment Stations have indicated that applying plant foods to the foliage gives no better results than those obtained from applying the same amounts to the roots.

CHAPTER *8.* *Watering and Mulching*

To win [the Rose lover] must woo, as Jacob wooed Laban's daughter, though drought and frost consume.

These two important items in the successful culture of roses are here considered together because they affect each other and because they both have the same objective—that of providing sufficient moisture to keep the plants at maximum growth and producing the greatest number of the finest flowers.

Among the many factors contributing to the end result of an excellent crop of rose blooms, there is none quite so often underestimated and neglected as that of providing an adequate supply of water; and yet in all the excellent volumes of the *American Rose Annual,* published by the American Rose Society, containing excellent information on almost every phase of rose growing, I do not recall ever having seen an article devoted to this subject. For our own rose garden we would rather have—if the choice were forced upon us—abundant water and too little plant food, than too little water and all the fertilizers that could possibly be applied.

As has been explained previously (page 42), but for the sake of emphasis is repeated here, plant roots can ingest foods from the soil *only when they are in solution.* In all our vast country there are few sections, aside from some parts of the lower southeast and the coastal northwest, where rainfall is sufficient and *sufficiently well distributed,* to assure maximum growth of roses of the several types usually grown in gardens.

HOW MUCH WATER?

To this question, in the very nature of things, there can be no definite answer; first, because the amount of water supplied by rainfall is not a fixed quantity, and second, because there is a very great variation in the capacity of different types of soil to "hold" water once they have absorbed it. The sandy soil of our present garden, even after being fairly well provided with humus, requires at least twice as much water as was needed in our previous location where the soil contained a fair amount of clay.

In unscientific layman's language, it may be said that the soil should be kept, as nearly as possible, constantly moist. The key word here is *constantly,* for both saturated, soaking wet soil on the one hand, and on the other that which is allowed to become so powdery dry that there is the least danger of wilting, interfere with steady, even growth, and lower the plant's resistance to various injurious insects and diseases. Dry surface soil to a depth of an inch or so, but moist in the root zone below it, will cause no damage; but it is a warning signal that the danger line may be near. A wet surface soil, on the contrary, particularly if it is of a fine-grained, clayey character that may interfere with the free penetration of air, is decidedly an obstacle to good growth.

In examining soil to see if water is needed, dig down with a trowel to a depth of at least four or five inches, and be guided by what you find *below* the surface.

How much water the soil needs is a question to which it is difficult to give a specific answer. Perhaps the reply made by an old New England farmer is as good a general rule as any. His advice was "as often as it don't rain." It might be more accurate to say, as often as the soil at a depth of two or three inches begins to feel dry to the touch. This may be once a week or once every other day, according to the type of soil and to *weather conditions,* for low humidity, hot sun, and high winds are all factors, and the combination of the three may suck as much moisture out of the soil in twelve to twenty-four hours as would ordinarily be lost in three days to a week.

The best time of day to water, ordinarily, is fairly early in the morning, for moisture on the foliage during the night, particularly in weather with high humidity, greatly encourages the development of that worst of all rose troubles, black spot.

There are however, occasions when watering in the late afternoon or evening may be advantageous, as when the temperature is moderately low but drying winds and bright sunshine make it difficult to keep the soil sufficiently moist. Under such conditions there will be much less loss of moisture through surface evaporation from water applied late in the day than from that applied in the morning.

METHODS OF WATERING

The one essential thing in watering roses, whether it be a whole garden full of them, a bed or border, or just individual plants, is to apply a sufficient quantity to moisten the soil to a depth of at least six inches, and preferably more. The deeper the penetration of the soil, the smaller will be the percentage of water lost through evaporation, with little or no benefit to the plants.

The method used to apply the water makes little difference, *provided only* that application is not so rapid as to cause runoff, or puddling, or compacting of the surface with the result that a hard crust is formed.

Subirrigation—that is, the application of water directly to the root zone in the soil—is the ideal method. This, however, is very expensive and requires a rather complicated installation and the risk of winter injury to the system, unless it is engineered for perfect drainage of the pipes. The use of the new plastic pipe makes possible a reduction in cost, and the job need not be quite so carefully done since this type will withstand some freezing without bursting. Nevertheless, subirrigation is not for the average amateur grower of roses.

Those who have seen the magnificent display gardens at the Jackson & Perkins Company at Newark, N.Y., may be interested to know that in the subirrigation system used there, the pipes are placed 24 inches deep and 36 inches apart.

Hose-and-nozzle watering is the least satisfactory of all because the water is applied too rapidly, and very unevenly unless carefully done. The soil-soaking type of porous canvas hose has the advantage of applying the water slowly and without getting it on the foliage, but it is cumbersome to use, and unless the ground is perfectly level, results in an uneven distribution of moisture.

Sprinkler-type plastic hose, now in almost universal use by home gardeners, does have the advantage of applying the water evenly if there is sufficient pressure, and slowly enough to get real soil penetration. Its two disadvantages are that in a rose garden it must

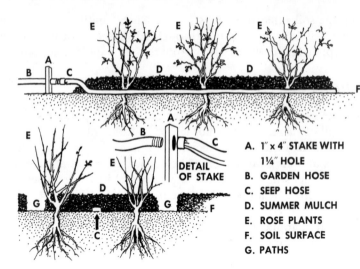

A. 1" x 4" STAKE WITH
   1¼" HOLE
B. GARDEN HOSE
C. SEEP HOSE
D. SUMMER MULCH
E. ROSE PLANTS
F. SOIL SURFACE
G. PATHS

DETAIL OF STAKE

GrayRock Watering System: *Seep hose (C) with perforations turned* down *is run length of each bed. Water is provided from garden hose (B) attached to seep hose through hole in stake (A) at one end of each bed. When each bed has been thoroughly moistened, garden hose is removed. Mulch reduces to a minimum loss of moisture from surface evaporation.*

The perforated hose type of sprinkler applies water in a mistlike spray, evenly and thoroughly, without leaving a muddy, hard-packed surface.

Sprinklers of the oscillating type are the most effective. They apply the water in droplets; and, as they swing from side to side, allow each "wave" to sink into the soil before more water is applied to the same surface. The largest sprinklers of this kind, such as the one illustrated, cover an area 50 to 60 feet square from one position.

be frequently moved; and that as the plants get their full summer growth it is almost impossible to do this. In watering a long, narrow bed or border of roses, of course, these objections do not apply.

The GrayRock method of watering—we call it that because we have never seen it used elsewhere—is both the most efficient and the least time-consuming of any we know that does not involve the installation of underground pipes.

This consists of laying a plastic sprinkler hose, *upside down,* along the center of each bed (4 feet wide) between the two rows of rosebushes. The open end of each hose is held permanently in place, above ground, by a firmly driven, 3-inch-wide stake, with a hole near the top. This hole is just the right size to accept a hose connection.

The lines of sprinkler hose, after being laid out, are covered with the same mulch—in our case pine needles—as that used throughout the rose planting. This remains undisturbed for the entire season. Individual lengths of sprinkler hose should be somewhat longer than the beds so that the ends—which distribute less water than the portion of hose nearer the supply line—can be doubled back along the end of the bed to help equalize the distribution over the entire bed. Water is fed to the sprinkler lines from a regular hose attached to a nearby faucet. When one bed has been thoroughly watered, the feed hose is moved to the next bed and attached to the sprinkler-hose connection.

Examination of the soil the first time the system is used, will indicate how long the water should run on each bed before the feed hose is moved to the next. Usually this requires from one to several hours.

Sprinklers are available in many patterns. There are three distinct types: those which rotate to distribute water in a series of concentric circles; those which oscillate, automatically turning a rainlike curtain of droplets from one side to the other; and the common type, which throws a spray up in the air in the form of an inverted cone to let it fall back, covering a circular area.

We prefer the oscillating type. It applies water to any one spot at short intervals so that it has time to soak in before the next "wave" strikes the same place. This type covers a rectangular area instead of forming a circle, so that when the position of the sprinkler is changed, another complete rectangle is covered. Oscillating sprinklers come in sizes which cover areas of 15 by 20 feet, up to 60 by 60 feet, an area of 3600 square feet.

In very sandy soil, such as is likely to be encountered in seaside or lakeside areas, it may be desirable to set the plants in depressions eighteen inches wide and six to ten inches deep, held in place by circular strips of aluminum or heavy waterproof roofing paper. This is for the purpose of concentrating the application of water to the soil about the roots, which of course should be especially prepared with a very generous proportion of peatmoss or other humus material designed to retain moisture as long as possible.

MULCHING

Good roses can be grown without mulching; but better roses can be grown with much less time and effort if mulching is employed.

Mulching, in simple terms, is covering the soil surface with some material which will be left undisturbed during the growing season, or even through the year. Winter mulching is employed primarily to protect plants from injury by low temperatures. It is applied, normally, after the ground has frozen to a depth of a couple of inches or so. Summer mulching is usually put on from mid-spring to early summer. This is the type with which we are here concerned.

Summer mulching benefits the rose garden in many different ways. Among these are:

In sandy soils that leach rapidly "wells," made of heavy roofing paper and filled with soil containing peatmoss or other humus materials, greatly help to provide an adequate moisture supply.

Conserving moisture by drastically reducing the amount of moisture loss through evaporation from the surface after rain or watering.

Lowering soil temperature; experiments have proved that the soil, under an adequate mulch, is eight to ten degrees cooler than adjacent soil exposed to hot, bright sunshine.

Controlling weeds; while not 100% effective in this respect, mulching frequently eliminates more than 90% of the weeding that would otherwise be required, and the few weeds that do manage to come up through the mulch are easily removed, with the *roots,* by the slightest pull.

Helping to control black spot, the most troublesome of all rose diseases, by preventing the splattering of infected soil particles over the foliage in case of a heavy rain or careless watering.

Enlarging the available root-run, because where the soil between plants must be cultivated or hoed, feeding roots cannot develop in the upper two or three inches, whereas under a mulch they can forage practically up to the surface.

Preventing compacting of the soil surface and thus shutting out the free admission of air, as happens when bare soil between the bushes must be trodden upon in cultivating, spraying, pruning, gathering flowers, etc.

Lessening the danger of damage to new growth from spring frosts; the soil beneath the mulch does not thaw out and warm up so quickly as bare soil and consequently delays the emergence of foliage.

Almost any one of these advantages would make mulching worth while. When you can get them all tied up together in one big economy package, there just is not any doubt about it: if you want to grow the best roses the easiest way—*mulch!*

MATERIALS FOR MULCHING

Over the years we have tried more than a dozen materials for mulching rose beds. The half dozen which we have found most satisfactory are described in the following paragraphs, in the order of our preference for them. The mulch which is most practical for use in a particular section of the country will depend largely upon what is available locally since transportation charges, in the case of mulching materials, constitute a very large percentage of their cost to the user.

Bagasse or shredded sugar cane, widely used as poultry litter under trade names such as Stazdry or Servall is available in most sections of the eastern United States. It is a rather coarse material put up in tightly compressed bales but readily shaken out and made ready for use; it is easily applied, stays put, and lasts through the season and the following winter. On the ground it forms a rather open, porous, springy mat which water penetrates readily even when the surface has become dry. Somewhat objectionably light in color when first applied, it soon darkens to an inconspicuous and not unpleasant dark brown. Or for an immediately pleasing color effect, buckwheat hulls or peatmoss may be spread over it in a layer a half inch or so in thickness.

The essentials of a good mulch for the rose garden are that it should be porous (non-matting), and free from weed seeds. We use pine needles. Many commercial types of mulch are available. These vary in different sections of the country.

Compost. To be of best service in the rose bed, this must be in just the right stage of decomposition, sufficiently far along to have become partly broken down and blended but not yet granular or powdery in texture. Sometimes leaf mold in just the right condition may be gathered from the woods. A compost mulch is an excellent soil conditioner but does not last as long as most of the other materials mentioned here; and it may contain some weed seed. It should be worked into the soil at the end of the season.

Buckwheat Hulls. Where obtainable, these are the easiest of all to apply as they may be poured onto the ground from a basket or bucket and, with a small rake or a stiff broom, spread about

Buckwheat hulls make a neat and attractive-looking mulch, but provide little humus.

to form an even, soil-brown carpet, the most attractive in appearance of all mulches. Water penetrates them readily even when they are dry, and yet, after the first couple of rains or waterings, they will "stay put" even in quite high winds. They last even well into the second season, when the addition of a much lighter application will make the mulch as good as new. They are of little or no fertilizing value in themselves, but plant foods of any type applied to the surface and watered in readily penetrate to the soil below.

Peatmoss. This old stand-by, while it has many excellent qualities and is a perfect soil conditioner, has two serious disadvantages as a mulch for rose beds. If once allowed to become thoroughly dry, it forms a mat that is impenetrable by any ordinary watering or even a heavy rain; and if kept constantly moist, it encourages fibrous root growth at or even above the soil surface.

Birch Chips is a promising new commercial product.

Wood Chips. This material consists of chopped and ground up branches, twigs, and foliage. It is becoming available in many localities at little or no cost, as it is a by-product of street cleaning and public utility maintenance. It makes a coarse, springy mulch of good physical qualities but is not attractive in appearance. Where it is used, extra nitrogen should be applied, as is now the standard practice when sawdust is used either as a soil conditioner or a mulch.

Sawdust, if sufficiently coarse, is excellent but rather unsightly until it has begun to decompose. Where both are available, a base of sawdust with a top layer of pine needles makes an inexpensive mulch which is about as fine as one could desire.

Pine needles alone are used in our own garden, as they are the easiest for us to obtain. (See page 144 for details.)

Other mulches frequently recommended are corncobs, cocoa-bean hulls, mushroom compost, and peanut hulls. Grass clippings, in our experience, have proved unsatisfactory. If applied in a layer thick enough to be effective, they decompose into a slimy mass.

APPLYING MULCHES

All of the materials suggested above are put on in an even layer two to three inches thick, forming a carpet sufficiently dense to leave no areas of exposed soil. It is important to spread the mulch evenly, and care should be exercised to prevent its being packed in closely about the stems at the bases of the plants. Our practice is to keep it at a distance of five or six inches, to make sure of free air circulation at this point, since a soggy mass about the canes during long rainy periods or when the plants must be constantly watered may cause injury. Where fresh wood chips or sawdust are employed, some high nitrogen fertilizer should be applied before the mulch is put on.

Maintaining the mulch is essential if its full benefit is to be realized. Bare or thin spots may develop as the season progresses and so it is well to keep on hand a sufficient supply of the same material to do any patching up that may be needed. Among its other advantages, an edging for rose beds extending two inches or so above the soil level is of great help in holding the mulch in place and maintaining a neat, attractive appearance.

[The Rose grower] must have not only the glowing admiration, the enthusiasm, and the passion, but the tenderness, the thoughtfulness, the reverence, the watchfulness, of love.

In all the literature on roses there is probably no one subject to which more space has been devoted than to that of pruning. The recommendations given by different authorities range all the way from "Don't be a whacker—just leave 'em alone!" to "The harder you cut them, the better your flowers will be." If all the paper upon which *rules* about pruning have been printed could be run through a shredding machine it would make enough paper excelsior to mulch all the rose gardens in the country—and perhaps accomplish just as much in the production of good blooms as it has in books, magazines, and newspapers.

There just is no one general rule that is best for all roses, or even for all roses of any one type, or even for the same rosebush for all seasons and conditions. So instead of starting out with a set of rules for pruning, let us rather attempt to get a general picture of what may be accomplished by pruning, and then adapt our practice to fit objectives and conditions.

What is "pruning"? If we turn to Webster's New International Dictionary we find: "To lop or cut off the superfluous parts, branches, or shoots . . ."

But what *is* superfluous? There is the rub—and until that point can be decided upon, we are completely at sea.

Let's first ask the question: What are we pruning *for*—what do we aim to gain by it?

The answer of course is "better roses." But by this we may mean

104

either a finer show of roses in the garden, or more roses of good quality for cutting, or the finest possible individual blooms—especially if we are interested in competing for prizes at a rose show. Or perhaps we have in mind a combination of all three of these objectives.

As a matter of fact all three are gained by a judicious system of general pruning. It is only in minor details that the methods need be varied in order to accomplish a particular end.

SOIL AND CLIMATE FACTORS

One of the troubles with most of the "general rules for pruning" given in articles and lectures is the failure to take into account the fact that differences in climate and in soil make a very great difference in how and when roses should be pruned.

In the South and along the Pacific coast most rosebushes, and particularly Teas and Hybrid Teas, attain two to three times the size they normally do in the Northeastern or North Central states. Plants grown under particularly favorable conditions with adequate protection from severe winds, and in well-enriched soil or with foliar feeding, often produce fully twice as much growth during a season as the same varieties growing in the same locality in an average soil and in an average exposure. Furthermore they start into growth earlier and continue to make growth later in the season.

The vigor of the individual plant has a great deal to do with the way a rose should be pruned. The aim in all pruning—except where it is desirable to control the shape or habit of growth, as is often the case with climbing roses—should be to produce the most vigorous plant we can grow. If that is done, the flowers will take care of themselves and a generous crop of fine quality blooms will follow as the night the day.

WHAT PRUNING DOES

There are five definite ways in which pruning is of assistance in the growing of better rose plants and, as a result, better rose blooms.

1. The removal of old wood.
2. The removal of surplus growth (page 106).

3. The removal of diseased or injured wood or parts that failed to develop normally.
4. The control of growth—guiding the plant in size, form, or the direction in which we want it to grow.
5. The control of bloom.

More than one, or even all, of these various objectives of pruning may be accomplished at the same time and in one operation. It is important, however, that every clip of the pruning shears be made with only one of these definite objectives in mind. Before you snap the blades shut, ask yourself "Why?"

Now let's take a little closer look at each of these purposes for which we prune.

Removal of old wood, including not only dead wood but canes or branches so old that they neither produce flowering stems themselves nor give rise to vigorous new lateral growths or branches that will bear flowers, helps in two ways. First of all it prevents the waste of such nourishment as would go to these parts if they were left on the plant and conserves this for the development of *new* growth; second it increases to some extent the amount of sunshine, air, and light which can reach the remaining parts of the plant; and also it reduces the chance of the introduction of diseases or plant pests from the old wood to new growth. There is also the matter of good looks, of course, for good roses on a well-groomed plant naturally make a better appearance than the same flowers would on a scraggling and unkempt bush.

Surplus wood differs from old wood in that it may be healthy and vigorous—in fact sometimes too vigorous!—but present in such quantity or in such a location that it is detrimental to the plant as a whole. The reasons for removing it are much the same as those mentioned above in connection with old wood. Dense crisscross growth keeps out sun and air; provides ideal conditions for the development of many diseases and pests; and also makes it much more difficult to do a thorough job of dusting or spraying.

Pruning to Control Growth. Here we have a problem to solve that is quite different from either of the preceding. It concerns not the general health and well-being of the plant, but persuading it to assume the size, form, or position which we may desire. I never think of this type of pruning without recalling an incident which occurred many years ago when, aiming to say something complimentary, I wrote concerning a neighboring orchardist, that he could "do anything with a fruit tree except make it jump through a hoop." Much to my surprise this individual, after having seen the piece in print, stormed into my office and in high Teutonic anger demanded to know what I meant by declaring that he could not make a fruit tree jump through a hoop. I pacified him as best I could and there the matter ended until nearly two years later, when he stopped again and asked me to get into his car because he had something he wished to show me. At his home he displayed with pride both a peach and an apple tree, each of which had several branches growing in the form of complete and very accurate circles!

There is no particular reason that I can think of why one should wish to train a rose in the form of a hoop but *Rosa* is particularly amenable to directional guidance, and this is especially true of the climbing forms; yet one seldom sees in a rose garden or planting around the home instances in which advantage has been taken of this fact.

The illustrations on pages 156 and 157 show examples of what may be done in leading a rose where you wish it to go.

Another type of pruning to control growth is that in which the desire is to reshape or rebuild the entire plant. The Shrub Roses, for instance, tend to grow tall and leggy but can readily be reshaped or entirely rebuilt from the ground up. The remaking of an old bush of Harison's Yellow in our own garden, (Plates 14–17 between pages 76–77) shows what can be done in a case of this kind.

In pruning to control growth, advantage is taken of what the botanists speak of as "apical dominance," i.e., the tendency of the top bud or eye on a branch or a shoot of a plant to make the most vigorous growth. The direction which new growth will take may be quite accurately controlled by selecting a bud which points in the direction one wants new growth to go. This, in combination with tying a branch or a shoot, at least temporarily, in the position you would like it to assume, makes it possible to persuade your rose plant to do exactly what you want it to do, even to jumping through a hoop!

Pruning to control bloom is of two distinct types: first, such treatment as may be given the plant as a whole; and second, the removal of flower buds. While the latter is, in a sense, a form of pruning, it may more accurately be referred to as disbudding, and as such is treated separately (see page 223).

Pruning may be employed to a large extent to control the quantity of bloom or number of flowers which a plant will produce; the length of the stems of individual blooms; and to a limited degree, the time of bloom, making it possible to have flowers spaced more evenly during the season instead of appearing in one big burst in June and another in autumn. This may mean sacrificing some of the early blossoms (when there are often more of them than you know what to do with) for the sake of having more during the period when they usually are scarce.

TYPES OF PRUNING

Speaking now of the garden or bush roses—Hybrid Teas, Floribundas, Grandifloras, Teas, and the like—garden literature is replete with arguments for and against "high pruning," "medium pruning," and "close pruning"; and there are, of course, those who advocate no pruning at all or "the less pruning the better." While there are no definitive definitions of these terms, high pruning implies cutting the canes back to a height of 2½ to 4 feet; medium or moderate pruning, to 12 to 18 inches; and close or hard pruning, to 6 to 12 inches.

Another way of attempting to visualize the difference between high, medium, and close pruning is to consider the number of growth buds or "eyes" left on the plant. In some respects this gives a more accurate picture because the normal height of individual varieties varies greatly and also because the length of the joints or internodes (between the eyes) varies greatly even in the same variety according to differences in climate, soil, and growing conditions. In general it may be said that a well-established, vigorous bush which has come through the winter with uninjured canes 3 feet or more in height may be considered high pruned if about 15 to 20 eyes are left on each cane; moderately pruned if 6 to 8 eyes are left; and closely pruned if only 2 or 3 eyes are left per cane.

An even simpler, but less accurate, method is to say that in high pruning about one third of the growth is removed; in moderate pruning about one half; and in low pruning at least two thirds.

Plant with new growth just beginning.

Pruned high.

Pruned moderately.

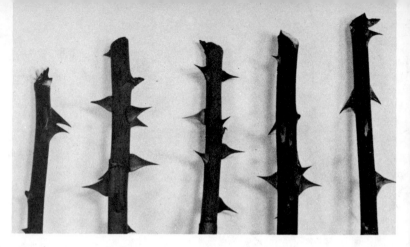

Pruning cuts: (1) ragged, made with dull shears; (2) too far above bud; (3) too close to bud; (4) too slanting; (5) right—correct slant, and about ¼ inch above bud.

HOW TO PRUNE

Concerning the technique of pruning—the mechanical details of just how the job should be done—there exists among the experts much more unanimity of opinion than in regard to how much or how little. As with any technique, however, it takes practice to make perfect, and so if the beginner can find an old rosebush somewhere on which to do some experimental cutting, he should take

Results of different types of cuts: (1) ragged cut has failed to heal; (2) too long stub has begun to die back; (3) cut too close to bud has left weakly attached new growth which has broken off; (4) correctly made cut has resulted in vigorous new shoot, firmly anchored to old cane.

advantage of the opportunity. The two basic essentials in rose pruning are:

1. Have an absolutely clean, sharp cutting instrument.
2. Cut just above an eye or bud.

That certainly sounds simple enough and yet it is remarkable how often, in going through a rose garden or looking at an individual rose plant or climbing rose, one can find ragged cuts with bruised or jagged bark, giving an open invitation to disease or decay to set in; or a long stub above the eye which has already begun to shrivel and die back.

Most of the pruning required in taking care of roses, particularly of the types grown in gardens, is done with ordinary hand pruning shears. For Climbers, and for very large old canes of Hybrid Teas and Bush roses, it often is necessary to employ long-handled pruning shears, or a keyhole saw. The pruning knife, too, occasionally comes into play, especially for the cleaning up of rough cuts. These tools are described in detail and illustrated on page 128.

In the spring pruning of garden roses (which is by far the most important pruning job of the year), whether the pruning is high, medium, or low, cuts should be made just above an outward-pointing eye on canes which are to be retained. "Just above" means about as close as you can get without actually cutting into the eye. This will leave a stub above the eye about ¼ inch long. The cut should be made on a slant, at an angle of about 30°, with the upper edge of the cut just above the eye.

The object in cutting just above an outward-pointing bud is to get a spreading, open-centered bush. (See illustration page 118.) The advantages of having such a plant are that the sun can readily reach all parts of it and a free circulation of air is possible—important factors both in the production of perfect flowers and in minimizing the danger of injury from insects and diseases. It is not always possible, however, to find an eye just where you would like to have it, and in such instances the grower must decide whether it is better to remove more of the cane than he would like to and cut above a less vigorous eye further down the stem, or to select a more vigorous one that does not point in just the direction that he would like the growth to take. The choice is not a matter of too great importance because future pruning will make it possible to avoid the thing which we do not want—a bush with thick, tangled growth at the center.

Removing Old Wood. The suggestions given above apply principally to garden-type roses in fairly cool sections, where winters are severe enough to kill back the tops at least part way so that nature does a large part of the gardener's pruning for him. There are other types of roses, such as Climbers and Shrub roses, however; and in warmer climates even the Hybrid Teas and Teas that grow to proportions which to northern gardeners seem almost incredible. With all of these the rose grower's pruning problems differ somewhat from those encountered in northern gardens.

The finest roses and roses in the greatest quantity are always produced on vigorous new growth. Hence, where dead, dying, and merely surplus wood accumulates, its removal must be considered if the rose plants are to put on their best possible performance. It is true that one often sees old and neglected plants, which for years have not seen so much as a glint of sunshine reflected from pruning shears or pruning saw, making a marvelous display. But for the best showing year after year, some attention to pruning is essential.

The first step in pruning such roses is to cut out all dead wood at the base; and the next to cut out, also clear to the ground, old canes which, while they may still be alive, have ceased to throw out vigorous laterals. Such wood merely draws upon the strength of the plant without giving any adequate return.

Have no worry about cutting out too much of such old or tired wood. I recall two occurrences which would have eliminated any doubt that I might have retained on this point. One happened many years ago when I was visiting a relative in New Jersey who owned a rose garden of which she was very proud. She confessed, however, that for the past couple of years, despite generous feeding and watering, the plants had failed to flower as well as formerly. She asked if I would prune them for her and presented me with some nice shiny new pruning shears which her daughters had given her for Christmas. Fortunately she was away at a bridge party when I undertook the job. What I found on that windy March afternoon was a complete jungle of vigorous plants that had received practically no cutting back for years. I decided that the only thing to do was to be ruthless. And I was, ending up with some neat beds of stubs few of which were over fifteen or eighteen inches high, and a pile of "brush" which towered above the garden fence. When the lady returned and went out to look at what I had done she burst into tears and wailed that I had completely ruined her beautiful rose garden; and she could hardly bring herself to speak to me during the rest of my visit. However on one June morning I received a long distance telephone call from her saying that her roses had never been so bountiful or so beautiful, and she was filled with apologies that she had so mistrusted me.

The other occasion was still more illuminating. This had to do with a long row of climbing and trailing roses which bounded one side of our former home at West Nyack, New York. They had been allowed to run at will and had formed a fence-high thicket which for several years had had very little pruning. One late spring day on my return from the city, my good wife—the coauthor of this book —met me at the station with tears in her eyes and informed me that something terrible had happened: she had started a grass fire which had got out of control and had burned fiercely in dry leaves and dead weeds along our row of big boulders, completely killing all of the Climbers, which were then well out in leaf. Not one cane survived, and we wrote them off as a complete loss. Fortunately we were too busy to dig them up, for the stubs sent up new canes, and two seasons later we had as fine a display as ever. I would not advise such drastic treatment as general practice but it just goes to show that you can't keep a good rose down—at least not by pruning alone.

Protecting Pruning Cuts. Some rose experts make quite a point of coating the cuts made by pruning with tree-pruning paint or orange shellac in order to protect the cut ends from fungi or stem borers. Except in the cutting of quite large canes—one-half inch or more in diameter—we never bother to protect the cut ends. When we have had occasion to we have found grafting wax easy to use, and it lasts almost indefinitely. A dab of it may be applied with a small, flat stick or with the fingers if they are first smeared with Quickee, a hand cleaner which prevents the wax, about the stickiest material you ever encountered, from adhering to them.

Since there is almost always some diseased wood removed in pruning, it is advisable to burn all of the clippings. A flat, open basket, of the type known as a strawberry-picking basket, carried along as one does the work, makes a convenient receptacle for moderate-sized clippings. Keeping the clippings gathered up is worth while, quite aside from its value as a sanitary measure, because any of them left on the ground will be a nuisance when one is working around the plants later on, cultivating, applying a mulch, or cutting flowers.

WHEN TO PRUNE

While the pruning of roses may be done at any time—and in fact should be a fairly continuous operation—there are certain seasons when the main job of pruning is best undertaken. This varies with climatic and growth conditions and also with the type of rose to be pruned. Garden roses such as Hybrid Teas and Floribundas, once established, receive their principal pruning early in the spring as soon as new growth has started sufficiently to indicate to what extent the tops have been killed back during winter and which eyes show signs of most vigor and therefore should be retained. Calendarwise spring will vary all the way from mid-January in the far South to mid-April in cold northern regions.

Following this first pruning it may then be well to go over the plants a second time, after the first big burst of bloom is over, to reshape them and to remove weak lateral growths that show little sign of producing flowers later on and merely overcrowd the centers of the plants.

Again in late autumn, especially in northern sections where near-zero temperatures and high winds are to be expected, another general pruning is desirable. At this time long canes should be headed back about one third. Chances are that these long growths would be killed back anyway during the winter, and their being blown about by heavy winds tends to loosen the roots in the soil.

Often, too, late in the summer, some varieties tend to send up very tall, candelabra-like growths with a burst of bloom—if Jack Frost doesn't get his icy fingers on them first—at the very tops. These should be cut back two thirds or even close to the ground. (See page 115.)

Climbers. Climbing roses of various types form the next most important group. In contrast with the garden roses, they generally

Abnormal "candelabra" growths like the one shown here should be discouraged. (This plant died during the winter following its late autumn burst of bloom.)

receive their most important pruning *after* they have flowered instead of before flowering.

Among the Climbers, of course, there are several quite distinct types. (See page 282.) Of these the first to become really popular were the Ramblers, starting with Crimson Rambler and followed by Dorothy Perkins, American Pillar, and many others, few of which are to be seen today except along the New England coast, where they are not subject to the blighting mildew to which they were subject in other sections. As the Ramblers bloom on one-year-old wood, the time for pruning them is immediately after flowering, in late June or July.

Large-flowered Climbers, with their very mixed ancestry and habit of growth of different varieties correspondingly varied, have no uniformly best time for the main pruning. In general they should be given a "once over lightly" pruning job in early spring (when the garden roses are being pruned) for the removal of dead, broken, or diseased wood, or to control shape; and a heavier pruning just after the first main blooming period.

Shrub Roses, which include species and varieties usually grown as individual plants, and also roses used for hedges—a purpose for which many of the taller-growing Floribundas are ideally suited— may be given their main pruning either in early spring or in late fall. With these the shape and vigor of the plant is usually quite as important as the production of individual blooms or even more so. As with most shrubs pruning can be done any time the plant is free of foliage so that one is best able to see what wood should be removed.

PRUNING HYBRID TEAS AND FLORIBUNDAS

The beginner with roses will soon come to realize that with each of the several types of roses there is some difference as to just what kind of pruning should be done as well as when it should be done. Some general suggestions on this point follow.

In general these two groups will require more pruning than any of the others. This is especially true if one desires to produce the finest possible individual roses rather than the greatest mass display. Many gardeners, of course, prefer a happy medium, and the following suggestions are aimed at procuring that result.

First Year. Forget about "the dozens and dozens of wonderful big roses by June 15 that you may have heard or seen promised in radio or newspaper advertising. A rosebush is or should be a long-term investment, and don't expect long-term dividends in a few short weeks.

The first pruning to be done, of course, is that given the plant when it is set out, as already described in the chapter on Planting. (See page 76.) Following this, any canes which may fail to begin to produce vigorous side shoots should be cut back to clean, live wood. Don't be alarmed if you find a few which have to be cut back clear to the base of the plant.

During the first burst of bloom, cut off fading flowers promptly. In fact it is better to cut them back to the second or third leaf on the stem as soon as they have developed sufficiently—that is, when they are showing plenty of color—and let them open indoors.

After the first flowering period it is well to look over the plants critically, not only to remove weak lateral growths that give no promise of ever amounting to much, but also to plan the directions which new growths will take by cutting above eyes which point outward, or toward an empty space within the plant where additional growth would be desirable.

Fall pruning the first season should be restricted to cutting back the taller canes moderately, as previously described. This is particularly true of varieties whose winter hardiness, under your own particular growing conditions, is still an unknown quantity.

Second Year. Early spring pruning will follow the suggestions given and illustrated on page 109. Naturally there will be very much more wood to be removed than there was the first season if the plant has made normal growth.

Begin by cutting out all dead or diseased canes or laterals back to live wood—that is, wood in which the underbark or cambium is still green and the pith white. When this has been done, examine the plant carefully for any signs of disease such as stem canker, or for insect injury.

Next comes the shaping of the plant. You will have to decide whether you are going to prune high, medium, or low—as illustrated on page 109. In general the more vigorous a bush is, the less pruning it will require *in proportion to its size.* If there are many laterals growing toward the center of the plant, some of these should be removed or cut back to an outward-pointing eye. As new growth progresses—the second spring it will begin considerably earlier and develop much more rapidly than it did the first spring after planting—and the first flower buds begin to show, there will occasionally be some snipping required here and there to prevent overcrowding in certain areas of the plant and to encourage clean, straight flower stems. The latter are particularly important if one is planning to have blooms for the local rose show. (See page 221.)

Some gardeners make a practice of carrying a pair of pocket-size pruning shears with them whenever they are working about their plants—cultivating, weeding, applying mulch, etc.—but it is our ex-

(Left) Hybrid Tea plant. (Right) Pruned moderately, to outward-pointing stems and buds that will form an open-centered plant.

perience that the job can be done more thoroughly and in less time if one makes a special pruning expedition.

Pruning by Disbudding. We now come to a type of pruning we have not heretofore stressed, that of *preventing* unwanted growth instead of removing it after it has been made. This should not be confused with the type of disbudding that is done to procure better individual blooms, which is discussed in the chapter on Rose Shows. It refers to the removal of growth buds in the leaf axils by rubbing them off when they have attained the length of a half inch or so. This method has the advantage not only of being quicker and easier, but also of saving the sap food and energy wasted in developing growth that is merely to be removed by the pruning shears later on. As someone has remarked, the rose grower's best pruning shears are his thumb and forefinger.

The after-bloom or midsummer pruning the second year will be much the same as that for the first except that there will be considerable more of it to do. Keep in mind that the period from mid-June or late June to mid-August or early September (it varies from season to season as well as from locality to locality) is the worst time for roses during their entire long growing season. Temperatures in the upper eighties or above, a mercilessly hot, beating sun, and drying winds will tend to frustrate their efforts to produce bloom; and such flowers as do develop open too fast, lose their color or "blue" so that it is often almost impossible to recognize even well-known varieties, and drop their petals quickly. Under such

(Left) Floribunda; new growth after low pruning. (Right) Same plant in bloom.

conditions it is mere folly to attempt to force the plants to continuous bloom. One's efforts in the rose garden during this period should be spent in the attempt to build up plants that will be as well prepared as possible to take advantage of cooler and more moist autumn weather when it does arrive.

To this end, the midsummer pruning in general should be a repetition of spring pruning except that it is much less severe, the plants being kept "high." Such flowers as do develop will give most satisfaction if cut when they *begin* to open and allowed to unfold indoors, where they will be of better color and last much longer. The spraying or dusting program, however, should be kept up religiously for there is no surer way to have a poor autumn display than to allow black spot or other diseases or pests to defoliate the plants.

Fall pruning the second year will be a repetition of that of the first year, but naturally there will be much more wood to remove, and by this time the characteristics of individual varieties will be more manifest.

Pruning Established Plants. Pruning the third year and thereafter will be much the same as for the second year except that by this time there will be old wood that has outlived its usefulness, even if it is not actually dead, to be cut back to the base.

Chief Differences in Pruning of Hybrid Teas and Floribundas. Insofar as pruning is concerned, Floribundas differ from the Hybrid Teas chiefly in that they tend to send up more canes from the base; and also, since the flowers are borne in large clusters, much more

*Grandiflora (Buccaneer)
pruned high.*

small, twiggy growth. The same is true, to an even greater extent, of the Polyanthas—one of the parents of the Floribunda type.

In spring pruning, therefore, there will be considerably more wood to be removed. For the best show of flowers not more than three to five stems should be left to form the frame of the plant. Don't be afraid of overdoing it. The plant illustrated on page 119 is a Floribunda that was pruned low the second spring after planting.

PRUNING TEA ROSES

Tea Roses, on the contrary, require the least pruning of any of the garden types, particularly in sections where winters are sufficiently mild to allow the tops to come through with little killing back. In colder sections Dame Nature is apt to take over and do the rosarian's pruning job, so far as the Teas are concerned, leaving him no alternative but to cut back to such live wood as may be left. And in really cold climates with temperatures frequently touching zero or below, unless the plants are given very careful winter pro-

Hybrid Perpetual: an old plant, moderately pruned.

tection, she will do a complete job of it and leave him nothing to do but to remove the dead roots.

In mild climates where the Teas can make their natural growth, all of the old wood is left until the plants become so overcrowded that it becomes necessary to cut out some of the overmature canes at ground level. Most of the new growth is in the form of laterals or side shoots from old canes and not—as is the case with most of the other garden types—at or near the base of the plant. In many old southern gardens, such as the very delightful one of the Hill sisters at Lynnhaven, Virginia, we have frequently seen Teas, shoulder-high or higher, loaded with glorious blooms, which apparently had had little or no pruning for years.

PRUNING HYBRID PERPETUALS

Here we have a horse—or rather a rose—of another color, for although these too, like the Teas, include many varieties which will attain great height, they flower best on wood that is one year old.

Second or third year growth can be cut out, three to five of the previous season's growths being retained, and these topped back to three or four feet.

The robust-growing Hybrid Perpetual varieties, such as that glorious old-timer Frau Karl Druschki, make excellent Pillar or Trellis Roses, in which case they will require very little pruning except such as is needed to make room for new canes.

PRUNING SHRUB ROSES AND HEDGES

Here the pruning problem is not so much determined by the character and habit of growth of the plant itself as it is by the desirability of making the plant assume and maintain the form we want it to. Many different types of roses are suitable for use either as individual shrubs or for making attractive hedges. In each group, of course, there are certain varieties which lend themselves better than others for these specific purposes. A number of these are mentioned in The Rose Grower's Rose Finder, page 303.

As with other shrubs, Shrub Roses appear at their best when allowed to grow naturally, pruning being confined, for the most part, to the removal of old wood. A rose kept clipped to a formal shape is no more graceful and attractive than a forsythia or a spiraea that has been given a crew haircut by some ignorant itinerant "landscape gardener."

Some types of Shrub Roses, such as *R. rugosa* and *R. spinosissima* and their hybrids, spread by surface or underground suckers and form clumps that soon become thickets. With these it is necessary to do persistent pruning unless one secures plants that have been budded on some other stock. In planting these, of course, the union or knuckle should be kept well above the soil surface.

There are others which do not spread but which tend to grow taller year after year, becoming leggy and scraggly, with most of the blooms, in increasing numbers, borne at the tops of the plants. *R. Hugonis* and that old but still very worth-while favorite, Harison's Yellow, which still is frequently to be seen in country dooryards or even around the abandoned ruins of old farmhouses, may be rejuvenated if the tall cane or canes are bent over and fastened down to induce the growth of vigorous new shoots from the base of the plant. An example of such an operation, performed in our own garden, is shown in Plates 14–17 between pages 76–77.

Roses for Hedges. Many species and varieties of roses serve excellently as hedge material. The important thing is to select from the many available one which in its natural growth will come nearest to giving you the type of hedge you wish. If you succeed in doing that, you will need to do very little pruning. It would be worse than senseless, of course, to set out a variety that normally would grow five or six feet tall where you wanted a three-foot hedge. A number of roses well suited for hedge plantings are suggested in the Rose Finder.

The kind and the amount of pruning to be given a rose hedge will depend largely upon whether one's prime objective is to get a neat and effective hedge, or an abundance of bloom. If the former, pruning will have to be more or less continuous, with the sacrifice of much new growth that would have produced bloom; if the latter, the plants must be given more latitude in following their natural habit of growth. In either case, after the second or third year, there should be the annual removal of some of the old wood, cut back to the ground, or just above it, to encourage new growth from the bases of the plants.

MINIATURES OR BABY ROSES

These little darlings, which are truly very minute forms of Hybrid Teas and Floribundas, are pruned in exactly the same way as their standard-sized relatives. After a burst of bloom, moderate pruning just above outward-pointing eyes sets the tiny plants on the road to shapely form and their next monthly blooming period. As they are inclined to produce less lush growth than regular garden varieties, the task is a light one. A few varieties, like Gold Star, tend to throw up very tall, erect canes which must be kept in check by rather severe pruning, but most of them are inclined rather to be low and spreading so that the removal of dead flowers can easily be combined with the necessary pruning back of branches.

The removal of overmature wood from the centers of the plants any time they are dormant will help to keep them in good form.

PRUNING CLIMBING ROSES

The pruning of climbing roses presents some problems not encountered with the bush types; and like the bush types they cannot all be handled in the same way because they include several quite distinct groups: the Ramblers, with dense clusters of small flowers; the modern Large-flowered Climbers, of mixed ancestry, many of which, unlike the Ramblers, bloom repeatedly throughout the season; climbing forms of Hybrid Teas; and climbing forms of Floribundas and Polyanthas.

Ramblers. Typical of these are the old Crimson Rambler and Dorothy Perkins and such newer ones as Chevy Chase and Torch. The Ramblers bloom on one-year-old canes. To make the best showing they should be pruned each year *immediately after flowering,* the old wood (which has just flowered) being cut clear back to the ground so that vigorous new wood, starting from the base of the plant, may take over to produce next year's bloom. If pruning is delayed even for a short time, the new canes quickly become entangled with the old, and the job of pruning is made infinitely more difficult. In any event, if the plants have been secured to supports, pruning is not easy. Cutting the old canes into several pieces and then pulling them down rather than out is advised for any gardener with high blood pressure. After removal of old canes, the new ones should be trained or tied to supports as they grow.

The Large-flowered Climbers. Of these there are two types or groups: those which, like the Ramblers, flower but once and are through for the season; and the "Repeaters," those which flower intermittently after the big June show, often ending up with quite a fine display in autumn in much the manner of the Hybrid Teas and Floribundas. A few recently introduced varieties are bettering this generalization by giving continuous bloom throughout the season. A list of some of the best of these may be found in the Rose Finder.

The once-blooming type—varieties such as Thor, City of York, and Silver Moon—need no pruning the first year except removing of the old flower heads after blooming, and cutting back of the stems to two to five eyes. The first concern must be to get a sturdy plant established.

To keep vigorous Large-flowered Climbers—such as Orange Everglow—flowering freely, oldest canes are cut back to the ground once every three or four years.

After the second, or more often the third year will be time enough to consider removing some of the older canes during spring pruning, if this seems necessary to keep the plant within bounds—that is, within the space you would like it to occupy. Climbers of this type, in contrast with the Ramblers, make very little new growth from the base of the plant, but form main canes that are almost like small tree trunks and send out laterals; these in turn send out sub-laterals, on which the flowers are produced. After each burst of bloom these blooming laterals are cut back to two or three eyes.

The really everblooming hardy Climbers, that is, Climbers which flower constantly and persistently as do many of our garden or bush roses, have been a long-sought goal that at last gives promise of being realized. In addition to the group of Large-flowered Climbers which bloom intermittently throughout the season, and which for greater accuracy should be termed "Repeaters," there is the famous variety Dr. J. H. Nicolas, which produces clusters of very large, double, globular rose-pink flowers almost continuously; and the new All America Rose Selections Award Winner, Golden Showers, which blooms constantly but is more accurately a Pillar.

In pruning, the Repeaters and Everbloomers receive treatment somewhat different from that accorded the Once-bloomers. In the first place most of them are less winter-hardy than the Once-bloomers, and therefore at spring pruning time there is likely to be considerable winter-killed terminal growth to be cut out. Faded flowers are pruned away, leaving three or four eyes on the flower-bearing sublateral. The next blooms will then be produced on shoots which start from the last eye. Neglect of this practice may lessen but certainly will not prevent recurrent bloom. The great arch of New Dawn Roses which was a much-admired feature in our old GrayRock garden was too massive for such pruning and flourished from year to year with little more attention than the removal of dead wood and the heading back of too rampant new growths.

Climbing Types of Garden Roses. In addition to the several types of real Climbers above mentioned, there are also the climbing forms of many garden roses. These are not the result of hybridizing but are natural sports or "breaks" which, when propagated, retain the tendency to climb. Most of them attain only moderate height and are better described as Pillar Roses than as Climbers. (There are a few exceptions to this rule, however, such as Climbing Peace, which easily reaches twelve feet or more.) This group includes many Hybrid Teas such as Climbing Crimson Glory and Climbing Etoile de Hollande; and also Floribundas such as Climbing Pinocchio and Climbing Goldilocks.

All of these require but moderate pruning, especially during the first two or three years while they are getting established. If you wish to gather flowers during this period, cut clusters, not sprays, leaving at least two eyes on each stem. Long, arching sprays are wonderful for house decoration but each one you take sacrifices future bloom.

For the rest these roses are treated much like their prototypes: in spring the removal of the tops of canes that may have died back during the winter and the occasional cutting out of old wood to make room for new growth. In removing faded flowers, leave a couple of eyes on each stem.

Trailers and Creepers. These include a somewhat heterogeneous collection of varied ancestry, all having in common two characteristics: the formation of long, willowy growths and the ability to withstand a great deal of neglect and abuse. Allowed to sprawl at will over a bank or a stone wall, they demand no attention whatever, although an occasional cutting and tearing out of some of the older growths—no job for a lady with nylon stockings!—will help to maintain an even mass of bloom. If grown on a fence or other low support, they will need some training and an occasional pruning to remove very old wood and to make the new growths go where you wish them to.

EQUIPMENT FOR PRUNING

Whether the job of rose pruning turns out to be an interesting and rather pleasant garden chore or becomes an unpleasant Herculean task will depend to a very great extent upon whether the tools used for pruning are adequate and kept sharp or are of mediocre quality and allowed to get dull.

The three most essential tools are pruning shears, long-handled pruners or loppers, and a sharp-pointed pruning saw or ordinary keyhole saw. (The usual type of pruning saw with a wide curved blade is not suitable for performing many of the cuts which will be required in removing old wood without danger of injuring the bark of adjoining live wood.) Almost every gardener possesses a pruning knife for this purpose and no other—and if he doesn't he should.

We also have found extremely useful the long-handled flower-cutting shears operated by a handle at the base of a fifteen-inch rod. While this is not strictly a pruning tool, its primary purpose being flower cutting, it is an extremely useful instrument for removing dead blooms from Climbers, and in other hard-to-get-at places, and for doing light pruning—stems up to a quarter of an inch in thickness. It is also extremely handy for removing cut sections of old or dead wood since the pressure on the blade can be so regulated as to hold and pull out a severed piece without cutting through it.

Pruning Shears are of two types: those which really shear, having two blades which pass each other like those of a pair of scissors; and the "anvil" type with but one cutting blade closing down upon a flat anvil made of bronze. Some gardeners prefer one type, some the other. We make use of both, finding the anvil cutters more convenient for removing dead or hard old canes of considerable size, and the shearing type—in some circles you will lose face unless you refer to them as "secateurs"—for removing smaller wood and particularly for cutting close to a bud. The most convenient shears

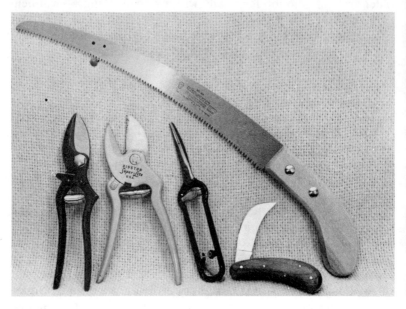

Sharp pruning tools save time and temper, and make possible more and better blooms. (For source, see page 324.)

to carry about, for general garden work, is the new Disston Super-Lite—really feather weight.

If you grow many roses and particularly if you do much exhibiting, you will find it convenient also to have a pair of narrow, sharp pointed shears of the "thinning" or "close-bud" pattern for getting into difficult places and for disbudding.

Pruning saws also are made in many designs. If you have many roses and like to do a careful job of pruning, you will want, in addition to a regular garden pruning saw with a wide blade and fairly coarse teeth, a smaller one tapering to a narrow point, and with peg or needle-point teeth, like that illustrated above.

Lopping shears you will find essential if you have much heavy pruning to do, as will be the case if you grow many climbing roses, bush roses, or Hybrid Perpetuals. Our preference is the type with all-steel handles which are very light in weight, easy to use, and practically indestructible.

Pruning knives come in so many shapes and sizes that you can, if you wish, acquire a whole collection of them. If you have but one, keep it for pruning, and use it for nothing else. We have found the Kunde or standard pruning pattern, with a curved handle and a curved blade terminating in a sharply hooked point, to be the most useful. It cuts as you draw it toward you. This is also made with a stationary blade. Another very useful type is the lightweight, hollow-handled aluminum knife which takes safety-razor-type blades that can be replaced in a few seconds.

Pruning tools make pruning much easier and also save bruised bark and bruised tempers if they are kept razor-sharp. For this purpose keep in your pruning kit, along with the pruning tools we have been discussing, a small carborundum sharpening stone such as that shown on page 215.

CHAPTER *10.* *Winter Protection*

> *[The Rosarian] is loyal and devoted; . . . not only the first upon a summer's morning to gaze admiringly on glowing charms, but the first, when leaves fall and winds are chill, to protect against cruel frost.*

Next to pruning, the most controversial subject in connection with growing roses is winter protection. There are those who believe that "the less protection the better," and act accordingly; others who go to the most painstaking extremes, mounding up soil about bush roses until only their multiple noses protrude, and disengaging climbers from their supports in order to peg them down and wrap them up as though in preparation for a trip through Siberia, or even going to the extreme of actually burying them alive.

The very first rule to learn about winter protection is that there can be no rules for it. There are too many variable factors involved; and even these may change from year to year and season to season. Take, for instance, the matter of winter hardiness in any particular variety. This will vary with the way the plant has been fertilized, the weather during the fall before winter sets in, the amount of snowfall, or lack of it; and the micro-climate (local protection from wind, air drainage, etc. (see page 29) in which it is growing.

Furthermore, a good many rose growers, including the authors of this book, believe that *cold,* as indicated by thermometer readings, is not nearly so decisive a factor in winter injury as it was formerly thought to be; and that alternate freezing and thawing, and exposure to wind, are much more important than was formerly supposed.

130

So before deciding just what should be done in the way of winter protection, isn't it logical to investigate:

1. What makes roses susceptible to winter injury?
2. How do winter conditions result in injury to rose plants?

Only when this has been done can we arrive at some sort of logical basis for methods of protecting them.

CAUSES OF WINTER INJURY

The primary cause of winter injury to roses lies within the plants themselves. Our native roses and the majority of other wild species are completely winter hardy, some of them even to arctic conditions.

Take a look at our native species, *Rosa carolina* for instance. The coldest winters fail to kill back even the tips of its many shoots. For weeks we've been fighting a stand of *R. carolina* plowed up in January and a little later disc-harrowed in two directions, exposed to zero temperatures, and still, by midsummer, in serried ranks of green holding its own against being tramped over and subjected to the most severe drought that has occurred in this area in more than seventy years. Could we have modern rose blooms on bushes with such stamina as these possess we would indeed have reached near perfection in the development of *Rosa*. But would there be quite as much fascination, and satisfaction, in growing them? I wonder; and I feel very sure that the American Rose Society would not boast its present membership of over sixteen thousand.

Some of the rose species used in creating the man-made roses of the Western world were quite as hardy as *Rosa carolina,* as for example *R. rugosa* and *R. Wichuraiana.* Many of the "old" roses which still survive are just as tough as were their progenitors; for instance, Queen of the Prairies, Harison's Yellow, and most of the Hybrid Perpetuals. It was not until the introduction of tender species from China and other Eastern sources that we began to get non-hardy sorts. The Pernetianas (one parent of which was *R. chinensis*), crossed with other hybrids, gave us a new range of colors and repeat-blooming characteristics—but at a sacrifice in winter hardiness. They made possible the wonderful roses of today—and of tomorrow—but with these glorious blooms came new problems in culture, decreased resistance to pests and diseases and, in many varieties, a decrease in vigor of growth. Even today you can grow roses that will leave you little to worry about on the score of winter injury, but not if you wish to possess roses in the greatest variety of color and the most perfect of flower forms. You can, however, restrict your roses to the varieties that are the most resistant to cold and also have very satisfactory blooms. (A group of these is given on pages 316–19.)

So much, then, for factor number one, i.e., the plant itself.

Now let's take a look at the other factors.

THE NATURE OF WINTER INJURY

Winter *injury,* as the term is commonly used, refers to the damage to the plant tissues from low temperatures. Parts of the plant, usually the upper portions, may be killed outright, dead as the proverbial doornail, or affected in such a way that the final results of the damage do not become evident until much later, often well on into the following year's growth. Winter *hardiness* is the ability of a plant either to resist injury from low temperatures, or to recuperate quickly if such injury is inflicted.

For a scientific explanation of what happens in the case of winter injury, we feel that we cannot do better than to quote from an article by Griffith J. Buck in the 1949 issue of the *American Rose Annual:*

There are several theories concerning the ability of plants to withstand freezing temperatures without injury, but the most plausible one is concerned with the desiccating effects of freezing and the carbohydrate content of the cells and tissues. In general, the capacity of the plant to resist damage by severe cold is associated with its ability to retain water within the cells against the extractive forces of freezing . . .

There are two kinds of water within the plant, (bound and free water): water that is held without freezing during sub-zero weather . . . called bound water . . . with all the characteristics of a solid and none of those of a liquid; (and) water that *is* readily frozen—"free" water . . . to all intents and purposes . . . the same as tap water. Those plants that have a high percentage of free water in proportion to the amount of bound water are usually less hardy than those with a smaller ratio between the two.

In a word and in nontechnical terms, this means that the more juicy and succulent plant growth is, the more likelihood there is of winter injury, when Jack Frost gets his icy fingers upon it.

In the culture of plants during the growing season, there are several things that can be done and that can be avoided to help plants go into the winter in the best possible condition to minimize the danger of winter injury. These are the ounces of prevention which will save pounds of cure. Observe them all, and your spring replacements will be cut to a minimum.

Unripened growth, (with its high ratio of "free" water) is first on the list of things to avoid. Feeding late in the season, particularly with nitrogenous fertilizers, tends to push the plants into the production of new wood instead of letting them follow their normal inclination to slow up and permit the hardening up of wood already produced. The time to stop feeding will of course vary with climatic conditions, from late July in northern sections to late August in the mid-Atlantic states, and even later further south.

The amount of water to be given during this period naturally will depend upon the season. In general, the less the better, *provided* the soil is kept merely moist enough to prevent actual injury from drought. In thoroughly mulched beds it is not likely to be needed except in extreme drought. Late season blooms from plants kept on the dry side may not be quite as large as from those watered abundantly, but they will be just as beautiful and will last longer when cut.

Weak Growth. Some varieties, of course, are normally much weaker growers than others. Since this is an inherited characteristic, there is nothing that can be done about it. Weakness that is due to inadequate feeding, mechanical injuries, improper pruning or disease, and particularly to premature defoliation such as is caused by black spot, is quite another matter; and a rose bush which has suffered from any of these goes into the winter with two strikes against it before the first touch of frost.

Late pruning is another potential cause of winter injury. If followed by a period of mild weather it may result in the initiation of soft new growth that will be in no condition to withstand freezing later on; if it is followed by cold weather the pruning wounds which are left will not heal quickly and will therefore be vulnerable to injury from many sources.

If very tall canes have developed during late summer and are in danger of being whipped about by winter winds sufficiently to cause damage to other growth or to loosen the roots of the plant, then these should be cut back. In this case we have to take the lesser of two evils. The earlier such pruning is done the better, even if a few late blooms have to be sacrificed in the process. The cuts made should be protected with paint or wax as suggested on page 113.

METHODS OF PROTECTION

Before describing the various methods of protection which may be employed to carry roses safely through the winter, we would like to quote again from the scientific paper already referred to:

It is not the steady cold with gradual temperature changes that kills well matured plants . . . but the rapid day to day fluctuations in temperature. It has been shown that the most rapid killing of cells is done by the freezing of ice crystals within the cell wall. A rapid drop in temperature will freeze free water within the cell instead of initiating its extraction by ice crystals forming in the intercellular spaces. . . . A rapid decrease in temperature will kill plants at temperatures several degrees higher than does a gradual decline. Our methods of winter protection must be designed *to level off the extreme fluctuations of our winter temperatures.*

The words above which we have taken the liberty of italicizing, we think, hold the key to effective winter protection. At least they have been borne out by our own experience over a great many years.

Here briefly are the various methods that are commonly employed for protecting roses through the winter.

Hilling Up. For winter temperatures from 20° above to 20° below zero, this has been and probably still is the method most commonly used. Earth is built up in a cone or hill about the base of the plant, covering the canes to a height of eight to twelve inches, depending upon the severity of the average winter temperatures. In actual practice the "hills" are often much less than their estimated height, particularly after being beaten down by a couple of heavy autumn rains. Frequently too, the inexperienced gardener attempts to get his soil for the hills by scraping it up from between the plants, thus making a corresponding series of "valleys" that leave very little soil over the roots. If soil from some other source is brought in, the gardener finds himself with a real job on his hands even if he has a nearby place from which he can dig it up. Furthermore the surplus soil must be moved again in the spring. If scat-

(Above) The type of winter protection most commonly employed is placing mounds of soil around the bases of the plants. This is done late in the season, just before hard freezing is to be expected. (Below) Hilling alone has a disadvantage in that sunshine striking the sloping sides of the mounds frequently removes the snow, which is Nature's form of winter protection. Furthermore, the soil mounds thaw out early in spring. A mulch, or evergreen boughs, put on after the mounds have frozen, makes them much more effective.

tered around between the plants when taken down in the spring it will soon raise the surface of the bed to too high a level. So he must select whichever, in his own case, is the lesser of two evils.

Another material for hilling up is well-rotted but rather coarse compost (the nearer the consistency of soil, the better). Being less dense than soil, this can be incorporated in the soil of the beds when

The soil mounds are raked down in spring, after the first pruning (which removes surplus long growths of plants) and an application of fertilizer.

removed from around the plants in spring, thus adding desirable humus to improve soil fertility.

To be effective, the hills must remain frozen. Otherwise buds at the base of the plants may be started into premature growth which is likely to be killed by a late frost after the hill is removed.

Hilling plus Mulching. Many gardeners hill up moderately with soil and then supplement this by filling in between and over the hills with a mulch of leaves, straw, or rough compost. We have found the latter the most satisfactory. Most of it by spring may be easily worked into the soil or left as a summer mulch. Another method is to spread well-rotted manure or broken-down compost between the hills and then cover the surface with leaves or straw, the purpose being to keep the mounds of soil frozen until later in the spring than would otherwise be the case.

Mulching. Because reports that have been made on mulching with various materials are so conflicting, it seems impossible to arrive at any definite conclusion. In many instances heavily mulched beds have shown a much higher percentage of winter injury than plants

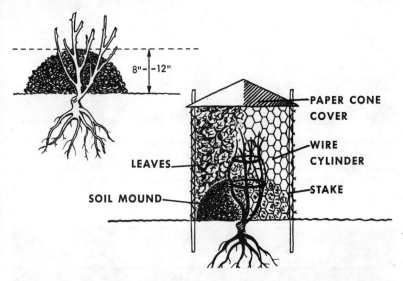

8"-|-12"

PAPER CONE
COVER

WIRE
CYLINDER

LEAVES

STAKE

SOIL MOUND

The method of protection most frequently used is a mound of soil at the base of the plant put in place before ground freezes hard. Leaves, held in place by wire cylinders, increase the protection afforded, especially for varieties of doubtful hardiness.

under similar conditions receiving no protection at all. Any mulch that remains soggy after winter rains or melting snows is likely to do more harm than good, particularly in climates where there are apt to be warm spells during the winter. Mulches of some nonabsorbent light material such as oak or other hardwood leaves, or clean, dry straw held in place by chicken wire around the edges of the beds, seem to have given the best results.

Burying. In extremely cold sections the method resorted to has been that of taking out the rose plants bodily—the branches being first tied up to make them more convenient to handle—and bury-

Effective winter protection in cold climates presents a difficult problem. Here is one method of solving it developed at Iowa State College. Bottomless boxes, 18 inches high, 18 inches wide, and 4 feet long are placed over the plants and filled with ground corncobs. Tops of boxes are then covered with heavy waterproof paper.

In spring boxes are removed; plants, which come through winter unharmed, are pruned back in usual way and give a full crop of bloom. Where corncobs are not available, straw, oak leaves, vermiculite, wood chips, or other light mulching material could be used.

ing them in a trench four feet deep. This has seemed to give complete protection even in extremely cold climates. But under such conditions it would probably be little more expensive and much more rewarding to build a greenhouse and enjoy one's roses in bloom during the winter!

Burying the plants in a box by the expedient of surrounding them with a wooden frame (in an experiment conducted at Iowa State College), seems to be a much more practical expedient for areas where temperatures in winter drop far below zero. Here is an account of it.

The ideal winter protection is a deep blanket of snow which remains all winter long. In cold climates where this snow cover is lacking, rose growers must improvise other methods which usually approximate an all-winter snow drift.

Such a cover should possess the same qualities of insulation and freedom from water-logging which snow possesses. It should conserve the soil's residual heat, while minimizing the rapid temperature fluctuations common to winter air. In addition, like snow, the good winter protection keeps the plants dry. Excess moisture around the dormant canes provides a condition ideal for the development of rot and mold organisms. . . .

We found that ground corncobs fitted most of these requirements. While ground corncobs do tend to hold water, which reduces their insulating value, this disadvantage can be overcome by using waterproof containers. . . .

[We used] boxes 18 inches wide, 18 inches high, and long enough to accommodate four rose plants, spaced 2 feet apart, allowing 1 foot at each end to permit the ground corncobs to completely surround the plants. . . . The boxes were placed over unpruned plants and were filled with coarsely hammermilled dry corncobs to within 2 inches of the top. The tops of the plants were bent [down] and held in place with a cover of waterproof paper. Krinklekraft paper, 40 inches wide, was found suitable for this purpose. The 40-inch width allowed a 12-inch lap down the sides which covered cracks left when the boxes were assembled. This lap, plus a small amount of soil pulled up against the base of the box, kept the contents relatively dry. This type of covering may be applied after growth has ceased in the fall, but before cold weather has set in. It should be removed as early in spring as possible.

This discussion of various methods of winter protection would be incomplete without reference to an exhaustive experiment made some years ago by the Chicago Regional Rose Society. The specific purpose of this survey was to obtain information concerning "the relationship and influence of methods and materials in rose culture to winter kill." The survey covered careful reports on a total of 8,464 roses in the gardens of the members of three rose societies, the gardens being fairly equally distributed over three types of soil —sandy, clay, and mixed. Here are some of the high lights on the resulting information obtained.

METHODS OF WINTER PROTECTION

	Percentage of Plants Winter killed
Hilling with soil alone	5.7
Hilling with soil plus straw	7.9
Hilling with soil plus leaves	9.1
Hilling with soil plus hay	9.3
Hilling with soil plus hay and straw	9.8
Hilling with paper	42.0
No protection	*2.4* !

OTHER FACTORS EFFECTING WINTER LOSSES

Effect of soil type on winter loss:	
Sandy	7.6
Clay	10.2
Mixed (loam)	4.7
Effect of type of fertilizer used:	
Organic	4.1
Inorganic	11.1
Spring versus fall planting:	
Spring	6.1
Fall	8.9

A survey made in Cincinnati, Ohio, however, showed—in a test of 2,658 roses of members of the Cincinnati Rose Society—that hilling the plants with soil alone resulted in only 1% loss while there was an 8% loss among unprotected plants.

GRAYROCK METHOD OF WINTER PROTECTION

With such wide divergence of opinion among the experts as to what method of protection from winter injury is best, one hesitates to recommend any particular method.

The system which we have worked out over the years and which we employ in our own garden with results that satisfy us, is as follows:

First, keeping in mind that health and vigor of plants are important factors in enabling them to resist winter injury, we do everything we can to have them in the best possible condition.

Our winter protection really begins in August with the last feeding, which contains little nitrogen. We avoid "pushing" plants in any way. Watering is continued for another month but tapered off as the period of normal heavy fall rains approaches. Spraying or dusting is continued, especially to guard against black spot, which often attacks suddenly and develops rapidly late in the season. Pruning is continued with the primary aims of having plants go into late fall with well-ripened wood and to prevent the development of too vigorous, tall growths which may be wind-whipped.

All this is *preliminary* work, done during the routine care which rose beds receive. Just before hard freezing, the actual "protection" is started. This includes the following operations:

Removal of Summer Mulch to the compost heap is the next step. If black spot has been present, old mulch is *burned*. A feeding of low-nitrogen fertilizer is then applied and cultivated in, after which comes:

Watering. If the soil is dry, beds are given a very thorough soaking. At this late date there is no danger that watering will initiate new growth. We want roots and stems well provided with moisture. Desiccation, caused by cold and wind, is a big factor in winter injury. Therefore this last watering enables the plant to store up moisture to replace that which will be drawn from it in freezing weather. The roots far below the surface of the soil remain active long after the mulching material and the ground beneath it are frozen solid, since the plant itself continues to function and therefore is capable of replacing lost moisture.

Hilling. Just before hard freezing, plants are hilled with good loam to a height of 6 inches. (The more severe the winter climate, the higher should be the hills—up to 12 inches in the northern Plains).

Winter Mulch. Over the entire surface of the beds a mulch is now applied. In our own garden on Cape Cod, we use pine needles alone, as they are easiest for us to obtain.

A Christmas present for our rose garden! Surplus Christmas trees—ordinarily burned or consigned to the dump—are procured to provide material for winter protection. Cut branches can be tucked in and around bushes to keep off chill drying winds, and to hold snow blanket in place.

Other suitable materials are discussed on pages 100 to 103. As pine needles make a non-packing mulch, we use a depth of from 4 to 6 inches in winter. Each spring this is raked off into the paths, while we take down the hills, work the loam into the beds, cultivate, give plant food and water. A depth of 3 to 4 inches of the pine-needle mulch is then replaced on the beds and added to as needed through the summer. Mulch is removed only when plant food is to be applied, as it remains *over* our watering system (page 97).

Other Protection. For many years we used evergreen boughs for protecting the tops of roses. At our former home in Rockland County, New York, an ample supply was obtained by making arrangements with men who sold Christmas trees to have the leftovers delivered to us on Christmas morning. Since these trees had to be gotten rid of in any event, the cost was nominal. In our present location we are surrounded by pines, and find the pine-needle mulch sufficient.

Short branches were tucked in around the bushes after hilling, and longer ones were laid over the tops. Heavy, curved branches were reserved for tree roses, and extra long ones for Large-flowered Climbers which were a bit on the tender side. (See illustrations on pages 145 and 146.)

When the ground is frozen a couple of inches deep it is easy to punch holes through this crust with a crowbar to receive the ends of branches that one may wish to place in an upright position.

When possible, this green mantle is put on after a heavy fall of snow, to prevent its being blown away. The snow often remains as a frost-resisting blanket long after it has disappeared from adjacent open spaces.

A further advantage of this evergreen protection is that in addition to covering the tops of the plants from winter winds in January and February, and the often too-bright sunshine of March, it keeps the ground frozen during the early spring thaws and warm spells, thus preventing or delaying premature sprouting.

This system gives excellent winter protection in severe climates.

PROTECTION FOR CLIMBERS AND TREE ROSES

Climbers. With Climbing Roses as with Bush Roses it is the inherited characteristics of the type, or even of the variety, which

Tree Roses and Pillars can be bundled up neatly and completely with branches or small trees.

will determine how much winter protection may be required. As a rule the greater percentage of Tea blood present, the greater is the necessity for such protection. In other words (but with less accuracy) the larger the flower, the smaller the plant's capacity for withstanding winter conditions. There are notable exceptions, such as those grand old veterans Dr. J. H. Nicolas and New Dawn.

In an earlier chapter we spoke of micro-climates (page 34). The amount of protection provided by its immediate surroundings has a great deal to do with how a Climbing Rose will come through. High Noon, sent to us as a test rose, in a location well protected from north and west winds by adjacent buildings and shrubbery, lived through four winters with zero or lower temperatures although it was left trained to its support with no mulching or wrapping whatsoever.

We have found that the Christmas tree technique seems to work excellently with Climbers as well as with Bush Roses. If the soil

Tall Climbers, such as Climbing Peace, are surrounded with larger trees—here partly removed to show rose plant. Straying evergreen branches are pruned away, leaving a neat temporary "tree" to decorate the winter landscape! And in June these well-protected rose canes give us blooms clear up into the sky. (See Plate 1 between pages 12–13.)

about the base of the plants is heavily mulched when the soil begins to freeze in the fall, by Christmas time there will usually be not more than two or three inches of frozen ground beneath the mulch. This can readily be punctured with a pick or a crowbar, making holes to receive the butts of evergreens "planted" close in around the rose, the plant itself having first been tied in compactly about its support with heavy, soft twine. Twine is also fastened around the evergreens after they are in place. The Climbing Peace Rose (Plate 1), several years old when this photograph was taken, never had any protection other than that just described although it was planted in a fully exposed location.

A method of protection for not-quite-hardy Climbers in extremely cold sections is to take them down from their supports and lay them out horizontally (or as nearly so as possible!), holding them in place with wire wickets or forked pegs. After this treatment, which necessarily is pretty rough on the plants as well as on the plantsman, they are covered with soil and/or mulch, topped off with a roofing of waterproof building paper held down along the edges with planks or stones. The covering should not be airtight and should not be put on until after really cold weather has set in.

Sometimes Climbing Roses are grown on trellises which are hinged at the bottom, a foot or so above the ground, so that the plant can be laid over without being untied.

We have never had occasion to use this type of protection, but where we have seen it employed, there were gardeners, rather than the owner, to do the work. It is no pastime for the busy week-ender.

Tree Roses. While these make possible landscape effects which can be obtained with no other plant, very naturally rose varieties that are growing three or four feet up in the air are much more exposed to possible winter injury than the same kinds grown normally as bushes near the ground. The most effective way of carrying them through the winter without damage to the tops (and a lopsided Tree Rose is no ornament at all) is to grow them in stout galvanized wire containers that can be lifted bodily in the autumn and stored in a cold, moist cellar or a deep pit.

Sometimes they are partly dug, tipped over and given burial in a trench dug for the purpose. This looks easy in an "artist's conception" sketch of how it should be done, but believe us, it is not.

The method we have employed with success—although not in an extremely cold climate—is to prune the top branches back moderately, enclose the top in a pliofilm sheet tied tightly around the stem, thus forming an inverted bag, and then enclose the whole in a bower of evergreens tall enough to be tied together above the top. This does not require too much labor in the fall, and in spring can be removed in five minutes.

As we said at the beginning of this chapter, there can be no definite, hard-and-fast rules for winter protection that will apply under all conditions. Anyone who grows a considerable number of roses should do some experimenting and decide for himself which, for him, seems to be the most advisable.

See to your stakes when the stormy winds do blow . . .

Supports of one sort or another are essential in the culture of many types of roses. They make possible effects which otherwise could not be attained; and they make much easier such operations as pruning, dusting, or spraying.

Along with the provision of supports goes an essential corollary —training the plants in such a way as to secure, first, the pattern of growth desired; and second, the maximum amount of bloom and the maintenance of healthy growth.

Let us consider first the matter of the supports themselves. To begin with, any supports for roses should be *substantial.* A Climbing Rose or a Pillar Rose is a long-term investment, not infrequently a lifetime one. It is false economy, therefore, to skimp on the original cost and then, in a few years, have to repair or replace the support. The flimsy ready-made arbors and trellises usually sold to the inexperienced gardener are hardly worth setting up, and are better suited to providing support for climbing nasturtiums or morning-glories than roses. A husky Climbing Rose, when in a high wind, or laden with rain or snow, requires a really solid structure to cling to or to be tied to. To provide anything less is throwing money away.

TYPES OF SUPPORTS

Most supports for roses are made of wood. Do not be tempted to use anything in the way of lumber which may happen to be handy. Obtain cedar (juniper), cypress, white pine, or "pecky" cypress which is still available in some sections. All of these are long-lasting, rot-resistant, and weather to attractive colors. None of them require painting. In fact, in our opinion, supports for Climbing Roses should never be painted. Contact with stems and foliage, not to mention sprays of dusts, will quickly discolor any painted surface. The work of taking down a Climbing Rose in order to do a paint job is both time-consuming and exasperating, and usually results in consider-able injury to the rose. This is true even when the rose is supported by a trellis hinged at the bottom so that it can be laid down flat.

For training a rose against a house, the best plan is to keep the supporting pillars three or four feet out from the house wall. The occasional pruning away of inside branches to permit painting, even if a somewhat drastic operation, will cause less damage to the plant than taking it down bodily and then trying to put it back again—a task usually about as successful as trying to reassemble Humpty Dumpty. And in any event the freer circulation of air between the rose and the house wall is of enough importance, aside from any question of painting, to make it desirable. Hinged trellises are advisable, of course, in very cold climates where Climbers must be laid down and covered in winter.

Wood Preservatives. All parts of any wooden structures which will be below ground should be treated to prevent or at least long postpone decay. The standard material for this purpose is Cuprinol. This is a liquid which can be painted on—at least two coats—although immersion application, allowing it to soak in, is even better. In addition to the standard brown color, Cuprinol can also be obtained in a not unattractive green which quickly weathers to a darker shade. We use this—one coat is sufficient—on wooden members above ground where the natural light color of the wood would be too conspicuous.

Another worth-while step in assuring long life for supports set in the ground is to pack crushed stone, pebbles, cinders, or coarse gravel in the hole around the base of the post up to four or five inches of the surfaces. Concrete, with enough water added to make it run freely, poured in over this, will bind the aggregate together sufficiently to provide a more or less monolithic base that will last indefinitely and hold the uprights immovable. This requires very little extra time or expense and gives really permanent supports.

While holes for posts can be dug with a shovel, it is much easier and quicker to use a post hole digger. This makes a neat, round hole.

If at all possible, all supports should be set in place before the roses are planted.

Supports for Climbing Roses. Sometimes we are asked what is the best way to support a Climbing Rose? There is no one best way, any more than there is one best Climbing Rose. The type of support to use is one that will give you, first, the landscape or garden effect you wish to achieve; and, second, adequate support for the type of Climber you are using. It would be foolish to provide a lightweight, ready-made trellis for a New Dawn or a Silver Moon that will eventually develop a mass of canes fifteen to twenty feet in length; and equally so to put up a substantial arch or pergola for a variety normally not growing more than six to eight feet high, such as Dream Girl or Golden Showers.

Posts. The most easily erected and least expensive support for a Climbing Rose is a post. It also requires less space than any other. Despite these practical advantages it is the least desirable if considered from the point of view of getting an artistic effect. To improve it, nail short crosspieces to a post or, better, insert in it at intervals of about two feet, eighteen- to twenty-four-inch pieces of some stout, weather-resistant wood such as oak, hickory, or locust. These are best placed at an angle sloping upward. Such a post will require little or no tying of the canes, will allow the rose to grow and bloom in a more normal fashion, and after two or three seasons will present much the appearance of a tree stump up which the rose has climbed.

Our own favorite support for a Climber standing free is a dead cedar with the branches cut back to lengths varying from one to four feet. We are constantly on the lookout for such specimens. An old-timer six inches or more in diameter and weathered to a beautiful silvery gray makes just about the ideal support for a vigorous Climber. Several such supports made a much-admired feature in our former rose garden at West Nyack. If a dead tree is not available, a living one, trimmed back in much the same way, will answer the purpose.

Post-and-Chain. For enclosing a specific area, particularly where a formal or semiformal effect is wanted, a post-and-chain support will prove eminently satisfactory. Stout posts of any desired height are spaced ten to twenty feet apart and connected by a single stout chain run across the tops; or by two chains, one at the top, and another eighteen inches or so below it. The end posts should be thoroughly anchored by wire cables to a heavy stone or a concrete

An arched gateway such as this—designed by the author for a garden in Cape May, New Jersey—provides ideal support for vigorous-growing, cluster-flowered roses. The double arch gives extra strength and reduces training and pruning problems to a minimum.

block buried in the ground, and it is a good idea to have a stout turnbuckle in each of the end braces so that any slack can be taken up. As the canes develop they are trained along the chain or chains, thus creating, when the plants are in bloom, a living festoon of roses on a grand scale.

Arches. The most pleasingly decorative of all types of support for a climbing rose is a well-designed arch. This is especially true if the variety chosen is of strong, vigorous growth. One great advantage of the arch—or arches, for of course they can be used in series as well as singly—is the limitless variety in design which is possible. Too often the support provided for a climbing rose bears no relation whatever to its surroundings and sticks out like a bandaged thumb at a game of bridge. An arch can and should be designed to harmonize architecturally with the house, thus becoming an important part of the whole picture, even during the winter months when it stands on its own without any glamorous covering of rose or rose foliage.

In designing or selecting an arch it is important to get it sufficiently wide and high, keeping in mind that, as the rose which is to embrace it develops, its inside dimensions will shrink rapidly. And above all it must be of firm construction, for nothing can give a place a run-down look more quickly than an arch or an arbor which is even slightly askew.

In all types of design the effectiveness of *repetition* is recognized. This is quite as true in landscaping, even on the smallest scale, as it is in painting or in music. Therefore two arches—one at either end of a long path, for instance—have much more than twice the visual impact of a single arch. The general principle of repetition is one which may well be kept in mind, but it must be practiced with care and skill or the end result may be anything but pleasing.

Arbors and Pergolas. Much of what has been said above applies also to arbors and pergolas. They offer a practical solution to the problem of growing a considerable number of Climbers in limited space. Where the primary object, however, is to obtain a well-shaded area, there are plants other than roses—grapes, wisteria, virgin's-bower (*Clematis paniculata*)—which better serve the purpose. It should be kept in mind, too, that roses flowering on an arbor or a pergola will be seen only from the outside. There are occasions when this can be turned to advantage. We once landscaped a place where the owner of the house wanted to be able to see "roses like waves in the moonlight" from her bedroom window—and the rose garden was on the other side of the house! A broad, flat-topped pergola and a dozen plants of Silver Moon which spread out over it provided a shimmering sea of the great saucer-shaped blooms that surprised and delighted her.

Fences. One of the least expensive, easiest to install, most enduring, and most effectual supports from the point of view of the display obtained, is the ordinary post and split rail fence. It can be used not only along boundary lines but, in shorter sections, in many other locations. It has the further great advantage that the roses

(Above) Ramber-type roses, with their dense, twiggy growth, are especially at home climbing over a picket fence. This is good old Dorothy Perkins (prone to mildew); a comparatively recent variety, immune to this curse, is Chevy Chase. (Below) No form of support shows off the modern Large-flowered Climbers to better advantage than a post-and-rail fence; and none makes maintenance, in the form of pruning and spraying, so easily attended to.

are readily accessible for pruning, cutting for bouquets, spraying, or dusting. If winter protection is required that can be accomplished without disturbing the plants.

Stone walls, too, have many of these advantages, with the added one that roses grown along a wall are much less likely to suffer from winter injury, even considerably further north than they could ordinarily be grown without protection. Our former rose garden in Rockland County, New York, was bordered, along the road, with a line of very large boulders, some of them three to four feet high, over which a collection of Climbers sprawled and spilled at will. In bloom they were a cascade of color that stopped passers-by, and in winter the leaves piled in around the roots of the plants and snow-drifts remained long after they had melted in other locations, thus giving as effective winter protection as could be desired.

Supports for Tree Roses, or more accurately, Standard Roses, should be sturdy enough to prevent the "trunks" or understocks from bending in high winds. If they are whipped about, the roots will be loosened in the soil or may even be broken, and the plant, if it survives, will be injured for a long time to come. Even the half-

Climbing Roses that have a tendency to sprawl or creep—such as Polaris, a lovely white—make a fine display if allowed to stray at will over a rough stone wall or down a bank.

Standard Roses, the stems of which are only two to three feet high instead of the three to four or more of a regular Standard, are the better for some support, particularly if in an exposed location.

The best support which we have found for a Standard Rose is a section of a reinforcing rod such as is used in cement work. These can be obtained at any lumberyard and may be cut with a hacksaw to any desired length. They are readily driven into the ground, and when rusted from weathering, are in appearance not unlike the stock on which the rose is growing. The top of the stake should be but little above the stem on which the rose is grafted so that during the summer it will be hidden from sight.

Securing Canes to Supports. Most of the supports which we have particularly recommended above will require little or no tying to hold the canes in place. Sometimes temporary tying is needed to start the growths, especially those from the base of the plant, until the wood has hardened enough to hold them where they are wanted.

The material we like best for tying is Twist-ems, which may be had in either the regular length or extra long, sixteen inches. One end may be secured to or around the support and the other around the branch or cane. If cord is used, it should be large in size and loosely woven so that it will not cut into soft new growth. The proper way to tie is shown in the illustration on page 158.

Against walls of masonry or wood, a simple little gadget known as a Clampum vine tie is just the ticket. These are substantial, well-designed hooks with long points that either may be driven directly into the supporting surface, or, in the case of hard masonry, into holes of suitable size made with a masonry drill. If the canes must be secured in place permanently, strips of lead about a quarter to a half inch wide, cut into suitable lengths, should be employed. Twist-ems, however are easier to procure and use, and will last for several years.

TRAINING

Much of the satisfaction to be had from climbing roses of all sorts will depend upon how they are trained—that is, upon the position the canes are made to assume. Left to themselves the wiry stemmed varieties such as Coral Creeper and Max Graf will sprawl over the ground horizontally; and others, such as Blaze, New Dawn, and

When using Large-flowered Climbers, exercise care to train many of the canes at an angle or horizontally, to induce the growth of flowering side shoots.

most of the Climbing Hybrid Teas, with some support, will tend to grow straight up as vertically as they can. Usually neither one of these positions provides the most desirable effect or produces the greatest number of blooms; hence, it becomes necessary for the rose grower to take things into his own hands and persuade them to do what he wants them to.

It may be recalled that in Chapter 9 on pruning we spoke of what is known as apical dominance, i.e., the tendency of a terminal bud on a branch or twig to make stronger growth than the buds below it. In a sense this term is misleading because it is true of roses (and of most other plants) that the bud which is *highest above the ground* will become the dominant one and produce the most vigorous new growth. In other words, if a new rose shoot—or even an old cane for that matter—is bent over so that its tip is lower than some other portion of the wood nearer the base, the dominant new growth will come from the bud which has the highest elevation. To coin a new term, this growth characteristic might be called "altitude dominance." It is due, of course, to the tendency of the sap in growing plants to defy the laws of gravity and flow up as well as down. It is so insis-

(Above) This curving cane of a Climbing Polyantha (Orange Orleans) shows how flowering laterals have developed along its entire length, to form a graceful, flaming arch. (Below) An example of "altitude dominance": Every eye along the base of this cane—which was trained in a curve—has grown, flowered, and set seed. Normally, with the cane growing vertically, most of these eyes would have remained dormant.

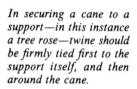

In securing a cane to a support—in this instance a tree rose—twine should be firmly tied first to the support itself, and then around the cane.

tent that it will often force the initiation of adventitious buds even on very hard wooded plants. We have a prostrate juniper (blown over by the wind) that sent up from its bare stem new shoots which have now become a hedge of tree-sized branches.

The Three "Tools" for Training. The knowledge of altitude dominance gives us the first of the three tools which may be used in training a climbing rose to do exactly as we wish it to. The second is *bud removal,* which refers not to flower buds but to the eyes or "breaks" indicating where new side shoots are starting to develop— shoots which, in the normal course of events, would form lateral branches. These, when they first start, can readily be rubbed off with thumb and forefinger; or if they have made too much growth, they may be cut out with a sharp knife. The third "tool," of course, is pruning, which has been discussed in detail in Chapter 9.

So when you plan to use Climbing Roses, the first step should not be—as it so often is!—to select varieties by running through the beautiful close-up color photographs in a catalog, but rather to picture in your mind's eye as definitely as possible the effects you wish to achieve with them. Then select varieties which you think are most likely to produce these effects. And last, provide the type of supports, and follow the system of training, that will bring them into reality.

CHAPTER 12

Roses in Pots

I could hardly believe that the grand Roses . . . could have come, like some village beauty out of her cottage dwelling, from such mean and lowly homes. But there were the plants, and there were the proprietors . . . pointing to various healthy and handsome rose-buds . . .

Roses are among the few flowers that may be had in bloom at any time of the year. The commercial production of "florists'" roses goes on during all of the fifty-two weeks—a fact which, of course, is of little interest to the amateur rosarian save as an indication that his favorite flower, with proper coaxing, may be persuaded to greet him with a smile at any time from New Year's Day to the Christmas holidays.

This is not to say that you can dig up in autumn a rosebush that has been flowering through the summer and expect it to continue flowering indoors all winter. You cannot do that with a geranium or a fuchsia, much less a rose. Somewhere in the year's cycle of growth there must be a rest period, and plants desired for winter flowering must be treated accordingly.

USES FOR ROSES IN POTS

Until recently, in any discussion of growing roses in pots, it would have been taken for granted that they were wanted for winter flowering in a greenhouse, or possibly for an attempt to get them to bloom in a window-sill garden. Now that picture has changed. With the modern trend toward patio and terrace gardens with plants in containers, a new and rapidly increasing use for roses in pots or tubs has developed.

The technique of growing roses in pots is in no way new—it has been in practice since early times; but only recently has it become something for the homeowner of moderate means to consider and put into use as a practical expedient of adding to the attractiveness of his intimate home surroundings. One of the greatest advantages of roses in this role is that they may be had in bloom more or less continuously for months on end, and do not have to be frequently removed and replaced with something else, as is the case with so many other shrubs if a continuous display of flowers is desired.

For Window-sill Gardens. Roses are among the plants least suited for this type of gardening. In the first place they require an amount of sunshine which is seldom available; and in the second, the temperature and moisture conditions are likely to be quite the opposite of those demanded if they are to make healthy, happy growth. Nevertheless there are enthusiasts who succeed with them.

By far the easiest and the most rewarding of roses to use as window-sill subjects are those of the Fairy or Baby group. (See Chapter 21.)

In a Small Greenhouse. Most roses that are grown under glass, either commercially or in large private greenhouses, are planted directly in benches of soil. The owner of a small hobby greenhouse, however, can succeed with them as pot or tub plants, Her Royal Highness being graciously willing to share bench space with more plebeian neighbors, although she will require a little special attention if she is to refrain from a bit of sulking. (Growing roses in beds for long-stemmed cut flowers is beyond the scope of this volume. Anyone contemplating trying this should procure a book giving all the details.)

CULTURAL REQUIREMENTS

In growing roses in pots or tubs, the general cultural requirements will be the same whether you plan to have them on a terrace, a window sill, or in the greenhouse.

Soil Comes First. If you have available only a rather heavy clay soil, add to it an almost equal amount (by bulk) of peatmoss and, if needed, enough sharp sand to make it friable. To a bushel of this mixture add two or three quarts of charcoal broken up into small pieces; this will not only improve drainage but help to keep the soil "sweet"; and it is advisable also to add regular superphosphate (20%) since this is a very slow-acting element. Other fertilizers can be added at the time of potting.

If you have to start with a light, sandy soil, you will need less peatmoss—about one half of the amount mentioned above. This may well be made up of equal parts of peatmoss and sedge or Michigan peat.

As with any potting soil, the ingredients should be very thoroughly mixed together. Keep your soil mixture in a tight container and well covered so that it will not dry out before you are ready to use it.

Containers. Any container that provides perfect drainage will do. Most of our experience has been with old-fashioned clay pots. If you are able to secure handmade ones, which have thicker walls and are not so symmetrical as the machine-made product, you will find that they give a great deal more character to your display of pot-grown roses. For this reason, too, wooden tubs are to be preferred to pots, particularly for plants of considerable size.

POTTING AND REPOTTING

Potting. Your initial success with pot-grown roses will depend largely upon the care you take in potting them. Drainage is even more important with roses than with most other pot-grown plants because the new, hairlike feeding roots that have to be developed are easily injured, if not actually destroyed, by either drying out or being kept too wet. Crocking should be very thorough. A curved piece of a broken pot over the drainage hole, covered with a layer of smaller pieces, will assure good drainage. On top of this we use a layer of sphagnum moss. This arrangement not only prevents fine particles of soil from being washed out but also forms a little reservoir to hold some moisture and at the same time admits air freely.

Do not jam or crowd roots down into the pot. It is much better to cut them back until they can be fitted into it readily. Then place enough soil in the bottom of the pot over the drainage material so that the plant can be held in position, with the knuckle or swelling where it was budded an inch or so above the rim of the pot.

The soil for potting should be moist but not wet—just moist enough so that a handful lightly squeezed will retain its form but can be made to crumble apart when pressed lightly between the fingers.

Aftertreatment. If plants are dormant when you pot them up, exercise care during the next several weeks to keep the tops at all times plump and moist. If only a few plants are involved you can do this most readily by covering each pot with a plastic bag and then watering, from the bottom, only when moisture ceases to condense on the inside of the covering. When new leaves begin to develop normally, your plant is safely on its way.

Procuring the Plants. While rose plants may be procured at any time of the year when the temperature is not so low as to endanger them in transportation, the two normal seasons are (1) late fall or early spring, when they are handled as dormant plants; or (2) late spring or early summer, when they are handled as growing plants in regular paper pots, tin cans, or other containers. For winter bloom plants may be potted up in December or January, after a two or three months' rest; in early spring, before growth has started; or at any time as growing plants. If much growth has been developed, the shock of changing them from the containers in which they are growing to pots or tubs, is likely to result in a severe setback. Dormant plants bought in the fall may be heeled in or buried in a trench to give them a longer rest before they are started into growth as specimens in pots or tubs to flower during the following spring and summer.

For planting in pots, the tops are cut back severely just as they would be for planting out of doors, but if in order to get the roots into the pots it is necessary to trim them back more than ordinarily, the tops should be reduced accordingly. Plants of the Miniature or Fairy group, received in growth in small pots, may be kept in them for the first season before being shifted to larger ones.

Feeding. The food contained in the potting soil will carry the plants on until they are well out in leaf. After that, an all-purpose liquid plant food such as Ra-Pid-Gro or Hyponex, provided every three or four weeks, will keep them going. It may be applied to the soil or as a foliar spray. Our preference is to use it both ways, putting it on the foliage only two or three times during the growing season.

Apply fertilizers only when the soil is moist since otherwise the roots may be injured. All feeding should be discontinued as the plants approach their rest period.

Repotting. At the close of the first season's growth, when the plants have gone completely dormant—some time after the last blooms have been produced—a shift to larger pots will be in order.

In making this shift, prune the plant back quite severely, remove the ball from the old pot and rub off any soil that comes away easily from the surface and from the sides, but without disturbing the main root ball. In repotting it is even more necessary than in the first potting to get the soil packed very firmly around the roots. This can best be done by filling in a little at a time and using a potting stick to firm it down into place.

It is seldom necessary to use pots more than eight inches in diameter, though possibly larger pots or tubs may be desired if the plants are to be kept on a terrace or patio, particularly in an exposed position where a smaller container might be in danger of being blown over by a gust of wind. The famous English rosarian Bertram Park speaks of having, by annual repotting, maintained roses in eight-inch pots for more than ten years without any lessening in the productivity of the plants. The use of foliar feeding makes it unnecessary to repot as frequently as when all nourishment has to be supplied from the soil.

Watering. Since the amount of soil in a pot, compared to the open ground, is extremely limited, particular care is required in maintaining the amount of moisture required by the root system. During periods of active growth, daily watering may be needed, and syringing or misting the foliage every day or two will help considerably, particularly where the humidity is low.

Keeping the surface of the soil in pots or tubs mulched with sphagnum moss or peatmoss will also aid materially in maintaining moisture in the soil.

The need for watering can be determined quite definitely by the old-fashioned practice of rapping a pot sharply with the knuckles or a piece of wood. If it "rings" the need for watering is certainly indicated. If only a heavy, dull sound is obtained, the soil is sufficiently moist. A little practice will soon enable the grower to distinguish clearly between the two sounds.

We are convinced from long experience that the best method of maintaining moisture in soil in pots is to water *from the bottom;* and we have found this to work equally well with very large pots and even tubs and flower boxes. Two precautions, however, are very important where a pot or other container stands in the open. There should be both very good drainage in the bottom of the container itself, and, in case of heavy rains, some way of immediately removing surplus water from the receptacle in which the container stands. A bulb sprayer, with the sprinkler head removed, or a short piece of one-fourth-inch rubber tubing, used as a siphon, will accomplish this.

SOME PARTICULAR PRECAUTIONS

The suggestions made above apply in general to roses grown in pots. There are other points in their culture which apply particularly to *where* they are grown.

On Terrace or Patio. Two of the most serious troubles with roses that are being grown on an open terrace or patio are sun and wind. While roses love sunshine, most of the modern varieties, particularly those with delicate coloring, cannot endure its beating down directly upon them during midsummer without suffering from it. Even though the plants themselves may stand up fairly well, the blossoms will be faded and short-lived. It is therefore desirable, if possible, to give them a location where they will get some shade during the midday hours.

Also, while roses thrive best where air flows freely about them, constant strong breezes keeping the branches disturbed and tossed about for hours on end cause them to dry out unduly; and opening buds whipped by the wind do not unfold normally to their full beauty.

Flooding. Another danger, under some conditions, is that during heavy rains the soil in pots or tubs becomes so saturated that it is merely a muddy mass which will not dry out properly for days even if it does not cake into a cement-like ball, as it may if exposed to hot sunshine after such a soaking.

A heavy mulch will help to prevent such a condition from developing, but it is far better to have available a sheltered corner to which the pots can be moved quickly in case of a threatened emergency of this kind. Or "ponchos" of heavy waterproof paper may be placed around the stems and over the tops of the pots or tubs when heavy rain threatens. These may be cut from a roll of SofTite building paper, obtainable at any lumberyard. SofTite is also useful for many other purposes about the house and garden.

On the Window Sill. Here the biggest threat to successful growth is exactly the opposite of that described above: in other words, lack of sufficient sunshine. The more sunshine the plants can get during the short days of late winter and early spring, the better. The Miniature Roses can be helped by artificial lighting but usually this is not feasible with bush varieties being grown in large pots.

Another threat to roses indoors is overheating. The nearer they can be provided with the temperature schedule for roses on a greenhouse bench the better; but ordinarily this is a very difficult thing to accomplish. Fortunately the tough little Miniature Roses, without suffering unduly, are capable of withstanding considerably higher temperatures and greater fluctuations in temperature than the garden types.

The third great obstacle to growing roses indoors is too dry an atmosphere. With hot air or steam heat it is almost impossible to overcome this. Frequent misting of the foliage and maintaining a supply of evaporating water near the plants will be of some assistance in combatting low humidity.

In the greenhouse one has the great advantage of having both temperature and humidity under much more accurate control. When the plants are first brought in from their winter storage in a frame, they should have a temperature of 55° to 60° at night. During the day the temperature should be increased about eight degrees more in cloudy weather, and ten to fifteen degrees more on sunny days. Later on, when the sun begins to get really strong— usually by mid-May—some shade should be provided, either by whitewashing the glass if many plants are being grown, or by attaching a double thickness of muslin or something similar to the roof bars above the plants if there are only a few. In late autumn —mid-September to October—the shading is removed.

Watering should be done early in the morning and, if possible, only on bright, sunny days.

Mulching the pots will help materially in lengthening the periods between waterings, as will also plunging the pots to their rims in cinders or a mixture of very coarse sand and vermiculite, if they are kept in a bench where this can be done.

Ventilation also is important. The more "air" the plants can be given without reducing the temperature below the required minimum, the better.

The growing of some roses in pots—even if merely a half dozen or so—will add another dimension to the pleasures which the rose lover can procure from his favorite flower. If you have never tried it, why not do a little experimenting this coming season?

Small plants grown from cuttings are excellent to experiment with; or a few plants can be obtained from a neighborhood florist who grows greenhouse roses.

CHAPTER *13.* *Rose Troubles:*
Pests, Diseases, Malnutritions

If May has been genial, June will be glorious. If not, we shall have the aphis . . . mildew, rust, larvae of saw-fly, swarming . . . until the poor Rosarian is nearly driven out of his wits.

The term "troubles" covers a lot of territory, as the sub-title above indicates, for it includes the insects and other living creatures which may injure roses, the diseases of many types that may attack them, and various environmental conditions that interfere with normal development of the plants or blooms.

Today's rose gardener, unless he has had many years of experience, can scarcely appreciate the fact that his plants may be kept free of insect pests and protected from diseases in a small fraction of the time that formerly would have been required. Both the effectiveness of the controls and the time required to prepare and apply them have been reduced to a very happy minimum.

While a hand duster will suffice if one has but one or two dozen plants, any owner of a real rose garden, even the smallest, will find the purchase of a sprayer of the type which attaches to an ordinary garden hose one of the most rewarding garden investments he has ever made.

Sprayers of this type automatically mix the spray, which is contained in a small glass jar, with the water as it comes from the hose. The

167

water, in the form of a fine mist, is applied continuously. The spray material is mixed with it, as wanted, merely by shifting the position of the thumb. And the *direction* of the spray—straight ahead, up, down or sideways—is guided by a mere twist of the wrist. There are no washers to wear out, no valves to stick or leak.

While a very light hose is adequate for use with sprayers of this type, as the water is not under great pressure, it is well to use a hose that is very flexible. A heavy, stiff hose, whether rubber or plastic, will be difficult to manipulate without injury to the rose bushes.

Needless to say—or is it?—a sprayer of this sort, like any other, should *immediately* be thoroughly washed out and cleaned every time it has been used.

The materials which we use in our rose garden are an all-purpose liquid rose spray *plus* the recommended amount of 75% Phaltan, or Benlate, a new systemic fungicide that will control Black Spot and powdery mildew, the best fungicides at present available. It is completely effective against black spot, if used weekly.

An important factor in the control of pests, diseases, and nutritional deficiencies is to be able to recognize them at the earliest possible moment. The illustrations in the following pages will help the inexperienced rose grower to accomplish this. Controls and remedies are given in detail later in this chapter.

GENERAL HYGIENE—A CLEAN ROSE GARDEN

The basic factor in having healthy roses is to have a clean rose garden. Most of the diseases and many of the pests are spread by actual physical contact. Therefore the first step is to practice sanitation in and around the rose garden.

Most of the waste plant material around our garden finds its way into the compost pile, but any and all debris from the rose garden, even the remains of old flowers and trimmings from summer pruning that have shown no indication of pest injury or disease, go directly to the heap that—unlike Christopher Fry's lady—*is* for burning. And where a winter mulch is to remain on the ground, it receives a dormant spray before growth starts in the spring. Dr. Massey, who certainly is an authority, doubts if this treatment helps in controlling black spot, but it certainly does no harm, and we believe it to be well worth while as a general sanitation measure.

INSECT PESTS

Such insect invaders as aphids, spider mites, rose bugs, and Japanese beetles used to keep the rose grower busy applying a succession of dusts or sprays. Practically every trouble of this type may now be kept at bay with one of the modern all-purpose dusts or sprays applied regularly at intervals of a week or ten days throughout the growing season. (Incidentally these same all-purpose mixtures include materials which control most rose diseases.) Only occasionally, when for some reason one of the troubles get a real start, is it necessary to resort to a specific. We sometimes find it worth while, for instance, to get after a colony of aphids that have appeared overnight, using a pressure can of Black Leaf 40 (nicotine sulfate) Pyrethrum, or malathion, with which they can be drenched directly; or to hand pick, into a can of kerosene and water, Japanese beetles that escape the regular spray. For the most part, however, the regular spray or dust program keeps everything under control.

It is well, nevertheless, to know what your rose enemies are. Here is a list of those most likely to be encountered; and of controls, other than the regular spray program, helpful in holding them at bay.

APHID. Aphids, or "plant lice," attack most garden plants and vegetables, and the rose is no exception. Two types, the Rose Aphid, green or slightly pink, and a much smaller green one, often infest roses. They appear in concentrated colonies which increase with amazing rapidity. Usually they are to be seen first on buds at the tips of new growth. Often the first sign of their presence is the flecklike white casts, more conspicuous than the aphids themselves because of their protective green coloring.

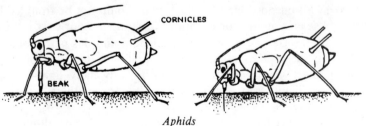

Aphids

Control is not difficult if undertaken in time. The old standard exterminator is nicotine sulfate or Black Leaf 40. Malathion is a specific, which also takes care of many other insect pests. These can be used for sudden local attacks. Complete sprays or dusts, if used regularly, usually keep aphids under control.

BEE, CARPENTER. A small bee, about half an inch long, which nests in tunnels made in the pith of rose canes. If an upper portion of a cane wilts, split it lengthwise. The presence of the carpenter bee is revealed by several yellowish maggots in the tunnels.

Control: Cut canes down to sound pith, and burn.

BEE, LEAF-CUTTER is readily identified by the perfection of its work in cutting very neat and perfect circles and ovals from the margins of rose leaves. She does not attack flowers and does little harm—unless she happens to pick a leaf on a bud being groomed for a rose show!

Leaf-Cutter Bee

Control: Methoxychlor or Sevin. Since it is one of the ingredients in your all-purpose spray or dust, you should not be troubled by these bees if you are conscientious in your spray or dust routine.

BEETLE, JAPANESE. Those who have encountered this pest probably need no description of it. The one-half inch long, copper and green adults arrive in June, devouring especially light-colored blooms. They continue until fall, being at their worst in midsummer.

Control: Specific: Sevin. As an ingredient of your all-purpose spray or dust, this will probably take care of your roses. If grubs are destroyed in lawns by treatment with 5 pounds of 5% chlordane dust* per 1,000 square feet, fewer adults will mature. Milky-spore

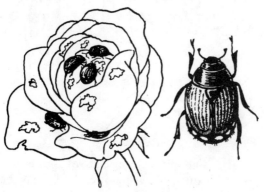

Japanese Beetle

disease is a long-term killer: inserted in lawns at 5-foot intervals with a corn planter, it spreads a bacterial disease among the grubs that progressively destroys the population over a period of several years. In an emergency, hand picking of adults into a can of kerosene may save the rose garden, but the regular spray or dust program is the best control.

BEETLE, LEAF. Very small, bluish-green beetles resembling flea beetles; attack buds and flowers.

Control: Methoxychlor or Sevin, as for rose beetle. See below.

BEETLE, ROSE. Also known as rose bug and rose chafer, this beetle is about one-half inch long, grayish-tan in color, with long, spiny legs. Usually appears in late spring, remaining for about three weeks and attacking flowers and foliage. Gregarious and almost omniverous, as it attacks flowers, fruits, and foliage of many species of decorative plants, vegetables, and fruits.

Control: Unless they are too numerous, knocking beetles, with a small wooden paddle, into a tin can about one-third full of kerosene, will keep them cleaned up. This should be done early in the morning while they are still a bit dopey. Methoxychlor— or Sevin can be used—follow label instructions on amounts to use per gallon of water.

* In some states chlordane can only be applied by a registered or licensed pesticide applicator.

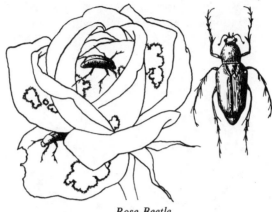

Rose Beetle

Once again, it or one of its close relatives is present in your all-purpose spray or dust. Choice flower buds may be protected from attack by being enclosed in small plastic bags.

BEETLE, SNOUT (Rose curculio) is a hard-shelled red beetle about three-quarters of an inch long with very prominent, curved beak

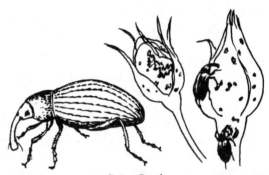

Snout Beetle

with which it drills punctures through the buds, making holes through the unopened petals.

Control: As for other beetles, methoxychlor or Sevin.

BUDWORM. Small worms (larvae), green with dark stripes, or with light-colored markings.

Control: Cut damaged blooms; look carefully for injured buds. Specific spray or dust; methoxychlor.

Earwigs are thin, hard, dark, beetle-like, soil-inhabiting insects three-quarters of an inch long, armed at the rear with a pair of pincers. They feed on foliage and flower petals, making unsightly

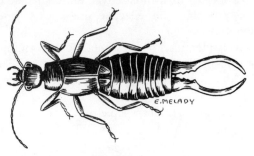

Earwig

holes. A rather new pest in this country, they are rapidly spreading. Here on Cape Cod they are a real problem, and they are also present on the Pacific Coast.

Control: Diazinon or Sevin is applied to the soil around the roots of plants.

Leaf Hopper. Small (about one-eighth inch long), yellowish, wedge-shaped, appearing in spring and again in late summer and fall.

Leaf Hopper

Characterized by "hopping"—to incredible distances for its size —at the least disturbance; feeds by puncturing the foliage, leaving irregular but conspicuous patterns.

Control: Spray or dust must cover undersurface of leaves. If regular spray program is not effective, use Black Leaf 40, methoxychlor, or Pyrethrum.

LEAF TIER. Easily identified by their method of forming leaves into protective rolls or tubes, inside which the larvae feed.

Control: Cut off and burn the "rolls." Specific: methoxychlor or Sevin.

MIDGE. A minute, almost microscopic pest, one of the most serious of all rose enemies, because of its "blitz," pin-pointed attack.

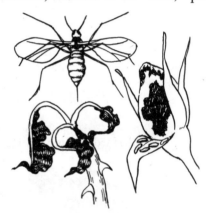

Rose Midge

Symptoms of its appearance are the sudden blackened, almost "burned-to-a-crisp" appearance of flower buds, leaf buds, and even tips of vigorous new shoots. There is no advance warning, and action must be immediate, as a new generation will develop in two to three weeks.

Control: Snip off into a pail and burn all infested buds and tips. Spray thoroughly—ground as well as plants—use methoxychlor and repeat twice at weekly intervals.

MITE, SPIDER (Red Spider). These tiny creatures, pinkish when young and yellow or green when mature, pierce rose foliage and suck, leaving a webby deposit on the backs of leaves. The mites

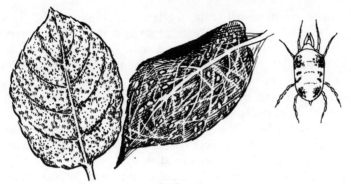

Spider Mite

themselves are all but invisible with the naked eye. A bad infestation may cause defoliation.

Control: Since Kelthane or Acaraben is an excellent control, and is an ingredient of the all-purpose spray or dust, there is little likelihood of mite trouble if plants are conscientiously dusted or sprayed weekly. Follow label instructions on amounts to use per gallon of water.

SCALE. Not likely to be found except on neglected bushes, especially old Hybrid Perpetuals and Hardy Climbers. Resembles the bet-

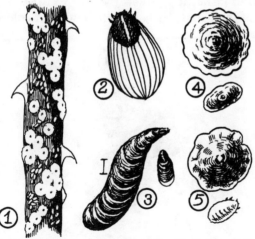

(1) Scale on cane (2) Cottony cushion scale (3) Oyster-shell scale (4) California and Florida red scale (5) Lecanium scale

ter known oyster-shell scale, the females being covered by flat white "shells" one-quarter inch or so in diameter. In neglected cases the multiplying scales form a scurfy incrustation.

Control: Cut out old badly infested canes to the ground and burn. Spray, while still dormant, with 70-second dormant oil or, during the summer months when crawlers are present spray with a combination of malathion and methoxychlor.

SLUGS (Rose Sawfly). Yellowish-green, tapering, soft-bodied, one-half inch or less long; skeletonizes leaves. The Bristly Rose Slug, somewhat larger, has distinct bristles.

Control: If slugs appear, remove and burn infected leaves. Regular spray program, *if started early,* usually prevents their getting a start. In case of a bad infestation, dust foliage and soil around plants with a 15% metaldehyde dust, applied at night, three or four times at weekly intervals.

STEM GIRDLER. Seldom appears in gardens; presence indicated by punctures in a spiral around the canes, causing swellings.

Control: Cut out canes, *below* injured areas, and burn.

THRIPS. This very minute—about one-twenty-fifth inch long—pest, makes up in numbers for what it lacks in size, as the life cycle is completed in two weeks, one generation overlapping another. First indication is distortion and browning of flower petals. Closer inspection reveals the thrips inside the flowers at the bases of the petals. Usually white and light-colored blooms are the first victims.

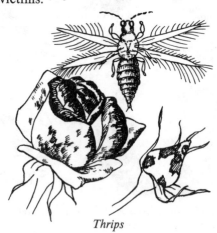

Thrips

Control: Difficult, as breeding takes place outside the garden. If regular spray program fails to control, remove infested buds, and keep fading flowers cut. Burn. Specific: malathion or pyrethrum, either of which may be used in a pressure "bomb" for emergency local applications.

DISEASES

Most of what has been said in regard to the control of insect pests applies equally to the control of diseases; but as climate and weather, in the case of diseases, are more important factors, we cannot be quite so sure that the all-purpose dusting or spraying program will be completely efficient in guarding against them. In general, however, *if applied regularly,* dusting and spraying are effective. Regular application is doubly important because most diseases, unlike the insects, must be *prevented,* instead of being treated after they appear.

Here are the diseases most likely to prove troublesome in the rose garden.

Black Spot

BLACK SPOT is the most widespread and the most troublesome rose disease in this country. Only in dry areas of low humidity such as California and the Southwest is it absent. The first symptom is the appearance of round black spots which are scattered over the lower leaves of the rose plant. It usually starts in humid weather and if it is not checked, the spotted foliage soon turns yellow and falls. Complete defoliation often occurs in susceptible varieties, especially yellows with Pernetiana blood.

Control: Because the spores of black spot are spread by water splashing from infected to healthy foliage, it is of prime importance to hand-pick affected leaves carefully, placing them in a bag to be burned. Gather up also any which have fallen on the ground or mulch under the plants as these are a source of further infection.

The new chemical Phaltan (Folpet) and included in most all-purpose rose sprays, is an excellent fungicide which makes the rose lover's life today much easier than it was a few years ago. Ferbam, sold as Fermate or Karbam Black, or Captan (orthocide 406) are also effective, but its soot-like appearance is most unattractive in the rose garden. All-purpose sprays and dusts are sure to include one of the new fungicides, and a regular program should prevent the dread disease from getting a start.

A comparatively new product, Benlate (1991) has recently been found most effective in the prevention and control of black spot.

CANKERS. There are several cankers which may attack rose stems, but the most common is Brown Canker, the first symptom of which is small purplish spots that soon become white in the middle, with a red-purple edge. Sometimes many small cankers develop on one cane. In other cases they join, causing long diseased areas. Hilled-up canes may develop the latter condition during the winter, especially if soggy-wet material surrounds the plant stems.

Control: In early spring remove all affected parts down to healthy wood, and burn prunings. Then give dormant lime-sulfur spray, such as Scalecide. After growth begins the regular spray program will prevent further infection.

CROWN GALL is a disease which usually appears on rose roots, though it occasionally appears above ground, or just above at the graft. Infection occurs through wounds or bruises, and this is one reason for root pruning of all injured parts before planting. The galls may be very small, round growths or, if neglected, may reach the size of a baseball.

Control: Purchasers should carefully examine all new stock before planting, and reject any stock which shows even small, spherical growths on the roots. Badly infected plants should be destroyed. Prune away injured roots on healthy plants before planting or transplanting to prevent infection.

HAIRY ROOT is less common than crown root gall. Its symptoms are great quantities of weak, fibrous, unhealthy roots, growing from swollen root areas.

Control: As for crown root gall.

Mildew

POWDERY MILDEW. This disease of humid weather is next in importance to black spot on roses. In gardens where the air circulation is poor around the bushes, mildew is almost sure to appear. Certain types such as the Ramblers are particularly susceptible. The layman usually recognizes the presence of powdery mildew when the young growth of a rose, including stems and buds, is covered with a white, powdery deposit. Before this appears, the leaves may curl a little and assume a blistery appearance. Infection occurs when the temperature is between 64° and 75°F., but the spores can develop in very high humidity.

Control: Once present, powdery mildew is not easy to control. Sulfur sprays or dusts were the standard for many years, but now new controls have been developed, including a dinitro chemical sold under the trade names of Mildex or Karathane and Benlate. Follow label instructions for rates per gallon of water to add to the regular all-purpose spray in humid weather if the temperature is not above 85°. Since 75° is the highest temperature at which the spores can develop, there is no reason for using it during very hot spells.

DISEASES OF ALKALINE SOIL

CHLOROSIS. This condition, characterized by lack of healthy, rich, green color in rose foliage, is a symptom rather than a disease. It may result from nutrient deficiencies (see page 182); from the fact that the ratios of the various nutrients and trace elements is such that some needed food is not available in soluble form which the roots can take up; from waterlogged soil; or (most common in areas of alkaline soil) the condition may be a lime-induced chlorosis.

Healthy   *Affected*

In mild cases young leaves have normally green veins with pale areas between. In more serious cases both veins and tissues between may turn pale green to yellow. In severe cases the leaves turn yellow while tips and edges brown and curl.

Control: Incorporate plenty of rotted manure or other acid humus in soil when preparing new beds, and add ½ pound of sulfur and 1 ounce of ammonium sulfate per cubic foot of soil (where soil is heavily alkaline). Give regular applications of complete plant food. In established beds where emergency treatment is indicated, apply ½ to 1 pound of ferrous sulfate per bush. Moisten the soil thoroughly, make holes 3 to 9 inches deep around each plant, and place an ounce of the ferrous sulfate in each. Cover with soil. One treatment is effective from two to four years.

ROOT-KNOT NEMATODE is a disease caused by the attack of microscopic nematodes on the roots of rose plants, especially in the Southwest. Symptoms above ground are stunting and yellowing of the foliage followed by dying of the affected plant. When dug, the fibrous roots are found to have small knots or swellings ⅛ to ½ inch in length. In extreme cases roots are often matted or decayed with fibrous roots largely lacking.

Control: Examine new plants carefully and reject any whose roots show signs of root knot. In the garden destroy infested plants. In ground which has been infected use Vapam or Nemagon. Follow instructions on the label for rates per 100 square feet. When using Vapam soil must lie fallow for three weeks before replanting.

TEXAS ROOT ROT is caused by a fungus native to semiarid, alkaline soils. Roses attacked by this disease die very suddenly during the summer months (June to September). Except that the leaves may tend to wilt in the heat of the day and the foliage to lighten in color, there is little previous warning. Strands of buff-colored fungus on the roots of a plant which has died in this way are pretty sure proof that this is the cause of death. Mats of white, cottony strands (filaments), later turning to buff, sometimes appear after rains or irrigation on the soil surface during the summer. The disease usually occurs where irrigation must be resorted to.

Control: Professor R. B. Streets, Head of the Department of Plant Pathology of the College of Agriculture, University of Arizona, has originated the following effective treatment. "Loosen the soil of the infected area . . . Then build a dirt bank about 6 inches high around it. Scatter ammonium sulfate evenly over the soil at the rate of 1 pound to 10 square feet. Then add an equal amount of agricultural sulfur to the same area and stir into the loose surface soil until the yellow color disappears. Fill the basin with water to a depth of three inches." In addition to the above procedure, which will not injure plants if directions are followed to the letter, one half to three fourths of the top growth of plants infected with Texas root rot should be removed. Add generous amounts of organic matter to the soil of the rose garden as another curative measure.

NUTRIENT DEFICIENCIES

Among other rose troubles sometimes encountered are abnormal growth characteristics due to deficiencies or surpluses of the various plant food elements. Ordinarily, if soil preparation and subsequent maintenance are carried out along the lines suggested in Chapters 4 and 6 instances of this sort will never occur. In case any of them do, here are the symptoms that indicate when something has gone wrong, and suggestions as to what to do about it, based on discussions of the subject by Dr. Frank A. Gilbert and by Col. E. H. Jenkins in *American Rose Annuals*.

It should be kept in mind that many deficiency symptoms are similar to those resulting from spray injury, which is much more common. A guiding difference is that the latter are usually *temporary,* while those caused by actual deficiences are *permanent;* and unless the deficiency is corrected, the extent of injury is likely to become progessively greater.

Boron is most apt to be lacking in alkaline soils. Leaves fail to attain normal size, become cup-shaped, and may appear scorched; terminal buds die, resulting in excessive branching at base of plant; such flowers as do form are usually misshapen. Boron deficiency may be corrected by applying *borax* at the rate of one level tablespoonful per 100 square feet. Mix thoroughly with 5 pounds of dry sand or dry sifted soil, broadcast, and scratch in lightly. Great care must be taken not to apply an excessive amount, which is quite as bad as a deficiency, causing the leaves to curl and twist and to assume a scorched appearance.

Copper is sometimes deficient in muck and peat soils. As with boron, such a shortage may cause the failure of growing tips to develop properly. If a deficiency is thought to exist, apply copper sulfate, one tablespoon to 100 square feet, mixed with 5 pounds of carrier, and applied as borax, above.

Iron. While this is usually present, in some soils it is "locked up" in such a way that the plant cannot use it. This happens when there is an excess of lime or when other elements present are out of proportion to the iron content; and results in such symptoms as a light chlorosis or yellowing of the young leaves. The veins of young foliage remain a darker green than the rest of the leaf, though in severe cases complete yellowing of the young foliage occurs, while mature leaves remain of normal color. Iron is applied either in the form of iron sulfate (ferrous sulfate or copperas) 1 teaspoonful per plant, applied dry to the soil and scratched in; or as a spray, 1 tablespoonful to 2 gallons of water, applied to the soil beneath the plants. It is also helpful to increase the humus content in soil which is lacking in this element.

Manganese. A deficiency of this element is most likely to occur in alkaline soils, and is indicated by yellowish or whitish mottling of the leaf tissue between the veins, more severe toward the tops of growing canes. The addition of manganese causes an increase of nitrogen in the soil because it oxidizes. A corrective application is manganese sulfate which is applied, 2 or 3 tablespoons per 100 square feet, mixed with 5 pounds of sand or other carrier, broadcast and scratched in.

Magnesium. Sandy soils, especially if lacking in humus, are most subject to this deficiency, which shows up as a chlorosis, with yellowing of the older leaves, which are often tinged red to purple. To correct, apply 1 pound magnesium (dolomitic) limestone per 100 square feet; or (if soil is already alkaline) 1 ounce of Epsom Salts, applied dry with carrier as above. The foliage may also be sprayed with 1 level tablespoon of Epsom Salts dissolved in one gallon of water.

Nitrogen. A rose plant suffering for want of nitrogen just looks and acts sick. The leaves—especially those lowest down on the plant—begin to turn yellow, but do not fall off. Growth gradually comes to a stop; foliage is light-colored instead of a deep, rich green; buds fail to develop properly; and flowers are undersized and pale or dull in color. Even all these symptoms, however, may not mean a lack of nitrogen *in the soil.* They do show that the plant is not getting enough nitrogen. It is a matter of how much nitrogen is available to the plant.

The addition to the soil of such carbon-rich, humus-forming materials as sawdust, ground corncobs, or straw (which temporarily use the available nitrogen in the process of decomposition) may rob the roses of the amount of nitrogen they need. This is why a high-nitrogen fertilizer is applied when such material is added to soil. In time, when decay has taken place, the nitrogen originally in the soil will again become available, but in the meantime the plants may suffer.

Where excellent drainage has not been provided in the rose garden, nitrogen may not be available to the plants, though present in the soil. In such a case, a prompt correction of the waterlogged condition is indicated.

Roses planted in very sandy soil—as at the seashore—may also need frequent applications of nitrogenous fertilizers because of the rapid leaching which occurs under such conditions.

Where nitrogen is lacking or unavailable, frequent applications of a fertilizer high in nitrogen content should be resorted to.

Phosphorus. Rose plants almost never suffer from a deficiency of this element when grown in the open garden. They certainly will not do so if regular applications of complete plant food are given. Symptoms are the dropping of mature foliage, though it does not turn yellow but a dull gray-green. Stems are weak, buds slow to develop, and the root system does not develop normally.

Potassium. Like phosphorus deficiency, that of potassium is never found in a rose garden where complete fertilizers are regularly applied, or where natural manures are used. When it does occur, leaves turn first yellow at the margins of the leaflets, and then brown, looking as though they had been scorched. As with lack of phosphorus, stems are weak and buds are not developed normally.

Sulfur. Lack of sulfur is most unlikely to affect roses in the well-cared for garden as sulfur is applied in the form of sprays in sufficient quantities to correct any possible deficiency. Chlorosis of the *young* foliage is a symptom. The application of superphosphate at the rate of one pound per 100 square feet is a corrective. Do not apply sprays when temperature is above 90°!

NUTRIENT EXCESSES

Too much of certain elements may cause as much trouble as too little. For this reason the novice should be most careful to follow exactly the directions on his package of fertilizer or nutritive element.

Lime. Where too much lime has been mistakenly applied to the soil, or in areas of high alkalinity such as occur in the Southwest, the pH in the soil is so high that other nutrients become unavailable because they are not soluble and therefore cannot be absorbed by plant roots.

Materials generally used to acidify soil of high alkalinity are sulfur or aluminum sulfate. The former, applied at the rate of 4 pounds per 100 square feet, will bring the pH down from 8 to 6 (slightly acid). Aluminum sulfate, which is sometimes used, requires 10 pounds to do the same work.

Nitrogen excess is apt to develop under garden conditions only if too heavy an application of high-nitrogen fertilizer has been applied to the rose bed. Symptoms are very lush, soft new growth, light green in color. Since such growth is particularly subject to frost injury, nitrogen is withheld from any application of fertilizer made late in the season when an early frost may occur within a few weeks. Heavy watering will carry off excess nitrogen, especially in light soils.

INSECTICIDES AND FUNGICIDES

BENLATE	fungicide (powdery mildew and Black Spot)	As directed on package.
CAPTAN (Orthocide)	fungicide (black spot, blights)	2 tablespoons per gallon water. Compatible with other materials.
DIAZINON	insecticide (caterpillars; beetles; earwigs; leaf miners)	Use as directed on package.
FERBAM (Fermate) (Karbam Black)	fungicide (black spot)	2 level tablespoons per gallon water; or as a dust. Leaves unsightly sootlike residue on foliage.
KARATHANE (Mildex) (Dinitros)	fungicide; insecticide; (mildew; mites.)	½ to ⅔ teaspoon per gallon water. (Use spreader. Do not apply over 85°F.)
LIME-SULFUR	dormant spray; fungicide; miticide; scalecide	Dormant spray: 1 part to 7 or 9 parts water. Summer spray: 1 part to 40 or 50 parts water.
METALDEHYDE	insecticide (slugs)	5 to 10% dust. Use 2 lbs. per 1000 square feet at night 3 or 4 times at weekly intervals.
MALATHION (Safe to use. Others of this group: Parathion, Tepp, and Hexatox are deadly.)	insecticide (aphids; mealy bugs; mites; scales; thrips; white fly)	50% wettable powder. 4 teaspoons per gallon water; or 4% dust.

METHOXYCHLOR (Methocide)	insecticide (canker worms; borers; Japanese beetles; rose midge, etc.)	50% wettable powder. 2 tablespoons per gallon water.
NICOTINE SULPHATE (Black Leaf 40)	insecticide (sucking insects)	Use according to directions on bottle.
PHALTAN (Folpet)	fungicide (the best preventive to date for black spot)	75% wettable powder. 4 teaspoons per gallon water.
PYRETHRUM	insecticide (aphids, beetles)	Use according to directions on label.
SEVIN	insecticide (beetles, caterpillars)	Use according to directions on package. Available in 5 and 10% dusts and 50% wettable powder.

COMBINATION ALL-PURPOSE SPRAY FOR ROSES

(Use every week to ten days in growing season.)

1 gallon water
4–6 tablespoons 50% wettable malathion
2 tablespoons 50% wettable methoxychlor (Methocide)
1 tablespoon 75% wettable Phaltan (Folpet)
   or 1½ tsp. 50% wettable powder Benlate

½ teaspoon Karathane   { Omit if weather is
                          above 85°F.

SPRAYERS AND DUSTERS

Ortho Hose-sprayer   California Spray-Chemical Corp.,
                              South Plainfield, N.J.
                              Pasadena, Calif.

Pressure sprayers   { Hudson Manufacturing Co.,
Dusters of all types   Chicago 11, Ill.
Trombone sprayers   { Sears, Roebuck and Company

Dusters (small rotary)   Jackson & Perkins,
                              Rose Lane, Medford, Oregon 97501
                            Wayside Gardens, Mentor, Ohio

APPLYING SPRAYS AND DUSTS

The effectiveness of any spray or dust depends upon the *thoroughness* with which the foliage is covered, and upon *keeping* it covered. Ordinarily this means an application every week when plants are making rapid growth, and every ten to fifteen days at other times, especially during rainy spells. As black spot is spread by splashing water, it is advisable to spray or dust before rain or watering, or *immediately* after.

Thorough and even application can be obtained only when the sprayer or duster is kept in excellent working condition. Uneven application may result in burning foliage, and in leaving areas that are not protected.

PLEASE NOTE:

In many states (New York, Maryland, Ohio) pesticides such as DDT and mercuries are banned. In addition materials such as chlordane, dieldrin, heptachlor are on a restricted list and can ONLY be purchased and used by a registered pesticide applicator. Check with your state cooperative extension for information concerning the use of pesticides.

> *"On each lopped shoot a foster scion bind,*
> *Pith pressed to pith, and rind applied to rind;*
> *So shall the trunk with loftier crest ascend,*
> *Nurse the new bud, admire the leaves unknown,*
> *And blushing glow with beauty not its own."*
> —*Charles Darwin, citing Vergil.*

If you love roses and have space for more of them, it is an easy matter to grow additional plants of your favorites. Or, if you have a friend who grows roses, you can produce new plants to "swap" for varieties you do not have.

Unfortunately in most articles about roses the art of propagation, if mentioned at all, has usually been played down, for many rose-growing concerns seem to have frowned upon the encouragement of this art. To us it seems that this attitude is a mistaken one, for the more roses there are grown in amateurs' gardens, the more roses will be bought by rose enthusiasts.

There are four methods of increasing one's stock of roses, three of them not at all difficult, and the fourth not beyond the scope of an amateur gardener who is willing to do a little experimenting until he masters the technique involved. These four methods are division; cuttings; layering; and budding.

DIVISION

Division is the procedure by which an old plant is separated into two or more parts, each of which is then treated as a separate plant. Division can be used with many species and with Shrub Roses that produce a number of stems from below ground, thus forming a clump, much in the manner of most perennials. It may be used with some types of climbers, but not with roses that grow from a single main stem such as the garden or bush roses included in the Hybrid Tea, Floribunda, and Polyantha groups.

The procedure involved in making divisions is very simple. The old tops are cut back severely leaving stubs eight to twelve inches long, and the remaining clump of roots and stubs is cut through, vertically, into two or more sections. An old, dull saw makes a suitable tool for this purpose. The roots are then dug up, pulled apart, and replanted, preferably in prepared holes in which a portion of peatmoss (or peatmoss and sand, if the soil is on the clayey side) has been incorporated. They can go in an inch or two deeper than they were formerly growing; they should be trodden in firmly, and of course kept well watered.

Single shoots from underground rooted stolons may also be severed and treated in the same way. Early spring is the best time for dividing, though we have been successful in using it in autumn and even as late as December. If done in the fall, the application of a heavy mulch is desirable in order to keep the ground unfrozen until new roots can become established.

CUTTINGS

Roses root readily from cuttings. Plants propagated by this method are known as "own root" roses. Most varieties grown on their own roots will grow as well and produce as fine flowers as those which are budded onto another stock. One advantage of "own root" plants is that there will be no undesirable suckers thrown up from the base of the stem.

Softwood cuttings are usually made in June or early July. They can be taken later but this somewhat lessens the chance of their coming through the first winter successfully, particularly in rigorous regions. The wood selected should be of new growth, but sufficiently firm to resist buckling when bent between the fingers. Firm, vigorous stems of flowers that have just dropped their petals are in the right condition. Such stems, originating near the base of the plant, are ideal. Needless to say they should be kept carefully labeled, and sufficiently moist to prevent any danger of their drying out between the time they are cut and their insertion in whatever rooting material is to be used.

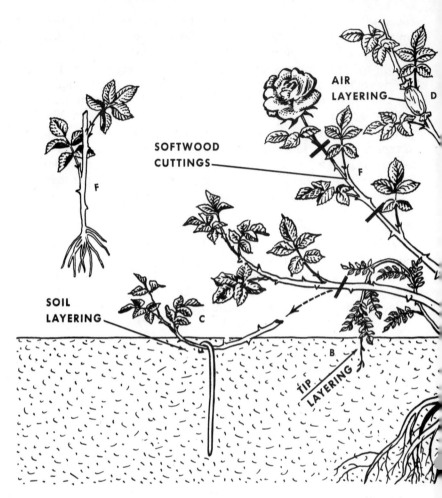

AIR
LAYERING D

SOFTWOOD
CUTTINGS

SOIL
LAYERING C

F

F

B

TIP
LAYERING

METHODS OF P

(A) DIVISION: *stolons (of some species) form roots and send up new shoots; merely need be cut off and transplanted.* *(B)* TIP LAYERING: *tips of fairly firm new growth are pushed down into ground, where they form roots.* *(C)* SOIL LAYER-ING: *wood near tip of lateral growth is partly severed, then pegged down and covered with soil. After roots form, new plant is severed from parent.* *(D)* AIR LAYERING: *firm new growth is cut part way through, surrounded with ball of moist moss held in place by airtight plastic wrap. When roots have formed in moss ball, stem is cut off just beneath it, and new plant is potted or set out.*

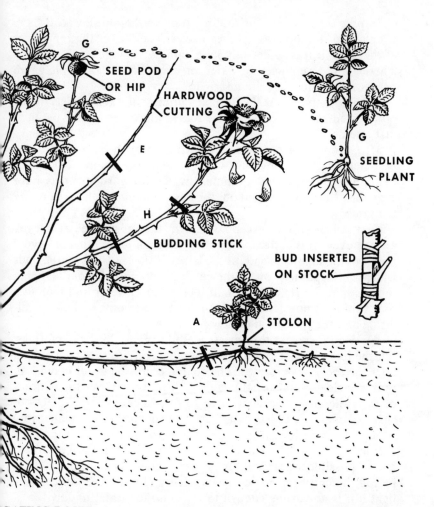

G

SEED POD
OR HIP

HARDWOOD
CUTTING

E

BUDDING STICK

H

SEEDLING
PLANT

G

BUD INSERTED
ON STOCK

A STOLON

GATING ROSES

(E) HARDWOOD CUTTINGS *are taken from dormant canes or laterals, placed in soil or rooting medium, and covered with glass or plastic film until new root system is well established.* *(F)* SOFTWOOD CUTTINGS *are taken from firm new growth, cut through or just below an eye, and treated as for hardwood cuttings.* *(G)* BY SEED: *parent varieties are "crossed," seed pods protected until well developed. These, when fully ripe, are gathered, processed, and later planted.* *(H)* BY BUDDING: *growth buds—at bases of leaves—are removed, and carefully shaped to fit into cuts made in bark on "stocks" (see page 206).*

To prepare the stem for rooting, remove the old flower, if there is any, and the top two or three leaves. Then sever the remainder of the stem, if it is sufficiently long, into five to eight inch sections. These should be placed in water, or wrapped in damp sphagnum or peatmoss until they are inserted.

It is advisable to make several cuttings of each variety to be propagated as there are apt to be some failures, especially on one's first attempt.

Methods of Rooting. Once the cuttings have been prepared, the best method of rooting to use will depend on the number of cuttings being handled and the equipment which the gardener may have available. In all of the methods, however, the preliminary steps are the same.

First, all the leaves except two or at the most three at the top are removed; it is better to snip them off than to pull them to avoid injury to the incipient buds at the bases of the leaf stalks—the buds which will begin to grow as the cuttings take root. Second, dipping the bases of the stems for a half inch or so in water and then in a root stimulant powder such as Rootone or Semesan will aid in callusing and the formation of new roots.

Rooting in water is the easiest method of handling the cuttings, but the least satisfactory as they are less likely to survive handling after the roots have formed. The container for the water may be an ordinary clear glass jar holding enough water to cover the bottoms of the canes to a depth of three to four inches. A few pieces of charcoal may be added to aid in keeping the water clear. More water must be added from time to time to maintain it at the original level. Keep the jar in a moderate temperature, out of drafts, and if possible where the air is fairly moist. During the rooting period the cuttings should receive plenty of light, even direct sunlight if it is not strong enough to warm up the water unduly.

Roots should begin to develop in four to six weeks. When they have attained a length of a half inch or so the cuttings are removed and planted very carefully in 2½- or 3-inch pots, in a mixture of half-sifted compost and half-sandy soil. The pots are then plunged to the rims in a frame or other protected place to keep them from drying out, and are regularly watered; after growth is renewed, they are given a bimonthly application of Ra-Pid-Gro or some similar liquid fertilizer.

For three weeks or so after being potted up the cuttings should be kept covered with a glass or plastic sash, or if only a few are being handled, with inverted glass jars or plastic domes. When good root balls have formed in the original pots the plants may be transferred to larger ones to be grown on into setting-out size. It is usually best to carry them through the first winter in a frame. In milder sections they can be transplanted to the open but should be well protected during their first winter.

Rooting in pots involves much the same procedure as the one described above except that the cuttings, instead of first being rooted in water, are placed directly in pots filled with a suitable rooting medium. Plain, gritty sand is often used, but we have had much better results with mixtures of sand and peatmoss, or sand and vermiculite, in proportions of about half-and-half. Individual cuttings may be placed in small (2- or 2½-inch) pots, but it is much easier to maintain an evenly moist condition of the rooting medium, which is quite essential, if four to six cuttings are placed in a 6- or 7-inch bulb pan. If the pots containing the cuttings are plunged to the rims in a bed of damp peatmoss, watering once a week or so

A softwood (green) and a hardwood (dormant) cutting. The former are usually taken in spring or early summer; the latter in fall, or at pruning time.

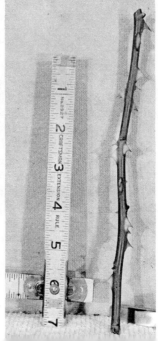

Softwood cuttings in bulb pan, covered with plastic dome. Saucer makes it possible to water from bottom, without removing dome.

will maintain the proper degree of moisture. Rooting may be hastened and made more certain by covering each pot with a plastic envelope held in place with a rubber band just below the rim. I find that the plastic bags in which my tobacco is packed (inside 1-pound tins) make ideal coverings for the purpose. *Do not be tempted to remove the covering until some new growth has been made.* To do so may result in the failure of your attempt to root them.

Subsequent treatment is the same as for cuttings rooted in water except that they may be allowed to make considerably more growth, in fact may be left until they begin to crowd each other, before being transferred individually to 4- or 5-inch pots.

Individual hardwood cutting, inserted in hole prepared with peatmoss and sand, and covered with glass jar (December 10). Same cutting, with jar removed, in spring. Vigorous new growth has started (April 15).

Rooting in Flats or a Frame. If a considerable number of cuttings are to be rooted they may be placed in flats or directly in a frame. If flats are used they should be at least 4 inches deep; if a frame is used be sure that there is excellent drainage under a 4- or 5-inch layer of the rooting medium. Otherwise the procedure is the same, including protection that will assure a moist atmosphere around the cuttings until they have struck. To be sure of this it may be necessary to mist-spray the tops frequently for the first couple of weeks. The cutting bed, however, must not be allowed to become soggy wet.

Hardwood Cuttings. Cuttings of hard or dormant wood are usually taken early in the spring before the foliage has begun to develop, or in autumn, after mid-August, depending on the climate, when little or no new foliage growth is being made. Except in mild climates spring is the preferable time because the baby plants have a full season in which to become established before going through their first winter.

The wood selected should be of one season's growth, the cuttings being made in the same way as softwood cuttings except that they should be considerably longer—six to ten inches. One of our correspondents—below the Mason and Dixon Line—writes that she gets best results with cuttings made eighteen inches long, inserted twelve inches deep in open ground.

The time-honored method of rooting dormant cuttings is to insert them in soil in a well-drained location, shaded from direct hot sun, with three or four inches of the tops left exposed, and then to cover them with inverted, wide-mouthed Mason jars. Results may be made somewhat more certain if a hole some four inches in diameter and five or six inches deep is filled with the rooting medium suggested above and the cuttings are "planted" in this before being covered with glass. In any case the soil about the cuttings should be watered frequently enough to prevent its becoming dried out.

Trench Method. While glass jars will serve if only a few cuttings are to be made, striking the cuttings in a prepared trench is much more convenient when a couple of dozen or more cuttings are involved.

The trench is made in a V shape, with one side perpendicular, the other at an angle of about 30°. If the soil is dry it should be thoroughly moistened before the trench is made so that the sides

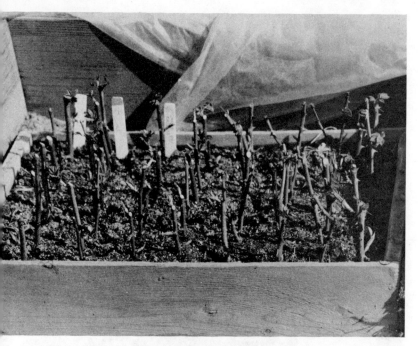

Hardwood cuttings, made in late February, placed in VisQueen-covered frame in shade out of doors. Of the 56 cuttings, all but three had started new growth when photograph was taken (April 15).

will not crumble. The bottom of the trench is then filled with a rooting mixture to a half to two thirds of its depth. A convenient tool for making the trench is an ordinary lawn edger or a sharp spade, the blade being thrust down vertically and then pressed over to one side, leaving an opening about five inches deep.

The cuttings, after being treated with a root-promoting powder, are inserted in the rooting medium and made firm, and the top of the trench is then filled full of soil, which also is thoroughly firmed about them.

A covering for the trench is then made by using a strip of fairly strong plastic, such as VisQueen, supported by pieces of wire bent to about the size and shape of croquet wickets. This strip should be of sufficient width to allow covering the edges with two or three inches of soil, thus forming an almost airtight, moisture-retaining tent.

September bloom on a dormant cutting made from a discarded March pruning.

LAYERING

In layering, instead of removing bodily a section of the old plant as in division, one develops a new plant by inducing the formation of roots near the tip of a branch or cane while it is still attached to the old plant. When this new baby plant has become established, it is cut off and transplanted.

While layering is used most in connection with Climbing Roses, it can be employed with bush types if canes suitable for the purpose are available. These should be young and vigorous, with healthy foliage, well matured but not hard. With climbers they can be young growths which have not yet bloomed; with bush roses, those which have recently flowered.

There are three distinct types of layering: soil, tip, and air. The first is the one most often employed, the easiest, and the one most certain to be successful.

While layering can be done at any time from June to September, the earlier it is undertaken the better (providing the canes to be worked have sufficiently hardened) because the new plants will have more time in which to become established.

Soil Layering. In soil layering the first step is to select the cane or branch which is to be rooted. Pick out one originating near the base of the plant; bend it over until it touches the soil at a point a foot or so back from the tip, and mark this spot. Dig out the soil here to a depth of five inches or so, and replace it with the rooting medium described on page 192. In good, loamy garden soil this may not be necessary, but it takes little effort and makes success more certain.

Next, at the point where the cane will touch the ground when it is bent over, make a clean slanting cut halfway through the wood, just above an eye, and then for an inch or two along the center of the cane under the bud. Insert a small twig or a matchstick to hold this cut open. Applying rooting powder at this point with a small brush will further assure success. Remove the adjacent leaves from both sides of the cut.

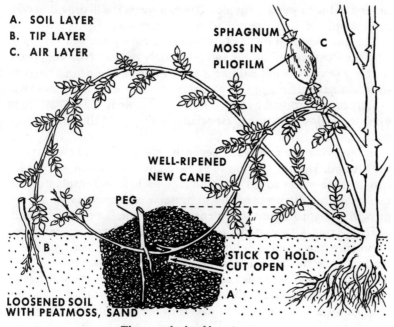

A. SOIL LAYER
B. TIP LAYER
C. AIR LAYER

SPHAGNUM MOSS IN PLIOFILM

WELL-RIPENED NEW CANE

PEG

STICK TO HOLD CUT OPEN

LOOSENED SOIL WITH PEATMOSS, SAND

Three methods of layering roses.

After being thus prepared, the cane is again bent down to the prepared spot of soil and secured *firmly* in place with a stout bent wire, or a forked stick, cut after the manner of those employed by small boys for carrying home fish; or a fairly heavy stone may be used in place of the stick.

Then cover the cane with a mound of soil about four inches deep after it has been thoroughly firmed down A stone or brick placed on top of the mound will help further in holding it securely in place. This is important because the least loosening or movement of the cane in the soil during the period when new roots are being formed may result in failure. It is advisable to leave a slight depression around the circumference of the mound so that water, when applied, will not run off to the sides and leave the soil dry at the center. Each mound should be watered thoroughly at the time of planting, and care taken to keep it moist, but not soaking wet, during the several weeks following. A time-saving way to do this is to punch a tiny hole in a tin can—just enough to make a leak—and place this next to the layer with the bottom an inch or two underground. If the can is filled with water a couple of times a week, it will provide a constant supply of moisture just where it is needed.

The time required for the layers to form new roots will vary both with the weather conditions and the variety of rose. New roots may start in a few weeks but nothing is to be gained by being in a hurry to sever the new plant from its parent. A June or early July layer will usually be well rooted by fall, but it is advisable to leave it attached until the following spring, especially in regions with fairly severe winters.

In removing the new plant, sever the parent cane where it enters the ground. Do not take up the new plant at once but leave it for two or three weeks to get along on its own before transplanting. In transplanting, dig up carefully to preserve all the roots, and if top growth is vigorous and succulent, prune it back a third or a half.

Tip layering is a variation of mound layering, sometimes employed to procure new plants of climbing roses of the Rambler type which send up from the base new growths that do not flower until the following season. When such new growths have become sufficiently ripened and hard, late in the season, they can be cut back at the tip, stripped of a few leaves, bent over and pushed into soil (prepared as described above) to a depth of about six inches, and firmly secured there by being tied to a short stake driven well down into the ground. When the plants have become well rooted, the parent canes are cut off a foot or so above the ground and the following spring may be transplanted to their permanent positions.

Air Layering. Still another method of getting new rose plants from old is that known as air layering. It differs from soil layering in that the part of the stem to be rooted, instead of being bent down to the ground, is left where it is and the rooting medium is placed around it. In former days this was known as Chinese layering, for the Chinese had made use of it for many centuries.

Formerly in air layering roses it was necessary to use the clumsy device of supporting a pot on a stick, in the right position to hold

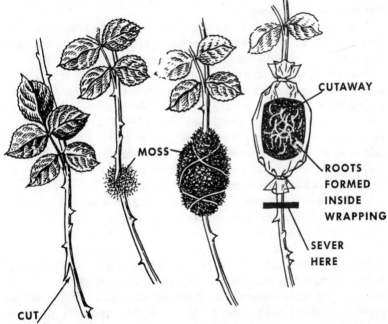

Air layering—a modern application of an ancient Chinese technique—is easily accomplished. Leaves are removed from a section of a young cane or lateral; a clean, deep, slanting cut is made a half to two-thirds through the cane; and in this a little sphagnum moss is placed to hold it open. A generous wad of moist moss is then tied around the cane, and this is wrapped in prepared plastic film and is securely fastened at sides and ends. When roots have formed in the moss, the stem is cut off, providing a good-sized growing plant.

the rooting medium around it, and it required constant and expert care in watering to keep the rooting medium moist. Now all this has been superseded by the simple method of using a fistful of sphagnum moss held in place by a sheet of plastic film which keeps the moss moist indefinitely without further attention.

The film best suited for this purpose is a patented one known as Airwrap. It is specially prepared with a root stimulant, plant food, and fungicide added to it. It may be bought in the form of a propagating kit that provides everything necessary for the operation—sheets of the special film about eight inches square, sphagnum moss, and ties.

In this modern method of air layering the procedure is as follows. With roses, the best time to operate is in late spring just after the first blooms are passing.

Select a cane that is of new growth but well-ripened, such as would make good cuttings. At a point fifteen to eighteen inches below the tip, remove leaves and thorns for a space of five or six inches. Then, with a sharp knife, make a cut similar to that used in soil layering and force a bit of sphagnum into the cut to hold it open. Or, instead of making a cut into the wood, remove completely a circle of bark and cambium layer about one-half inch wide. It is best to remove this strip just below an eye and it should be clean and neat, leaving no bruised edges. Then wipe the cut portions and *the edges of the bark* clean with the treated side of a sheet of Airwrap.

Next dip a handful of sphagnum in water and squeeze it out until it is fairly damp but not dripping wet. Wrap the moss around the wound in a ball extending about two inches above and below the cut, and two to three inches in diameter, pressing it fairly tight. The final step is to wrap this ball in a sheet of Airwrap, making sure that it is entirely enclosed, as the plastic film must contain the moss tightly at both top and bottom. Next pull the vertical edges of the sheet together, lapping them about an inch, and refold until the plastic is drawn tight around the moss. The ends are then tied tightly around the cane. It is very important that no water, from rain or from sprinkling, be able to penetrate to the moss and make it too wet.

After a few weeks roots should begin to show through the ball of moss. When several are visible, or when you can feel the root ball by gently grasping the wrapped moss, cut the cane off at the bottom of the wrap and remove the rooted section to a convenient place for potting. Use a good potting soil containing about 25% peatmoss and, having removed the wrap, *but without disturbing the sphagnum,* pot firmly and plunge pot to rim in a shaded place, cutting any new growth back one third to one half. An occasional syringing or misting may be required to keep the foliage from wilting. The plant should become established within a couple of weeks and, after a good root ball has been formed in the pot, may be transferred to its permanent position. In cold sections it is advisable to carry the potted plant over the first winter in a frame.

BUDDING

Propagation by means of budding involves a technique considerably more complicated than the preceding, but one which is not beyond the scope of the patient and careful amateur.

Understocks. The first step in propagating by means of budding is to provide the understocks (young rose plants) upon which the buds are to be inserted. Sometimes these may be obtained from a local nursery; if so, this will save a year. Otherwise the would-be propagator will have to grow his own. This is not a difficult operation as he can easily root cuttings of *Rosa multiflora* or of the Climbing Rose Doctor Huey, both of which make good understocks by the time they have made a year's growth. Cuttings made in June should be well rooted by fall, and the following spring, as soon as frost is out of the ground, can be transplanted to stand about ten to twelve inches apart in rows two or two and a half feet apart. In transplanting do not set them too deep because the closer to the roots the buds to be "worked" on them can be placed, the better.

Preparing the Buds. The understocks or root systems having been provided, the next step is to select and prepare the buds which are to be placed upon them to develop the plants of the varieties desired.

This is done in midseason, usually late June or early July. As in making cuttings, the clean pump stem of a rose that has just shattered provides the ideal material for a "bud stick," so called because each such stem, if a foot or more in length, will provide several good buds. The top of the stick is cut off just below the first five-petaled leaf, and the rest of the leaves are snipped off, leaving a half inch

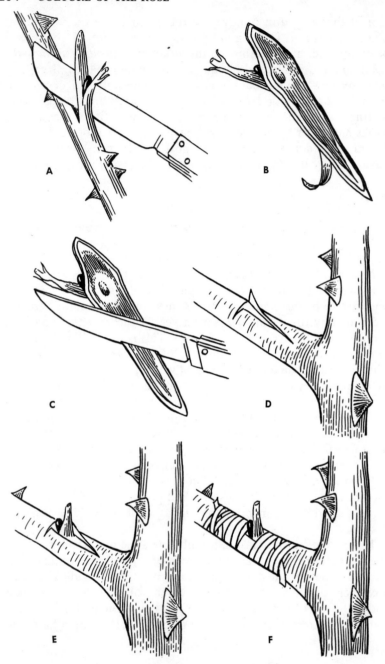

of the stem to serve as a handle when the bud is to be inserted. The bud sticks—carefully labeled—are placed in water or wrapped in damp sphagnum moss.

When the bud sticks have been prepared, the next step is to proceed to the actual operation of budding. For this job a budding knife (see illustration page 215), designed particularly for the work to be done, is desirable. With the bud stick and rubber bands or strips of raffia at hand for tying the buds in (it is convenient to carry them in a small basket) we are ready to begin our exciting experiment.

With a damp cloth, wipe clean the lower part of the stock down to the ground, for the lower the incision into which the bud is inserted, the better.

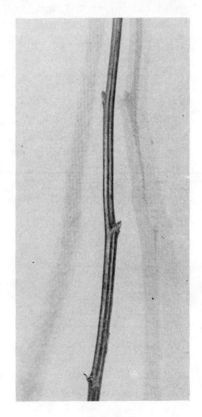

BUDDING A ROSE. (Illustration on opposite page) *(A) Growth bud, or eye (at base of leaf stem) of variety to be propagated is cut out with a long sliver of bark and wood attached. (Stem of leaf is left to serve as a handle.) (B) Sliver of wood is very carefully removed, leaving eye attached to the piece of bark, termed the "shield." (C) Base of the shield is then trimmed to a point, and cut off square just above the eye. (D) A T-shaped slit is made in the bark of the plant (known as the "stock") to which the bud is to be transferred. This incision should be in clean, live bark that will heal quickly. (E) The trimmed shield is inserted into the cut, until it fits snugly under the flaps of the cut and across the top. (F) The inserted bud is then bound firmly in place with a rubber band. When the stock is a one-year-old whip, the bud is usually placed at the base—the nearer the ground the better. It may, however, be placed higher up, or on a young lateral.*

Bud stick

Bending down on one knee to get close to your work, make a horizontal cut one half to three quarters of an inch in length. This should be just deep enough to penetrate the bark without cutting into the wood. Next make a perpendicular cut an inch or slightly less, upward to meet the horizontal cut, leaving a T-shaped incision. Next, with the blunt end or blade of the budding knife—made of bone or stainless steel—very carefully loosen and lift up the two right-angled corners of the bark just below the horizontal cut.

Cutting Out the Bud. Now, from the bud stick, starting at the bottom, select a plump, vigorous-looking bud and cut it out. To do this, place the forefinger of the left hand under the bud selected and, starting about half an inch above the bud, cut down under it to about half an inch below, but without cutting it off. Instead of finishing the cut, place the right thumb firmly over the bud and pull down with a quick, firm motion which will remove it with a tapering strip of bark attached.

Next, holding the severed bud in the left hand, carefully pull back the long strip of bark from the wood beneath it. Now comes the most critical step—to remove this bit of wood without damaging the eye. If the eye comes with it, or is bruised, the operation is a failure and the patient will not live. But fortunately there are plenty of other patients so you can start over again.

The strip of bark with the leaf stem and the bud attached, is known as the "shield." The eye, if uninjured, should remain firmly fixed in the shield with its base showing clearly on the inside. The section of the shield below the eye is now trimmed to a point, and is slipped down into the T-shaped incision already made in the understock. It is pushed well down so that the eye is slightly below the horizontal cut. Then the section of the shield above this line is carefully cut off and removed so that the shield itself will make a smooth union with the edge of the bark above it, and press firmly against the wood underneath it.

The shield is now ready to be tied in with a strip of raffia or a rubber band. We prefer the latter not only as being more convenient but as holding the shield more firmly in place and at the same time, due to its elasticity, allowing for future growth without constricting the bark. If raffia is used, it should be cut off before this occurs. Dr. Brownell, of Sub-zero rose fame, found that he got a much higher percentage of "takes" in budding by placing a ball of thoroughly moistened newspaper at the base of the stem, enveloping the bud after it was tied in.

If the bud graft is successful, the shield and the leaf stem keep their normal color and the bud remains plump, in fact should show indications of swelling in a week or ten days. The bit of leaf stem that was left with the bud then gradually turns yellow and will drop off at a touch. If the shield turns black and the shriveled stem adheres to it, you may be sure that the bud has failed to "take," and another may be inserted at a different point on the same stock.

Aftercare. Needless to say the stock plants should be maintained in vigorous growth for the balance of the season. It is especially important that they never be allowed to suffer for lack of moisture. If in soil that has been well fertilized they will not need further plant food until the following spring, as overluxuriant soft new growth is undesirable.

In late autumn the stock plants may be trimmed back, and on the approach of freezing weather, if they are in an exposed, windswept location they may be provided with a shelter of pine boughs held in place by wire as suggested in Chapter 10. In spring the top growth should be cut back to within five or six inches of the buds that were worked upon them.

CHAPTER 15. *Hybridizing:*
Creating Your Own New Roses

*Words fail me to picture dreams of hope, expectations, surprises—
yes, disappointment, sometimes despair, that are the lot of the
hybridizer . . .*

DR. J. H. NICOLAS

One is tempted to begin this chapter with the short but
pithy advice given by Puck to people contemplating matrimony—
"Don't!"

The chance that even a trained and experienced hybridizer has
of obtaining a better or a distinctly different rose, when he crosses
two varieties, is one in many, many thousand. With the amateur, it
is even less. However, the rose grower who feels the urge to try his
hand at the game, and who will derive from this interesting venture
sufficient pleasure to be its own reward in growing roses which he

*Modern rose breeding is done on a scale involving hundreds of thousands of
trials—all but a very few of which are discarded.*

himself has created, even if they are not gold medal winners, will find it a fascinating gamble.

The technique involved in creating a new rose is by no means beyond the grasp of the amateur—or even of the rank beginner. If he wishes to take a ten thousand to one shot that he will obtain something worth while, that is his own affair. In any event it will be his baby, and no matter what others folks may think of it, in his eyes it will probably be the fairest in the land. Personally we have always found it more rewarding to test and to try to grow well the roses which other people have created than to attempt to produce any of our own, but it's all a matter of one's point of view. The fact remains that many excellent varieties have been bred by amateurs. The late Doctor Brownell started as an amateur and achieved his big family of Sub-zero varieties; and John deVink, not a special hybridizer, hit upon the happy idea of doing something with Miniature Roses, and using the very old variety Rouletti, attained the Miniatures Tom Thumb and Pixie, thus starting the distinct new group that has already gained a prominent place in rosedom, with full color pages assigned to them in leading rose catalogs.

HAVE A GOAL

If you should decide to attempt any hybridizing, do not go at it blindly. The first step is to set up an ideal of a rose you would like to create and then use parents which possess these characteristics. Some of those you should consider are hardiness, vigor, constant bloom, color, fragrance, form, and disease-resistance. Do not, however, make the mistake of thinking you can pick out these characteristics and, at will, pass them on to the next generation. Our modern roses are of such very mixed ancestry that you will get all kinds of throwbacks to ancestors in the long, long line of descent. Almost anything can happen—and usually does! Don't be surprised if from two double flowers you get a batch of singles; but a rose that is subject to black spot or mildew is more likely to transmit that characteristic than one that is not. And above all, don't attempt rose breeding as a one-shot gamble. It is only when you have a batch of new seedlings coming along every year, and you have begun to feel your way from previous experiences, that the game really becomes exciting enough to be worth while.

Bloom at right stage for emasculation: sepals turning down and petals about ready to open.

THE MECHANICS OF "CROSSING"

Equipment. The equipment required for hybridizing is very simple. Most of it can be found in any household, the rest being readily obtainable. Here is the list:

A pair of tweezers, preferably with curved points.
Small, pointed scissors.
A small magnifying glass—unless your eyesight is excellent.
A number of glassine or plastic envelopes.
A notebook.

For convenience during the hybridizing season these should all be kept in a small box or a basket with a handle.

Rose Anatomy. Rose blooms are monoicous; that is, both the male and the female organs (stamens and pistils) are contained in each flower, the stamens forming a ring around the pistils. Consequently each flower is likely to self-fertilize unless the hybridizer takes means to prevent it.

To get a "cross" between two different varieties, it is necessary to take steps to prevent self-fertilization, or accidental fertilization from neighboring flowers. This is done by removing the stamens from the flower selected as the female parent before the pollen "ripens" and becomes ready to fall off onto the pistils of the same blossom. To do this proceed as follows.

OPERATION "CROSSING"

(1) On a plant of the variety selected as the female parent, choose a bud which is fully developed and ready to open, but with the petals still tightly closed.

(2) The next step is to remove all of the petals, starting with the outside row and pulling them sideways until the heart of the flower —the central group of pistils surrounded by rows of stamens—is exposed. An examination with the magnifying glass will show the tips of the pistils (the stigmas) still dry; and the tips of the stamens (the tiny moccasin-shaped anthers) without the dustlike pollen which will appear when they ripen.

(3) Next, with the tweezers or the scissors, *very carefully* so as not to injure the pistils, remove all of the stamens by pulling or cutting them off at their bases. This operation is known as emasculation.

(4) The emasculated flower is then tightly covered with a plastic envelope which is secured around the flower stem at the bottom with a rubber band, or a short piece of the paper-covered wires known as Twist-ems. In two or three days the group of pistils inside the bag

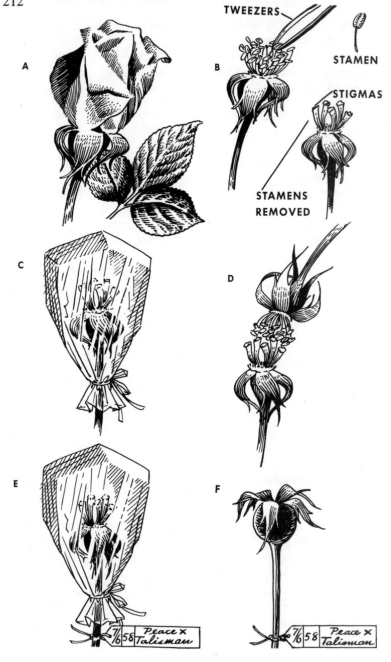

A

B

TWEEZERS

STAMEN

STIGMAS

STAMENS
REMOVED

C

D

E

F

Peace ×
Talisman

Peace ×
Talisman

Rose hips or "apples," matured and ready to be gathered—the harvest of the rose breeder, to him more precious than gold.

HYBRIDIZING. (Illustration on opposite page) *(A) Flower of female parent at right stage to be emasculated. (B) After petals are removed, stamens are cut or pulled off, leaving stigmas exposed. (C) Flower is enclosed in bag to prevent accidental pollination. (D) Stamens of male parent (with petals removed) are brushed across stigmas of female parent. (E) Pollinated bloom is again enclosed, and securely tagged with record of cross. (F) Seed pod or hip (rose apple) develops, and—when fully matured—is removed from plant.*

will have matured, and the stigmas will have developed a slightly sticky coating indicating that they are ready to receive the pollen from a bloom of the variety selected as the male parent. At this time they will also have turned somewhat darker. Here again the magnifying glass will be of help to the beginner in determining just when the stigmas are ready to receive the pollen.

(5) The flower that is to be used as the male parent should be selected at the same time as the female parent, or a day earlier—according to its development. It takes about the same time from the bud stage for the pollen produced on the anthers to develop and be ready to shed as it does for the stigmas to be ready to receive it. The male parent flower may be tagged and left on the plant, or cut and kept in water until it is needed. Under the magnifying glass the pollen grains may readily be discerned when they are ready to shed. The petals are removed, and the cluster of stamens, with two or three inches of stem left on the flower to serve as a handle, are brushed back and forth over the cluster of pistils that were left on the female parent, the protecting bag of course having been removed.

(6) The bag is immediately replaced and made tight to prevent unwanted pollen from reaching the pistils, and also to protect them from hot sun and drying wind. After a week or so the bags are removed.

If the cross has taken, the hip—the round base of the flower with the sepals still attached—will stay green and begin to grow like a small apple, to which as a matter of fact it is very closely related. If the cross has not taken, it will shrivel, decay, and drop off.

If the hybridizing was done in June or very early July, as it should have been in order to give the hips time to mature properly, they will begin to ripen in three months or so, gradually getting darker and changing color to red, yellow, or brown, the sepals usually falling off as they become fully mature. The ripened hips are cut off before freezing weather and autumn rains turn them black and mushy.

GROWING THE SEEDLINGS

The tiny seeds, much the shape of apple seeds but infinitely smaller, are removed from the hip by cutting it in two with a sharp knife and squeezing them out between thumb and finger. There may

Tools and materials used in rose propagation and hybridizing. (For source see page 324.)

be a dozen to two dozen or more in each hip. Only the hard, plump seeds should be saved for planting. Each lot of seed, needless to say, should be kept carefully labeled in a separate container. Small glass tubes or vials are ideal for this purpose.

While the seeds may be sown at once, better germination is usually attained if they are first placed in slightly moist vermiculite or peatmoss, kept for two months in a fairly warm temperature. *and then two months longer in a temperature between 32° and 40°.*

If sown at once, they may be placed in ordinary flats in rows about three inches apart. Seeds should be spaced individually about one inch apart in the row and one-fourth inch deep. It is advisable to treat them with Rootone or Semesan and then sprinkle the surface of the flat lightly with captan or finely sifted sphagnum moss, as precaution against possible damping off. As not all of the seeds will germinate on the first round, the flats should be carefully held over, without allowing them to dry out completely, for at least a year, when another round of seedlings may be expected.

Soil for growing the seedlings may be made up of one part gritty sand, one part peatmoss, and two parts sifted loam or rich compost.

Seeds sown soon after harvesting in November or early December, and kept in the greenhouse (or in a very sunny window indoors) will usually germinate in March or April. If sown later, or if the flats are overwintered in a cold frame, germination will of course be correspondingly later.

The little seedlings quickly develop vigorous taproots. As soon as the second true leaves develop they should be transplanted to three-inch pots, in which they can be grown on until ready to go out into open ground after danger of late spring frosts has passed. At all stages watering should be done in the morning to avoid plants going through the night with damp foliage which is likely to encourage mildew.

The first blooms will appear when the plants are surprisingly small. These flowers will be of miniature size and do not give any accurate idea of what later normal blooms, which often do not develop until the plants are two years old or even later, will be like. By that time most of them will be ready for the compost heap or the brush pile but the few which may seem to be worth keeping will be the hybridizer's reward. At least he will have the satisfaction of knowing that there are no other roses in the world quite identical with them. Additional plants of any of these new creations may be obtained by making cuttings or by budding as described in the preceding chapter.

CHAPTER *16.* *Rose Shows*
and Showing Roses

*Go to one of our great exhibitions and you must surely bring the
conviction home, that true love, seen seldom in the outer world, may
be always found 'among the Roses.'*

Sooner or later most gardeners who achieve fairly good
success in growing roses will yield to the temptation of trying their
luck at entering blooms in a local flower show, or even in a real rose
show devoted particularly, if not exclusively, to the queen of flowers.

They soon discover, however—too often only after heartbreaking
experiences—that growing fine roses is one thing, and being able
to capture prizes with them is quite another. It is our hope that this
chapter may show the neophyte showman how to get a running
start and how to avoid many of the mistakes and resulting disap-
pointments too often experienced.

So, on the supposition that the reader is a beginner at this fascinating form of competition, we shall attempt to guide him step by
step.

THE ROSE SHOW SCHEDULE

The schedule, or list of classes in which roses may be entered,
comes first. In a general flower show the rose "section" is usually
short and very simple. (A typical one is given on page 242.) Even
so, the prospective exhibitor should take pains to be certain that
each entry he makes conforms *exactly* to what the schedule calls
for. If it is "3 specimen Hybrid Teas," for example, an entry of two
Hybrid Teas and one Floribunda would immediately be ruled out.
Or if a "spray" of a Large-flowered Climber is called for and he

217

brings in a beautiful arching *branch* with several sprays on it, he is equally out of order.

Obtain a copy of the schedule well in advance, study it carefully, and if a description of any class in which you might wish to make an entry is not perfectly clear, *check,* in advance, with the committee in charge.

Next, the *date.* This is important because there are a number of things you can do to keep possible prize winners for a few days longer than they naturally would last; or to hasten their development if it looks as though they might be too late. (This is known as "timing" and is discussed later on in this chapter.)

WHAT THE JUDGES WILL LOOK FOR

The judges at a local amateur flower show may or may not be fully qualified for the job when it comes to the rose section, but there is likely to be at least one among them who is acquainted with the rules and the official scale of points adopted by the American Rose Society and used at all important rose shows. This scale of points is as follows:

> Form....................25 points
> Substance...............20 points
> Color...................25 points
> Stem and Foliage........20 points
> Size....................10 points

Even if this official method of scoring is not strictly adhered to at an amateur show, the judges, who presumably will be good gardeners, will just naturally more or less adhere to it, for it is merely a codification of the results of good culture. Point-by-point scoring is resorted to when competition is keen and the judges must really "get down to cases."

GROWING THE PRIZE ROSE

As the rose grower, once bitten, becomes more and more interested in flowers that are destined for this specific purpose, he will learn that there are many tricks of the trade to be picked up. Personally we feel that one who becomes a real show addict eventually

What the judges will look for: (A) a flower of perfect form, one-half to two-thirds open—25 points; (B) substance and quality (of petals) 20 points; color (depth and purity) 25 points; (C, E) stem (strong and straight); and (D) foliage (unblemished, clean, and of good color) 20 points; size (for the variety shown) 10 points. (Mere size, in this scale, is relatively unimportant.)

comes to miss a great many of the pleasures to be had from growing roses. His enthusiasm becomes a lopsided one, and to his rose-colored but jaundiced eye, a silver trophy or a blue ribbon in a show case is more beautiful than a whole gardenful of blooms spreading their color and fragrance for the enjoyment of every passer-by.

Blue ribbons, nevertheless, have their place in rose economy. The rose section in any local flower show usually draws more than its share of attention and helps greatly to stimulate an interest in the growing of roses. And not the least reward, from the exhibitor's point of view, is the pleasure of becoming acquainted with other rose enthusiasts in his neighborhood. Many a local rose society has had its origin in just such meetings.

General Culture. Insofar as the care of the plants is concerned—fertilizing, watering, mulching, pruning, etc.—there is little difference whether the blooms will be wanted for showing, for display out-of-doors, or for bouquets and arrangements in the house. There are, however, a few things which may be kept in mind.

Special Feeding. Usually the dates for rose shows have to be set a long time in advance. If, as spring draws on, continued cold or gloomy weather makes it look as though your plants will not begin blooming at as early a date as usual, and therefore might be too late for the show, an extra feeding with a quick-acting, high-nitrogen fertilizer such as nitrate of soda, ammonium sulfate, or a plant starter solution may help to speed them up a little. So also will a delay in applying the usual summer mulch, permitting the ground to warm up faster.

Careful spraying, too, is of the utmost importance. Keep in mind that good foliage alone counts for quite as much toward that coveted blue ribbon your heart is set on as does the *size* of the flower you show. Most first-time exhibitors forget or refuse to accept this fact and many an irate green showman has cussed out the judges for being either prejudiced or not impartial because his great big, beautiful rose—with its accompanying spotty foliage and possibly a weak stem—did not win a prize.

Another method of making sure that you will have roses when you want them, if you are seriously going into the show game, is to grow plants of the same variety in two different exposures. A bed facing south or east, and fully exposed to the sun, will begin to produce blooms a week or ten days earlier than one facing north or

To get good sprays (of several flowers) keep the plants pruned sufficiently to avoid entangled canes and laterals.

west and receiving some shade, especially during the morning hours.

Pruning. Formerly it was a pretty generally accepted belief that low or hard pruning produced fewer but better blooms. Most rosarians today, however, consider this theory as having been thoroughly discredited, at least so far as modern garden varieties (most of which have in their veins a much smaller percentage of Tea blood than did the older ones) are concerned. And in any event, mere size of bloom is not so important a factor in winning blue ribbons as it formerly was.

It is interesting to note here, as pointed out by Mr. Charles

F. Leon of Portland, Oregon, in the *American Rose Annual* for 1955 that the only persons who had won grand sweepstakes *two or more times* at the great Portland Annual Rose Show, held for sixty-six consecutive years, were Mrs. Nat Schoen of Vancouver, Washington, and Professor Paul Miller of Oregon State College, and himself. He also quotes Professor Miller's statement that "the proper pruning of roses is another important operation in the production of prize-winning blooms. From my experience I am convinced that high pruning will give a greater number of better quality flowers than low pruning. By high pruning I mean cutting back the canes to two and one half to four feet from the ground line."

Furthermore, in a series of pruning experiments in England (where, incidentally, the hard pruning theory originated), results showed that "the larger the rosebush, the bigger, more shapely, more highly colored and more numerous the blooms."

It must be kept in mind of course, that the climates in our own Northwest and in England, which are quite similar, are different from that in most other parts of the United States; winter killback for one thing is less serious, and plants make much more vigorous growth. Nevertheless this evidence is not to be disregarded.

In our own experience we have obtained the best results, so far as show material is concerned, with moderate pruning, particularly in producing clean, straight stems and perfect foliage. And undoubtedly these qualities have won us many ribbons which we would not otherwise have obtained.

When to Prune. In general the pruning schedule will be about the same whether you are growing roses for exhibition or not. The time of pruning, however, can have some influence on blooming dates. Bear in mind that, as a general rule, the higher you prune, the earlier your flowers will be; the lower you prune, the later they will be. This is the influence of our old friend apical dominance, for the top bud or eye on a cane is all set to make the earliest and the fastest growth: if, by pruning, you remove it, a bud lower down the stem will require a little time to catch up and take its place.

If you are attempting to "time" for show purposes, keep in mind that the time between pruning and the opening of the flower is longer for a variety with many petals than it is for a single or a semi-double, up to twenty-five or thirty petals. If you allow seventy to ninety days for the former, and sixty to seventy-five for the latter you will hit it about right. But of course it must be remembered that individual varieties vary greatly in this respect and that weather conditions also will make a big difference; so this method must be used merely as a general guide that is better than none at all.

Another practice—one easily followed—that will aid in producing roses when you want them is to prune some stems somewhat higher than others, thus spreading the period during which the blooms will open.

Disbudding. Single blooms that are to be shown in exhibition classes must be disbudded in order to qualify for competition. If there is any telltale evidence that the disbudding was done recently, this counts against the exhibit.

The ideal time to remove any side buds is immediately after they have developed sufficiently to show a rudimentary stem. At this point they can be snapped off sideways with the thumb and forefinger, and by the time the flower opens, the scar that is left will have healed enough to be scarcely visible. Or they may be cut out with thinning shears or a pointed, very sharp knife blade. If they are not removed at this time, the sooner thereafter the better.

If, as frequently happens when one does not make a business of showing, a flower to be exhibited is not selected until after the side buds are fairly well developed, they may be carefully cut out and the tiny scars touched with a drop of light green ink on the tip of a camel's hair brush to make them less conspicuous.

Protecting. It often happens that very promising show blooms are injured by high winds, stormy weather, or blazing sun, causing colors to fade or "blue" just preceding the show. Various devices are employed to protect them from such injury.

The simplest method is to cover the bloom with a bag or envelope of light plastic. After being placed over the bud or flower this can be partly closed at the bottom with a paper clip or a pin—just enough so that it will stay in place while still permitting free circulation of air.

A better method, but one which will require somewhat more time in its preparation, is to make up conical caps or cones of plastic or heavy black paper, about eight inches in diameter at the base, with an opening of an inch or so at the top. These may be held in place over individual blooms or sprays by being secured to plant stakes of bamboo or stiff wire. In England such shades, with appropriate

To protect flowers from wind and rain, a plastic dome may be secured by clips to an ordinary adjustable plant support. Dome can be moved up or down as desired without changing stake.

adjustable supports, may be purchased, but we know of no manufacturer who has produced them in the U.S.—very likely because there would be less demand for them here due to the fact that American exhibitors much more generally have available facilities for refrigeration to keep blooms in condition for a considerable time after they have been cut. Nevertheless there are occasions when the flower protectors decidedly have their use if one is going in seriously for showing.

Dark-colored protectors are used for two purposes. They will retard to some degree the opening of a bud which threatens to unfold ahead of the time when it will be wanted, and they are decidedly effective in holding the color of varieties that tend to "blue" in direct, strong sunshine—and remember that in the scoring scale color counts for one fourth of all the points which an entry can possibly win.

The form of protection which we have used, but have never happened to see employed elsewhere, is a plastic dome or tent in the eight-inch size, secured to one or two plant stakes that make possible its being adjusted as to height. (See photograph page 224.) If shading as well as protection is desired, the upper part of the dome may be given a coating of whitewash or of dark water paint.

Cutting. As the date for the show draws near, the rose exhibitor must decide the critical question of just what to cut and when to cut it.

Too often the novice, in a burst of enthusiasm over the beauty of the flowers in his or her own rose garden, decides at the last moment, and without having given any previous thought to the matter, to make some entries. We know of one case of this sort where the would-be prize winner delayed cutting until the morning of the show, cut the biggest roses he could find, plunged the stems into buckets of ice water, rushed them to the show, was fortunate enough to get some experienced help in entering them in the proper classes, where for the moment some of them looked quite well. By the time the judging started, however, two hours or so later, most of them were hanging their heads in shame, a few had actually shattered, and only a small number—principally because of lack of competition in their particular classes—succeeded in winning even yellow ribbons. Our friend was so incensed (not at himself, as he should have been, but at the judges and the show management) that he swore he would never again exhibit—an oath that he has religiously kept even though his garden every June produces dozens of roses which are potential prize winners.

Best Time to Cut. Contrary to the belief of many gardeners, the best time to cut roses either for exhibition or for decoration in the home, is during the two hours following four or five o'clock in the afternoon. This has been demonstrated not only by the experience of many rosarians but also by scientifically conducted tests. The reason for this fact is that at this time of day the sugar content in stems and buds is at its highest and consequently best preserves the flowers. If for any reason cutting cannot be done at this time, the next best period is *very* early in the morning.

Bud Stage to Cut. The keeping qualities of the blooms depend also on the stage of development they have reached before they are severed from the plant. On the average and for most varieties, the best time to cut is when the sepals have definitely turned back and the flower is one-fourth to one-third open.

Roses which are to be exhibited are best cut when not more than one-third open. If they are to be kept longer than overnight, cut when just starting to open, as illustrated here. Buds open very rapidly once sepals turn down.

"Tight-flowered" varieties—those with a great many petals which open slowly—should be taken when they are about one-half open.

Singles unfold very rapidly, and these should be taken while the buds are still tight, but showing full color.

Semidoubles, with twenty-five to thirty petals, the center ones shorter than the others, are cut when they are just beginning to unfold—a stage somewhere between tightly closed and one-quarter open.

Timing for show. Don't cut too far in advance, especially if weather is cool. In sequence on this and following page, note that there has been little change in seven days, while in another three days (after sepals have turned down) flower has opened fully. Variety is Buccaneer.

It will take only a few moments' time to do a little experimenting, well before the show, with buds of these various types, all cut at the same time, so that from experience you will gain a more accurate idea of just when to take them in order to have them at their best when they reach the show table. And you will find it a lot of fun too! We received our own first jolting lesson in the importance of bud-timing when we took a collection of Single Hybrid Teas to a show only to have them well past their prime, and in some instances minus a petal or two, by the time they were judged. The following year we captured the coveted "Best Rose in the Show" award with a bloom of Dainty Bess which opened up just in time to display her pristine but fleeting charms in absolutely perfect condition for the admiring eyes of the judges.

How to Cut. First of all make sure that your knife or pruning shears are absolutely sharp. Next check the *length of stem* you will take with the bud: the longer the better, up to eighteen inches (which is usually the limit allowed) provided the stem is clean, fairly straight and well clothed with foliage. Remember that stem and foliage count twenty points—*twice the maximum allowed for size!*

When you are ready to cut, hold the stem firmly with one hand while you cut with the other, and be careful when removing it from the plant, for a leaf may easily be torn by an unobserved neighboring thorn.

When you cut each variety, secure to it a label with the name of the variety and also the class in which it is to be entered at the show. This will avoid possible cases of mistaken identity and also save a great deal of time when you are packing your roses in boxes for transportation to the show.

Treatment after Cutting. The treatment accorded the flowers immediately after cutting is important. When you go out to cut, carry with you a pail containing five to six inches of water, to which may well be added, if it is a hot day, a trayful of ice cubes. While an ordinary metal pail will serve for collecting the cut blooms, we like better a plastic bucket with rolled edges. If a considerable number of blooms are being cut, more than one container will be needed because any crowding of the cut stems is almost certain to result in injury to the foliage if not to the blooms themselves.

As soon as the container is filled, it should be removed at once to the coolest available storage space, such as a cellar. Above all avoid a drafty location, for the treatment of the flowers from the moment they are cut until they are placed on the show table should be concentrated at every step on avoiding the loss of moisture from buds, stems, and foliage.

Do not syringe or sprinkle the cut stems and flowers. To do so will lessen the amount of moisture that will be drawn up through the stems; and moisture on the foliage, furthermore, creates conditions favorable to the development of bacteria that will cause spotting or decay. A slightly wilted condition soon after cutting is nothing to worry about.

STORING, PACKING, AND TRANSPORTING

Rose growers who exhibit at local shows are usually content to exhibit varieties which may happen to be ready at the time of the show. Those who wish to exhibit at more distant points, or who are anxious to make the greatest possible number of entries, are faced with more serious problems, and often have to cut their blooms a number of days in advance of the time when they will be

Holding blooms for show: two buds of same variety, at equal stage of development, were selected (October 9); one at left was cut and placed in refrigerator; the other remained on plant. Photo was taken October 12.

shown. To all such, experimental work which has been done, particularly at Cornell and at the University of California, is both of great interest and of practical value.

It has been demonstrated, for instance, that the three most important factors in maintaining flowers in fresh condition after cutting are

1. The sugar content at the time of cutting.
2. The temperature at which they are kept after being cut.
3. The degree to which the drying out (loss of moisture) can be prevented during the period of storage.

The last two conditions are intimately related.

The best time for cutting—that is, when the sugar content is highest—has already been discussed.

The ideal temperature at which to store is the lowest that can be maintained without actual freezing of the plant tissues. This ideal temperature would be 31°, but this would have to be maintained with absolute accuracy as a drop of one or two degrees below this point would result in actual freezing. For all practical purposes the ordinary home refrigerator which maintains a temperature of 34° to 38°, if in good order, will provide storage conditions that are just about perfect.

In experiments at Cornell, roses stored at 31° for fifteen to eighteen days, when they were removed and the stems were placed in water, opened normally and for four or five days after they were taken out of refrigeration kept in as good condition as freshly cut blooms of the same varieties. As the storage temperature of the cut blooms was increased, in these experiments, the length of time they could be kept after removal was proportionately reduced.

There remains much to be learned concerning the time that flowers, under proper storage conditions, may be kept. Many years ago when I was in charge of the flower bulb division of Seabrook Farms and we were shipping tulip blooms to New York by the carload and flooding the market, we tried extending the shipping season by keeping fairly tight buds in the model cold storage plant used for vegetables. They remained in good condition until we stopped shipping. A few dozen, as an experiment, were retained. I removed some of these every two weeks. The last lot were taken out on July 4, and were still in perfect condition—opened normally and lasted for two days even in a very warm room temperature.

In the Cornell experiments the only two flowers that failed to keep under cold storage were gladiolus and orchids.

Moisture. In keeping cut flowers fresh, the retention of moisture in the stems, foliage, and buds plays an important part. As moisture is lost, through evaporation, the flower begins to die; but if this lost moisture can be retained in the adjacent atmosphere until this becomes fully saturated, then further loss of moisture from the cut flower is reduced to a minimum and thus its life is prolonged. This condition is achieved if the container or wrapping in which the flowers are placed is made as nearly airtight as possible. Plastic bags such as are used for frozen foods are suitable for the purpose, if all openings are *sealed tight* as soon as the flowers are placed within them.

With flowers so stored, *it is not necessary* to have the stems placed in water. On the contrary, in the Cornell experiments, flowers wrapped in packages immediately after cutting—without being placed in water even temporarily—kept the best. Red roses, so treated, held their natural color instead of "bluing" as they did when the stems were kept in water during the storage period.

Roses stored by this method may appear slightly wilted when removed from storage even though they have been kept near the freezing point. If the stems—an inch or so at the bottom having first been snipped off—are placed in warm water (80 to 100°F.), five or six inches deep, and kept in a cool place (about 40°F.) for six to eight hours, they will regain their original crispness. This warm-feet-and-cold-head combination hastens the absorption of water at the stem ends, and at the same time reduces evaporation from foliage and blooms. After this revival treatment they will keep practically as long as freshly cut flowers.

Packing for Transportation. Even for a local show, in the neighborhood or only a few miles away, careful packing pays off not only in getting your flowers to the show table in better condition, but also in an actual saving of time in handling them, setting them up at the show, and getting all exhibits properly entered in the correct classes.

Our own practice is to use regular florist's cardboard boxes in several sizes. These come in the flat, with matching covers, but are readily assembled. They can be obtained from a local florist. They cost little, and if handled with reasonable care, will last for a number of years. A supply of waxed paper, which retains moisture, should be procured with them.

With the show schedule and the number of entries we have available in mind, we begin packing. The cover of one box, for instance, may be marked "Cl. H. Teas"; another "Red Hybrid Teas"; still another "Singles," etc. Or two or more of these groups may be placed in one box with a sheet of wax paper separating them. All this is to save time and trouble when setting up at the show—and it certainly does.

In preparation for packing, the boxes are lined with wax paper, and a few loose rolls of slightly moistened newspaper are made of just the right length to be laid crosswise in the box. One of these is placed near each end, underneath the wax paper, to form cushions

Singles and Semi-doubles open very rapidly. With these, storage at low temper-ature is especially important. Bud at left, refrigerated overnight; right, similar bud, kept in cool cellar.

which will support the roses at or just below their necks so that the flowers themselves will not be crushed against the bottom.

In packing, the longest-stemmed flowers are put in first, indi-vidual flower heads, where it seems necessary, being further pro-tected by a sheet of soft tissue paper. After all blooms have been placed at one end of the box, a similar row is placed at the other end, the stems meeting or overlapping in the center. These may be covered with a sheet of wax tissue, and a second row with shorter stems (so that none of the flowers will rest directly upon each other) may be added. These in turn are supported on newspaper rolls placed beneath their necks.

After the boxes are packed, if it will be several hours before they reach the show, we place three or four packages of eight or ten ice cubes wrapped in newspaper (or enclosed in plastic bags) in the bottom of the box.

When all is secure, the boxes are tied with soft, stout cord ready for the trip to the showroom. Needless to say they are carefully kept in a horizontal position.

Along with the roses there are a few accessories which should accompany the exhibitor. Our show "kit" includes extra labels, a waterproof pencil, pruning shears, a list in duplicate of the entries we are making (one copy for the person who will be making out the entry cards at the show), a small brush (which may be needed for "dressing" a blossom at the last moment); and also a quantity of some material such as chopped fern, carrot tops, or other fine foliage that may be required to hold a stem upright in its container: a rose leaning over at a drunken angle from a can or a bottle may be just as fine as its neighbor standing straight and erect, but it will not make quite as good an impression, even on the judges.

HOW TO SHOW ROSES

Under the rules of the American Rose Society, judges must disqualify specimens that are not named, incorrectly named, or of such poor quality that they do not merit recognition.

Exhibition types, i.e., Hybrid Teas, Climbing Hybrid Teas, Teas, Climbing Teas, Hybrid Perpetuals, and Climbing Hybrid Perpetuals, must be disbudded.

Single Hybrid Teas, which often grow in clusters, are not disbudded. A large, single, perfect bloom, if it can be found at the time of the show, is likely to be scored higher than a cluster, unless the latter is of unusually high quality.

Floribundas, Grandifloras, Polyanthas, and Climbers (other than Climbing Hybrid Teas) are not disbudded. One stem or lateral with its cluster of bloom is shown as a specimen. Faded blossoms may be removed before showing but the spray is judged on its number of perfect blooms in show condition. The ideal spray for showing has a number of perfect, open flowers, several half open, and a few buds.

Exhibition types should be shown in their most perfect phase. This

Judging: flower at left is a little tight, that at right slightly too open. In close competition either condition may result in loss of a prize.

is usually when the bloom is two-thirds to three-quarters open, though those with fewer petals may be at their most beautiful when only one-third open. If you know your varieties—as what rose lover does not—you will know at what stage each is most perfect. There is no hard and fast rule as to how far open exhibition roses should be when shown, but only the general one that they must be at their best.

The scale of points on page 218 gives you the exact number of points which may be won for each characteristic. A fine exhibition rose should have the most perfect form which may be found in the variety; crisp, velvety petals; the deepest and most vivid color characteristic of the variety; a straight, sturdy stem of adequate length clothed with healthy, unmarred foliage of good color. If the specimen is extra large, so much the better, but it may win a blue ribbon without being outsize.

Crimson Glory, long a consistent prize winner. This bloom took top honors at the New England Rose Society's 1957 show in Boston.

STAGING THE EXHIBIT

Plan to get to the showroom early—and not only plan but actually do it.

If you are making a considerably number of entries try to get someone to help you in filling containers with water and placing exhibits in the classes where they belong. This will give you more time to attend to the making out of entry cards, checking labels, and attending to other details which only you yourself can handle.

If you have wrapped any individual blooms, leave covered until the last moment those which look as though they might open too rapidly. Keep these in ice water as long as possible. The same holds true for Singles and for few-petaled, open-centered varieties.

"Dressing." To use a term which is familiar in all English rose

literature, each blossom should be "dressed" if there is any method by which its appearance may be improved before it is moved to the show table. If your entries have been properly handled up to this point, little dressing will be required, but there may be an occasional outer petal which has begun to "go" and which can be removed; a damaged leaf or leaflet that can be snipped off; a reluctant bud that threatens to remain too tightly closed, which you can open up by gently blowing into it a number of times; or an occasional speck of foreign matter on the petals that should be removed. For the latter purpose a camel's hair brush is usually employed, but we have found still better the combination bulb-and-brush which is used by photographers for cleaning lenses and negatives and which can be bought for a quarter or so at any camera supply house.

Staging. This term refers to the general arrangement of the show and the placing of the individual exhibits. Most of these matters are in the hands of the show management or, in larger shows, of the staging committee, and the individual exhibitor will have little or nothing to say concerning them. He can, however—particularly in local, nonofficial shows—have some control over the way his own entries are set up.

He may, for instance, provide some of his own containers, if not for all his entries, at least for the more important ones. I recall a case in point in connection with the first bloom of Peace which we ever exhibited (and which, incidentally, in order to get to open in time, I had kept overnight in warm water on top of our heater under a 100 watt light bulb). Even with this treatment, I had considerable difficulty blowing it open after I got to the show. Its only possible competitor for the coveted "Best Rose" award was a magnificent bloom of that half-century-old prize winner, Frau Karl Druschki. As I looked at them both in the containers provided by the show committee I had serious doubts as to which would win the award. As there was a little time left before the hour set for judging to begin, I hurried out, procured a tall glass bud vase, and substituted it for the other container. As a result Peace stood up straight and tall with every leaf showing, head and shoulders above its neighbors, unquestionably "Queen of the Show" from any point in the room. As a result I had the pleasure of wiring Robert Pyle, the American introducer of this splendid variety, that our very first bloom of it had won top honors.

PLATE 23

Genial Gene Boerner has to his credit as a hybridizer such fine varieties as Vogue, Fashion, Spartan, and Sterling Silver. Here we find him critically examining some of his "maidens." BELOW: *Three generations of Brownells appraising Yellow 84, one of the new group of Everblooming Pillars.*

PLATE 24

PLATE 25

Anyone who grows fine roses is likely to become interested in showing them. To win blue ribbons he should familiarize himself with the methods of keeping bloom in the best condition and with the scale of points (see page 218) by which roses are judged.

PLATE 26

Peace, an all-time record breaker as a prize winner, is usually placed in a class by itself, to avoid "unfair competition" with other varieties. Rose on facing page is Confidence, one of the many excellent direct descendants of Peace. If there is no rose show in your locality, why not get your local garden club interested in starting one, or at least in having a rose section in its annual flower show? There is no better way for one to become more proficient in the growing of roses than to exchange personal experiences with other rose growers who have the same problems with local conditions concerning soil, climate, prevalent pests and the like. And—of course—you will want to become a member of The American Rose Society!

PLATE 27

Shrub Rose, The Fairy, is a delightful everbloomer of low spreading habit, with flower sprays and delicate foliage that are ideal in mixed flower arrangements. Below is a vigorous Hybrid Tea, grown as a single bush at the edge of a flower border.

PLATE 28

Setting up the show: Usually it seems impossible that the exhibits can be placed and everything made ready in time for the judges, but somehow they always are. The arrangement classes are usually well filled.

"Roses in Alabaster" (A prize-winning arrangement by Mrs. Percy Merry, Needham, Mass.)

In the showing of a collection of roses in any class, the exhibitor may have an opportunity of displaying them to best advantage by providing a background. Our regular arrangement in such a case is to place dark-colored varieties at the front, with the lighter colors at a slightly higher elevation back of these, and at the rear a drapery of dark blue velvet which makes them stand out in clean-cut silhouette.

Individual varieties to be placed in containers with unsuitably wide mouths may be made to stand up straight, and to face the right way, by packing chopped ferns or other pliable foliage around the stems in the containers.

Final Inspection. Before abandoning your entries to the mercy of the judges, make a tour of the show tables for a final look to see that nothing has been omitted or gone awry. In some shows the absence of a name tag may mean disqualification; a bloom still too tightly closed may be opened up a bit, or a previously overlooked undesirable outer petal removed. Imagine that *you* are the judge, look critically for anything that might downscore your exhibit, and if possible correct it. I recall another experience, again with Peace —after a special class had been created for this variety alone—in which we had selected at the last minute a bloom that had not been disbudded. I had fully intended to remedy this, but in the confusion of getting a large number of entries ready at the show, neglected to do so. My chagrin may be imagined when, immediately after the judges had finished their work, one of them hunted me up and asked irately "Why in h—— didn't you take that bud off your Peace? It was the best of the lot, but we just had to disqualify it; couldn't give it even third place. And it might have made 'Best Rose' in the show even with one mark against it." That was one prize we didn't take—and the lesson was never forgotten.

And One Thing More. Don't grouse about the awards your exhibits failed to win and get the idea that the judges have been unfair or prejudiced in favor of some other exhibitor. Even if the judges are not experts they will have done the best they could in carrying out a thankless task, often under pressure of having to meet a deadline for the opening of the show. You can turn your losses to good account by trying to determine just why your entry failed, keeping in mind the official schedule of points which the judges must use in reaching their decisions.

ORGANIZING A ROSE SHOW

Where a group of rose growers develops in any locality, sooner or later someone is sure to suggest a rose show. If a garden club exists, this is the logical group to sponsor it, at least until such time as a local rose society may be organized and take over.

A Rose Show will usually draw a larger attendance than a rose section of a general flower show. Often a rose show with "sections for other flowers," is the best combination, for it attracts the general public and also encourages gardeners with other flower hobbies, or even accidentally good specimens of some other flower, to participate.

In any event, the project will have its beginning in the appointment of a show committee; and one of the first acts of the committee will be to appoint a show manager.

At this point it should be kept in mind that it is very important to get someone with previous show experience. The best gardener in the vicinity, or even the best grower of roses may not be—and in all likelihood is not—the best person to organize the show. And

The judges judged. If the ears of some of them do not tingle it is not for want of comments by exhibitors who haven't won awards.

Correct degrees of flower development for a "three-of-a-kind" class.

next in importance, if not equally so, is that the appointee should possess tact in human relations, for differences of opinion, conflicts of interest, and temper-trying incidents are certain to arise along the thorny path to a successful show.

Setting the date for the show is one of the first questions to be decided. Rose growers in the vicinity should be consulted as to when they are likely to have blooms in the best condition to exhibit. Probably the date finally decided upon will have to be announced some time in advance, but the longer announcement can be delayed, the more accurately the date can be timed to assure plenty of exhibits. If, as spring progresses, there is evidence that the rose season will be unusually early or unusually late, the date may be changed, but this always involves a good many undesirable complications.

American Rose Society rules and suggestions as to classes, scoring, etc., should be followed. At least one member of the committee should belong to the American Rose Society. Information concerning the staging of the show, and possible A.R.S. awards that may be available for it, can be obtained from the Secretary of the Society, Mr. James P. Gurney, American Rose Society, 4048 Roselea Place, Columbus 14, Ohio.

TYPICAL ROSE SHOW SCHEDULE

SCHEDULE OF POINTS FOR SWEEPSTAKES

All classes for single specimens: 1st, 3 points; 2nd, 2 points; 3rd, 1 point; times the number of entries in the class up to 20.

All classes for three or six blooms; 1st, 5 points; 2nd, 3 points; 3rd, 2 points; times the number of entries in the class up to 20.

Queen of the Show, 5 points; King of the Show, 4 points.

SPECIMEN ROSE CLASSES

SECTION A.   HYBRID TEA ROSES

One Exhibition Bloom

Named varieties only. Rose shown in Section C may not be exhibited in Section A. Figures in parenthesis denote American Rose Society's official color classification. (This guide may be obtained at the Entry Desk at the Rose Show, or in advance from the American Rose Society, 4048 Roselea Place, Columbus 14, Ohio.) To determine in which class to exhibit a variety, please refer to this official guide.

Class
1. White or near White (1). Example, White Swan.
2. Light Yellow (2). Example, Isobel Harkness.
3. Medium Yellow (3). Example, Eclipse.
4. Deep Yellow (4). Example, Golden Masterpiece.
5. Yellow Blend (5). Example, Sutter's Gold.
   (Classes 6 to 14; continued as above, through entire color range.)

SECTION B.   HYBRID TEA ROSES

One Open Bloom

Class
15. White or near White (1).
16. Yellow (2, 3, 4).
17. Pink (8, 9).
18. Red (11, 12, 13).
19. Any Blend (5, 6, 7, 10, 14).

Section C.   Hybrid Tea Variety Class

One Exhibition Bloom

Class
20. White Knight.
21. Peace.
22. Sutter's Gold.
23. Golden Masterpiece.
24. Confidence.
25. Helen Traubel.
    (Classes 26 to 34; continued as above, through entire color range.)

Section D.   Hybrid Tea Roses

Three of a Kind

35. Three Roses of one variety, named, in one container, showing one bud that has begun to open, one bloom about half open, and one flower three-fourths to fully open.

Section E.   Hybrid Tea Roses

Collections

36. Three exhibition blooms, different varieties, in one container.
37. One bloom each of six different varieties, to be shown in test-tube rack provided by committee.

Section F.   Single Hybrid Tea Roses

38. Three blooms or one spray, any color; must not be disbudded.

Section G.   Unnamed Hybrid Tea Roses

39. White or near White.
40. Yellow or Orange.
41. Pink or Pink Blend.
42. Red or Red Blend.

Section H.   Grandiflora Roses

One Stem to a Vase, not disbudded

43. Any color (examples, Buccaneer, Carrousel, Queen Elizabeth, Roundelay).

Section I.   Floribunda Roses

One Spray to a Vase

44. White or near White (1).
45. Yellow (2, 3, 4).
    (Classes 46 to 51; continued as above, through entire color range.)

Section J.   Polyantha Roses (Small Flowers)

One Spray to a Vase

52. Margo Koster.
53. Any other Variety.

Section K.   Collection

54. Six sprays, all different varieties of Floribundas and/or Polyanthas and Grandifloras, to be staged in a test-tube rack.

Section L.   Hybrid Perpetual Roses

One Bloom to a Vase

55. Frau Karl Druschki.
56. Any other variety.

Section M.   Climbing Roses

57. Climbing Hybrid Tea, one specimen bloom or spray.
58. Large-flowered Climber other than Cl.H.T., one specimen bloom or spray.
59. Climbing Floribunda, one spray.
60. Any other Climber, one bloom lateral (a stem coming from a main cane).

Section N.   Miniature Roses

61. Miniature Rose, one spray, exhibitor to furnish container.
62. Miniature Rose, one plant, grown in pot.

SECTION O.   OLD, SPECIES, OR SHRUB ROSES

63. Any Species, Shrub, or Old Rose not included in Classes 1 to 60. More than one entry may be made in this class.

ROSE ARRANGEMENT CLASSES

SECTION P.

64. Roses for Breakfast. Tray, furnished by exhibitor, set for one.
65. Roses for Coffee. An arrangement suitable for a low table.
66. Roses for the Hospital. Small arrangement for a bedside table, not to exceed 8 inches overall.
67. Roses for your Home. Arrangement for the home:
    A. In glass.
    B. In china or pottery.
    C. In metal.
68. Men's Class. Composition not to exceed 24 inches overall.
69. Roses for Adornment.
    A. Tuzzy-Muzzy. Old-fashioned, fragrant Nosegay.
    B. Corsage for Daytime.
    C. Corsage for Evening.
    (Add as many classes as may be desired.)

SECTION Q.

Open to Commercial Florists Only.

70. Best Wishes on Your Anniversary.
71. For the New Baby.
72. With Love.

ROSES FOR EDUCATION

SECTION R.

73. Exhibit: planning a Rose Garden. (Photographs and/or drawings)
74. Exhibit: planting a Rose Garden. (Photographs and/or materials)

CHAPTER *17. Calendar of Operations*

WITH REGIONAL NOTES

> *The cavalier of the Rose has* semper fidelis *upon his crest and shield.*

The rose grower's annual cycle of operations in the rose garden, so far as it can be based on the calendar, depends primarily on where he lives. But even in the same locality it will change from year to year according to the vagaries of the season.

The dates accorded the following list of tasks to be undertaken are for an average season in the northeastern section of the United States, and the quite similar conditions throughout Zones 5, 6, and 7, according to the Rose Zone Map we are using. (See pages 10-11.)

Calendar dates can be only approximate, because even in the same zone—in fact even in locations separated from each other by but a few miles—such phenomena as the last killing frost, the beginning of new growth, the formation of the first flower buds frequently vary by as much as one to three weeks. *The order in which they occur,* however, is generally the same. This fact serves to make a calendar of operations of some practical use to the amateur at rose growing. On this basis the following schedule is presented.

Pre-spring. (Feb. 15 to Mar. 15)

Before leaf buds start, apply *dormant* spray (pages 165, 185).

Examine winter protection for any disarrangement due to storms, and replace or repair as necessary.

Set out new plants as soon as frost is out and soil has dried sufficiently to permit working.

Early Spring. (Mar. 15 to Apr. 15)

As leaf buds begin to swell, remove mulching and/or hilling; if possible, do this gradually.

246

Proceed with annual spring pruning (page 114).

Finish planting if this has not already been done.

Transplanting—if required to rearrange varieties so that taller ones may be kept to the rear of beds, or overvigorous varieties given more space—is in order now if it was not attended to the previous fall.

Apply second dormant spray.

Cut back stocks of roses that were budded previous summer (page 207).

Spring. (Apr. 1 to May 1)

Apply fertilizer and work into soil lightly; water in thoroughly if weather is dry.

Examine pruning cuts made previously. Where a top bud has failed to develop, cut back to a live bud. A dead stub is likely to keep on dying back down the cane.

Watch for buds starting to grow toward center of plant and rub these out (page 118). This is especially important with Standard (Tree) Roses.

As soon as foliage begins to develop apply first all-purpose spray or dust.

Late Spring. (May 1 to June 1)

Continue spraying or dusting at weekly intervals.

Apply mulch if this has not already been done.

Examine foliage as growth develops for any sign of nutrient deficiencies (page 182).

Watch for "suckers" (those with seven leaflets instead of the usual five) starting from below the knuckle, or below heads on Standards. Prune close, or cut out with pruning knife.

Begin to tie up or train new growths on Climbers.

If soil is getting dry, water copiously.

If exhibiting at shows is contemplated, begin to select buds and canes that appear to be promising material (pages 218–25).

Disbud as soon as side buds begin to develop stems.

Early Summer. (June 1 to July 1)

Keep soil moist as plants are now making their most vigorous growth.

Winter injured wood that was not killed outright will now

begin to die back. Prune back to live wood with no discolored pith at center.

Make final selection of specimens for showing (page 225); continue disbudding; and cut according to "timing" for show (page 222).

Keep all faded blooms cut off.

Roses in pots that have flowered indoors should gradually be dried off for a summer rest.

Softwood cuttings may be taken now; and toward the end of the month or early the following month, budding is in order (pages 189–96).

Midsummer. (July 1 to Aug. 15)

This is the midsummer rest period after heavy bloom: don't try to "force" flowering by heavy feeding and watering. During periods of high temperatures and bright sun, cut buds in late afternoon and allow to open indoors; but do not take them with extra long stems as plants need all the foliage they can develop during this period.

Avoid spraying and dusting when temperature is 85° or more; or apply only in late afternoon. Covering the foliage with dust or spray, particularly if sulfur is included, under these conditions may cause more injury than the pests or diseases they are supposed to control.

Watch for first signs of black spot and *burn* any affected leaves.

Prune out errant canes and also crisscrossing growths to maintain open-centered plants.

Prune Rambler-type Climbers, the new canes of which will now be making very rapid growth.

Large-flowered Climbers also are best pruned at this time, although in their case the pruning may be postponed until later on (page 124).

This is the most propitious season to undertake layering to obtain new plants of roses readily propagated by this method (page 198).

Late Summer. (Aug. 15 to Sept. 15)

Give last application of fertilizer, avoiding high-nitrogen combinations.

Maintain adequate moisture, but avoid late-afternoon watering, especially in humid weather.

Select promising specimens for fall flower shows.

Continue regular spray program.

Early Fall. (Sept. 15 to Oct. 15)

Order new roses now, with definite directions for delivery date.

Prepare beds and/or planting holes for plants to be set out in fall. Do this early so that the ground can settle. If early hard freezing is usual in your locality, mulch the prepared ground to keep out frost.

Put in posts or other supports for roses to be planted later in the fall, or next spring.

Continue spraying or dusting as long as foliage remains.

If an early frost threatens while plants are still in bud and bloom, cover buds with VisQueen held with rubber bands; or cover entire plants, holding plastic down with planks or stones: this may give you an extra fortnight of beautiful flowers during Indian summer.

Late Fall. (Oct. 1 to Nov. 1)

Plant new bushes as soon as received.

If changes are to be made in the location of plants you already have, do any required transplanting.

Make provisions now for winter protection; obtain supplies of extra soil, mulching material, etc., that may be required.

Prune back long canes, candelabra growths, etc.

Prune Large-flowered Climbers if this has not been done earlier.

Gather rose hips (seed pods) resulting from crosses you may have made (page 214).

Slow-acting fertilizers (such as superphosphate, sulphate of potash, wood ashes, and lime) may still be applied if soil analysis indicates that they are needed.

Continue spray or dust program until leaves fall.

Early Winter. (Nov. 1 to Jan. 15)

Just *before* ground is likely to freeze, hill up around plants (page 134) if you are going to use that system.

Tie Climbers securely; or lay them down or bury them for winter protection.

After ground freezes a couple of inches deep, apply winter mulching material, if any is to be used; and covering of evergreen boughs or other protective material (page 136).

Late Winter. (Jan. 1 to Feb. 15)

Examine bushes occasionally for possible injury by rabbits or other winter-starved rodents. Rabbits do not particularly like roses but we have had them do serious damage. One-inch mesh chicken wire two feet wide will keep them off; it will also hold mulching material securely in place.

Snow shoveled from driveways or paths may well be spread over the rose bed as snow is an ideal mulch.

If rose plants in pots have been stored in a frame, some may be brought in now to start growth for indoor bloom.

Seeds which have been stored for preliminary chilling before sowing can be planted now (page 215).

REGIONAL NOTES:

WHAT TO DO IN THE ROSE GARDEN AND *WHEN* TO DO IT

In giving regional advice, the conscientious writer on rose culture is faced with a very real problem. The United States is a vast area, with all sorts of conditions of temperature, humidity, soil, rainfall and wind, to mention but a few of the many important factors. After compiling and discarding several elaborate charts giving dates for cultural operations in various temperature zones we have finally decided upon the following method as the simplest, clearest, and most comprehensive way of indicating what the rose grower should do, and when, in the more difficult areas where the preceding "Calendar of Operations" does not apply.

In the Rose Grower's Rose Finder (page 303), lists of varieties for special climatic conditions will be found.

PREPARATION OF NEW ROSE BEDS

One, or preferably two, months before planting date in your area.

In sections of *high rainfall,* raise beds 6 to 10 inches above ground level.

In sections of *low rainfall,* sink beds 6 inches below ground level, to help hold water when beds are irrigated.

In alkaline soil, treat beds spring and fall with commercial sulfur 4 pounds per 100 square feet or other soil acidifier (page 180).

Where *summer heat* or *drying winter sun* is extreme, locate beds where they will receive afternoon shade. In areas where heavy prevailing winds may be expected, locate rose bed in sheltered but airy position. See also Chapter 3.

PLANTING

Zones 3 and 4. As early in spring as ground can be worked. Usually early April in Zone 3 and late March in Zone 4.

Zones 5, 6, 7, 8, 9. In late fall or early winter; as soon as established plants have become thoroughly dormant (November-December-January). If spring planting must be resorted to, the longer before normal growth begins the better.

Zone 10. January-February.

Zones 3, 4, 5, 6. Place knuckle just below soil level. Hill up until growth starts.

Zones 7, 8, 9, 10. Place knuckle at or just above ground level. See also Chapter 6.

SUMMER MULCH

Desirable in all zones. See Chapter 8.

FERTILIZING

In fertile, heavy soil: just before growth begins in spring; just before June bloom; and again in late midsummer.

In poor or sandy soils: monthly when plants are in growth. See Chapter 7.

WATERING

Beds must maintain moisture, but need perfect drainage.

In sections of *high rainfall,* water deeply during *dry spells,* once a week or every ten days. In sections of *low rainfall,* irrigate weekly during dry season. See Chapter 8.

PRUNING

Main pruning of bush types just before spring growth begins.

Climbers may be pruned just after bloom. See Chapter 9.

WINTER PROTECTION

Hill after first freeze: Zones 3 and 4, 8 to 12 inches; Zones 5 and 6, 6 to 8 inches.

    Mulch over hills when ground has frozen, to cover plants: Zones 3 and 4.

    Mulch only (no hilling) of strawy manure or evergreen boughs: Zone 7 and warmer portions of 6.

    Lay down and cover Climbers: Zones 3 and 4.

    Wrap Climbers, Tree Roses, in straw or evergreen boughs: Zone 5. See also Chapter 10.

DORMANT SPRAY

    A month before growth starts. In sections where complete dormancy does not take place, monthly through rest period.

ALL-PURPOSE SPRAY

    Every week or ten days (except when temperature rises above 85°F.), starting when leaves begin to unfold. See Chapter 13.

Part Three

ROSE TYPES AND VARIETIES

Born in the East [the Rose] has been diffused, like the sunlight, over all the world . . . It is found in every quarter of the globe—on glaciers, in deserts, on mountains, in marshes, in forests, in valleys, and on plains.

The "Renaissance of the Rose," from which came the impetus for modern hybridization, occurred early in the 1800s when the Empress Josephine became a devotee of *Rosa* and her progeny. At Malmaison she endeavored to collect every rose known in her time, and from the 250 species and varieties brought together in her garden, she encouraged the botanists, nurserymen, and gardeners of France to create new hybrids. André Dupont, Cochet, Laffay, Prevost, and Vilmorin were among those who participated in this great movement.

The species and varieties in Josephine's garden,* available for hybridization by this galaxy of gifted men were: 8 varieties of *R. alba; alpina; arvensis; banksiae;* 22 varieties of Bengals; *carolina;* 27 varieties of *centifolia; cinnamomea; clinophylla;* 9 varieties of *damascena;* 107 varieties of *gallica; laevigata;* 3 varieties of *lutea;* 3 varieties of Moss; 1 variety of Musk; *rubrifolia; rugosa; sempervirens; setigera;* and 4 varieties of *spinosissima.*

Many of these Old Roses—Species and early Species Hybrids—have survived until the present day, and are to be found not only in the botanical collections but occasionally in the gardens of amateur rosarians. Several firms now specialize in Old Roses. A few specimens, even in a very moderate-sized planting, are always of interest and make excellent conversation pieces.

It is by no means true, however, that they are to be treasured for sentimental reasons only. Some of them are unsurpassed in fra-

---

*According to Dr. J. H. Nicolas, in his *Rose Manual.*

grance; some are exceptionally early to bloom; others, like the Moss Roses, of unique character; and practically all of them can be grown with less attention than even the hardiest of our modern garden roses require.

So here we present

A PARADE OF OLD ROSES
(with some modern varieties of similar type)

ROSA ALBA

ORIGIN: Southern Europe. Cultivated by the Romans. Described by Pliny. Introduced in England before 1600 and brought to America by the very early settlers. Usually believed to be a cross between *R. corymbifera* and *R. gallica*. (Svend Poulsen in his book *Poulsen on the Rose* states, however, that *Rosa alba* always comes true from seed and that therefore he believes it to be a species rather than a cross.)

FLOWERS: Small, pure white, single, opening flat to show yellow centers; borne in small clusters; petals tissuelike. Hyacinth fragrance. Hips large, elongated, scarlet. All known hybrids are of light coloring; many large and double or semidouble.

FOLIAGE: 5 to 7 leaflets, blunt, downy, gray-green, disease-resistant. Canes stout, clear green with hooked prickles interspersed with bristles.

HEIGHT: 5 to 7 feet.

HABIT: Vigorous, arching.

REMARKS: Very hardy and persistent.

SOME VARIETIES AND HYBRIDS:

Celestial: Light, fading blush pink, 4-inch, semi-double; 6 feet.

Great Double White (A. maxima): Blush buds turning white as double 4-inch flowers open flat; grayish foliage; 8 feet; often seen in Renaissance paintings.

Great Maiden's Blush: Very double, globular, light pink 3-inch flowers in clusters; 5 feet.

Mme. Plantier: Large, double creamy white opening flat, changing to pure white; in long-stemmed clusters; fragrant; hardy; persistent; 5 feet.

Queen of Denmark: Pink double with dark centers to 4 inches; fragrant; floriferous; grayish foliage.

ROSA CENTIFOLIA CABBAGE OR PROVENCE ROSE

ORIGIN: Persia and Asia Minor. Described by Herodotus in 45 B.C. and by Theophrastus in 300 B.C. Often appears in Dutch still-life paintings. Reached European gardens about 1600.

FLOWER: Very double, globular, pale pink, about the size of a small Hybrid Tea. Very fragrant. Hips round.

FOLIAGE: 5 leaflets to 2 inches long, deeply cut; green shoots, large down-curved thorns.

HEIGHT: 5 to 6 feet.

HABIT: Shrub-like.

REMARKS: Very hardy; easy to grow in any soil.

SOME VARIETIES AND HYBRIDS:

Königin von Dänemark: Flesh-pink, dark centers; very fragrant.

Red Provence: Clear rose-pink, deeper centers; very fragrant.

Rose des Peintres: Rose color to deep purplish rose-pink; large; vigorous. Rose pictured by old Dutch painters.

Variegata di Bologna: Largest striped rose; white with purplish-red veins; fragrant.

Vierge de Cléry: Large, white; very fragrant. Considered to be the best Cabbage Rose in existence.

R. centifolia muscosa *(communis)* MOSS ROSE

ORIGIN: First recorded in Holland about 1720 and in Southern France before 1700, the Moss Rose is believed to be a natural mutation of *R. centifolia.*

FLOWERS: Large, globular, pale rose-pink.

FOLIAGE: Buds and stems are covered with a mossy growth. Leaflets 5, similar in appearance to *R. centifolia* but red-edged when young. Wood red, with large, straight thorns.

HEIGHT: 5 to 6 feet, or taller if espaliered.

REMARKS: A must-have for every collector of Old Roses.

SOME VARIETIES AND HYBRIDS:

Cristata: A variety found first in Switzerland in 1820 and of unknown origin. The moss in Cristata is to be found only on the edges of the sepals; large rose-pink blooms.

Golden Moss: Double yellow, tinged with peach; moderately mossed; a shy June bloomer.

REMONTANT VARIETIES:

Blanche Moreau: Large, white blossoms in clusters; heavily mossed.

Deuil de Paul Fontaine: Very dark red, black and brown shadings; very spiny; free rebloom.

Mme. Louis Lévêque: Fragrant, large, double shell pink; occasional rebloom.

Mousseline: Medium-sized, cupped, pink to white; double; reblooms like a Floribunda.

Robert Leopold: Peach-pink, yellow and orange; profuse moss.

Salet: Rose color, opening to a very large, flat, double bloom. Well mossed, especially on buds. Reblooms freely in fall.

ROSA CHINENSIS *(indica)* CHINA ROSE

ORIGIN: China; introduced into Europe in 1768 as garden roses, long in cultivation in Orient.

FLOWERS: Double, red to almost white, 2 inches in diameter in few-flowered clusters; oval hips.

FOLIAGE: 3 to 5 leaflets to 2½ inches long, coarsely toothed, glossy, almost evergreen; green stems; hooked thorns.

HEIGHT: 2½ to 3 feet.

HABIT: Low, erect.

REMARKS: Tender; *chinensis* blood is in all Hybrid Perpetuals and Hybrid Teas, and in many other strains.

R. chinensis borboniana BOURBON ROSE

ORIGIN: First found on the island of Réunion (Bourbon) in 1817, and is considered to be a natural hybrid of *R. chinensis* and either *R. gallica* or *R. damascena,* probably the latter.

FLOWERS: Medium-sized rose-pink semi-double with an apple fragrance; in small clusters or singly.

FOLIAGE: Leaflets 5 to 7, large and thick, bright green with purplish edges.

HEIGHT: Low.

HABIT: Compact; vigorous.

REMARKS: Though few Bourbon varieties are available today, the Bourbon hybrids were widely used in creating the remontant Hybrid Perpetuals.

SOME VARIETIES AND HYBRIDS:

Bourbon Queen: Cupped pink; fragrant; flowers continuously.

Gipsy Boy: Dark crimson, medium blossoms. Blooms once only; 6 feet.

Hermosa: One of the most famous of the Old Roses, is still grown. The small, double, cupped blossoms are beautifully formed and fragrant; of a clear delicate pink known as Hermosa pink. Bears generous clusters throughout the season.

Louise Odier: Flesh-pink flowers of good form. Continuous bloomer; 3 to 4 feet.

Souvenir de la Malmaison: Another great old rose, very fragrant, of flesh pink color, large and opening flat; remontant.

R. chinensis Manetti *(chinensis x moschata)* NOISETTE AND TEA NOISETTE

Champney: The first Noisette was created by John Champney of Charleston, S.C. about 1817. Its large pink clusters are semidouble and it grows rapidly into a ten-foot pillar. Strong, hooked thorns and smooth, oval foliage with 7 leaflets, prickly on the petiole, are characteristic of early Noisettes, all of which are tender.

Old Blush Noisette: Bred by Philippe Noisette, also of Charleston is said to be a child of Champney. More double, the pink flowers are large and borne in large clusters, the growth quite low.

More recent varieties, comprising the Tea-Noisettes, include:

Chromatella: Creamy yellow with darker center, globular; climbing, vigorous; 1843.

Comtesse du Cayla: Copper-orange, semi-dwarf; spreading; vigorous; 1902.

Lamarque: Large double fragrant white golden center; climbing; 1830.

Maréchal Niel: Large, golden yellow, globular, very fragrant double climber; 1864; a famous variety; tender.

Rêve d'Or: Medium-sized soft yellow double pink reverse; climbing; 1869.

William Allen Richardson: Small, irregular flowers of buff to bronzy-orange; quite hardy in protected positions; 1878.

R. chinensis minima *(R. Rouletti)* BABY OR FAIRY ROSE

This dwarf form, to 1 foot in height, with 1½-inch rose-red blooms is the species from which a whole race of Miniatures has recently been bred. See page 289.

R. chinensis mutabilis

ORIGIN: Confused, but most authorities agree that it is a variety of *chinensis.*

FLOWERS: Single, medium-sized to large, of yellow, buff, orange, and rose-pink on one plant, colors deepening with age; a continuous bloomer.

FOLIAGE: As in *R. chinensis.* Young leaves dark red.

HEIGHT: 2 to 3 feet.

HABIT: Spreading.

REMARKS: From this variety have been created such modern Floribundas as the justly famous Masquerade, and newer Circus.

R. chinensis odorata See *Rosa odorata.*

R. chinensis semperflorens BENGAL ROSE

ORIGIN: Introduced to England from Calcutta in 1789 by a captain of an East India Company ship. Discovered in the wild in Central China in 1885.

FLOWERS: Solitary crimson blooms. Remontant.

FOLIAGE: Leaflets 5 to 7, smooth and glossy; occasional hooked thorns.

HEIGHT: Medium.

HABIT: Erect.

REMARKS: From the original import many early crosses were made in England in the eighteenth century, and in France during the first decades of the nineteenth century. These early varieties and hybrids with the precious characteristic of monthly bloom, were called Bengal Roses.

SOME VARIETIES AND HYBRIDS:

Birdie Blye: Pink, diffuse clusters; fragrant; remontant; large bush; quite hardy.

Old Blush: Bright, sparkling pink, informal, semi-double, in clusters at tips of canes and side branches; bloom almost continuous; habit erect; stalks with straight red thorns. This fine old rose is the ancestor of all pink Chinas.

ROSA DAMASCENA DAMASK ROSE

ORIGIN: Asia Minor. Referred to by Virgil in 50 B.C. Introduced to Europe by the Crusaders. Reached England in the 1500s.

FLOWERS: Semi-double, rose-red to pink with 18 or more petals and golden stamens, in clusters; very floriferous and fragrant; remontant; hips large, ovoid; bristly; scarlet.

FOLIAGE: 5 leaflets to 2½ inches long, light in color and softly hairy; disease-resistant; many hooked thorns; stalks, pale green.

HEIGHT: To 8 feet.

HABIT: Tall, arching.

REMARKS: This very hardy, intensely fragrant, ancient rose and its varieties are mentioned in old literature and often pictured in early still-life paintings.

SOME VARIETIES AND HYBRIDS:

King George IV: Double, loose, cupped crimson blooms; June-blooming but with the habit of a Hybrid Tea.

Marie Louise: Double, deep pink; intensely fragrant. Grown at Malmaison in 1813.

Portland Roses (Damask Perpetuals): Remontant varieties very popular up to the middle of the nineteenth century when their later descendants, the Hybrid Perpetuals, took their place.

Oratam: Large double blossoms of rosy orange-pink with Damask fragrance; June bloomer; 6 feet. A modern hybrid (Jacobus 1939).

York and Lancaster: semi-double, irregularly marked pink or white with a few reddish petals; fragrant.

ROSA EGLANTERIA *(rubiginosa)* SWEETBRIAR OR EGLANTINE

ORIGIN: Europe. Naturalized in some parts of the United States. This is the wild rose of song and story.

FLOWER: Medium-sized bright pink single. Hips small, round to oval, orange-scarlet.

FOLIAGE: Leaflets 5 to 7, 1½ inches long, roundish dark green above, grayish beneath, with an apple fragrance when crushed.

HEIGHT: 8 to 10 feet.

HABIT: Graceful, much branched with a good spread.

REMARKS: This wild rose, which has been cultivated in English gardens since the fourteenth century, is noted for its longevity. Very ancient plants have been found on the grounds of old castles and estates.

SOME VARIETIES AND HYBRIDS:

Brenda: Peachy-pink single.

Green Mantle: Bright rose-red single with white eye and golden stamens; fragrant foliage; tall and vigorous.

Lady Penzance: Copper with yellow base; single; fragrant; dark, scented foliage; vigorous, with arching branches.

Lord Penzance: Single, fragrant buff-tinted lemon in clusters on strong stems; dark, fragrant foliage; vigorous.

Refulgence: Bright scarlet semi-double, aging to cinnabar; fragrant foliage; vigorous.

ROSA FOETIDA *(lutea)* AUSTRIAN BRIAR

ORIGIN: Asia. Arrived in Europe late in the sixteenth century.

FLOWERS: Single, deep yellow, 3-inch, solitary blooms with an unpleasant odor. Round red hips.

FOLIAGE: 5 to 9 leaflets to 1½ inches long, brownish-green in color; wood, brown and spiny.

HEIGHT: To 10 feet.

HABIT: Arching sprays.

REMARKS: Prefers poor soil and resents pruning, but is quite hardy in sheltered locations. From the Austrian Briar came several of the Pernetianas, including Soleil d' Or, and modern Hybrid Teas like Peace and President Hoover.

SOME VARIETIES AND HYBRIDS:

Austrian Copper: Single copper red blooms with golden yellow reverse.

Austrian Yellow: Single yellow bicolor, streaked red.

Persian Yellow: Double, small deep yellow blooms borne along arching canes.

Soleil d' Or: A yellow, fragrant double of Hybrid Tea habit; one of the first of the Pernetianas; susceptible to black spot.

ROSA GALLICA *(provincialis)* FRENCH ROSE

ORIGIN: Europe; Western Asia. Ancient.

FLOWERS: Large, single or semi-double dark rose-red, opening flat, with golden stamens; solitary; fragrant; June-blooming. Hips large, round, red.

FOLIAGE: 5 leaflets to 2½ inches long; thick, brittle, smooth above; stems with weak, straight, prickly thorns.

HEIGHT: 2½ to 4 feet.

HABIT: Erect, bushy. Requires pruning and thinning.

REMARKS: There is some iron-hardy *gallica* blood in most modern hybrids as in the old roses bred at Malmaison by the Empress Josephine.

SOME VARIETIES AND HYBRIDS:

Belle Isis: Small double flesh-pink.

Belle of Portugal: Long, pointed bud to 4 inches; semi-double, 4- to 6-inch flesh-pink blooms; to 20 feet with glossy foliage; profuse, long spring bloom; *tender.*

Boule de Nanteuil: Large, very double, deep rose-pink blooms, silvery in reverse.

Cardinal de Richelieu: Double, medium-sized, dark purplish red blossoms; in demand by collectors of Old Roses.

Coupe d' Hébé: Rose-pink to flesh, very fragrant, cupped blossoms.

Damask Gallica: Large, semi-double, fragrant rose-red flowers.

Marie Tudor: Cherry or salmon, marbled blooms.

Rosa gallica conditorum: Good sized, tawny pink single flowers; free-blooming, hardy and intensely fragrant.

Rosa Mundi: Quite large semi-double white or pale pink flowers, striped dark red or rose; or half white, half red.

ROSA HUGONIS

ORIGIN: North Central China, in rocky, arid land.

FLOWER: Light yellow, single, very early; closely set along the canes. Small black hips.

FOLIAGE: 5 to 7 leaflets; light and dainty, remaining late in the fall. Canes very prickly.

HEIGHT: To 8 feet.

HABIT: Graceful; arching; can be trained to a wall or trellis.

REMARKS: Very hardy. Prefers poor soil but requires excellent drainage.

ROSA INDICA See *Rosa chinensis.*

ROSA LUCIDA See *Rosa virginiana.*

ROSA LUTEA See *Rosa foetida.*

ROSA MACROPHYLLA RUBROSTAMINEA See *Rosa Moyesi*

ROSA MOYESI

ORIGIN: South Central China. Brought to this country in 1894.

FLOWERS: Deep blood-red, through rose to light pink; 2 to 3 inches, velvety. Hips oval, coral-red.

FOLIAGE: 7 to 13 leaflets, dainty, pale green beneath. Stems with few thorns.

HEIGHT: 6 to 14 feet.

HABIT: Strong, shrubby, much branched.

REMARKS: This very hardy rose was first found at a very high altitude near Tibet by E. H. Wilson, who brought seeds back to England.

Sealing Wax: An English selection of the species is very hardy and bears many rose-red blossoms in June; large bright red hips suggesting sealing wax.

ROSA MULTIFLORA (*Polyantha*) JAPANESE ROSE

ORIGIN: Japan and Korea. Brought to England 1875.

FLOWERS: Large trusses of small, white, single, very fragrant blooms. Small coral-red hips.

FOLIAGE: 5 to 11 leaflets to 1¼ inches long; light green; on stout canes.

HEIGHT: To 8 feet.

HABIT: Erect; vigorous; spreading, making dense thickets.

REMARKS: Can be kept pruned. Very hardy. Used as understock for grafting and budding. Ancestor of Polyanthas and many other garden roses, including Crimson Rambler.

ROSA ODORATA TEA ROSE

ORIGIN: China. Introduced into Europe about 1809, as cultivated garden roses.

FLOWERS: White, pale pink or yellow; loosely formed double, 3 inches in diameter, fragrant, solitary or in few-flowered clusters; petals translucent; hips round.

FOLIAGE: Leaflets 3 or 5, pointed and finely toothed, evergreen. Reddish, straight thorns.

HABIT: Low.

REMARKS: Tender.

SOME VARIETIES AND HYBRIDS:

Duchesse de Brabant: China pink, tulip-shaped, fading to flesh pink; very fragrant; quite hardy; disease-resistant; vigorous, bushy; 1857.

Harry Kirk: Straw-yellow with pointed buds; 1907.

Lady Hillingdon: Deep yellow to apricot, semi-double; pointed buds; fragrant; bronzy foliage and bushy habit; considered the best yellow Tea.

Maman Cochet: Large, double clear pink flower; pointed buds.

Mrs. Herbert Stevens: Double white with lemon center; very fragrant; growth moderate.

Mrs. B. R. Cant: Large silvery rose, buff base, reverse deep rose; long stem.

Safrano: Long, pointed, apricot to orange-red buds. Flowers semi-double buff-apricot, fading to buff-pink; vigorous; profuse bloomer.

ROSA PROVINCIALIS See *Rosa gallica.*

ROSA RUBIGINOSA See *Rosa Eglanteria.*

ROSA RUGOSA

ORIGIN: China; Korea; Japan. Used in Japan as early as the twelfth century as a source of perfume. Was first recorded in Europe during the latter part of the eighteenth century.

FLOWERS: Purplish-red to white single, 4 inches, solitary or in small clusters. Fragrant. Remontant. Very large, round, fleshy red hips.

FOLIAGE: 5 to 9 leaflets to 2 inches long; rough and wrinkled, dark green, shining above; disease-resistant. Stems very prickly.

HEIGHT: To 6 feet.

HABIT: Forms dense shrub or hedge. Suckers freely.

REMARKS: Very hardy and adaptable to adverse conditions. Especially good for seashore where it often naturalizes itself. Does not blend well with other roses.

SOME VARIETIES AND HYBRIDS (See also Hansen Hybrids page 319):

Agnes: Double, open, fragrant, pale amber; center deeper; on short stems; foliage glossy, wrinkled; 6 feet.

Belle Poitevine: Long pointed buds and large, semi-double, open, deep rose-pink flowers; dark, wrinkled foliage; remontant; 4 feet.

Blanc Double de Coubert: White, fragrant semi-double; blooming from June to August; 5 feet.

Dr. Eckener: Large, semi-double, cupped, fragrant copper-rose, turning soft pink; recurrent bloom; 10 feet.

George Will: Clusters of deep pink flowers; 3 feet.

F. J. Grootendorst: Clusters of small, rich red, frilled flowers; everblooming; 4 to 6 feet.

Pink Grootendorst: Pink form of above.

Rose à Parfum de l'Hay: Large, dark crimson to carmine, very fragrant single flowers throughout the season.

Rosa rugosa plena: Very double, dark purple-red, intensely fragrant flowers with prominent stamens.

Sir Thomas Lipton: Double, cupped, white, fragrant flowers; recurrent bloom; 4 feet.

Sarah Van Fleet: Vivid rose-pink, cupped, semi-double, fragrant blooms throughout the season; 8 feet.

Stella Polaris: Large, single, silvery white in sprays; bloom throughout the season; 4 feet.

Vanguard: Large, double orange-salmon; fragrant; 6 to 8 feet.

Wasagaming: Double, fragrant, clear rose-color; 3 feet.

ROSA SETIGERA PRAIRIE ROSE

ORIGIN: United States from the Atlantic Ocean to the Rocky Mountains.

FLOWERS: Single, rose-pink 2-inch blooms fading to blush. Blooms later than most other roses. Scentless. Hips round, red, of medium size.

FOLIAGE: 3 to 5 leaflets, 1½ to 3 inches; blackberry-like, grayish-green. Stems very prickly.

HEIGHT: To 12 feet.

HABIT: Drooping or semi-climbing with long, arching canes.

REMARKS: Hardiest of our native roses, this species is a parent of many of our older ramblers.

SOME VARIETIES AND HYBRIDS:

American Pillar: A justly famous variety with deep rose-red, single, white-centered blooms 3 inches across. A June-bloomer; to 20 feet; very hardy.

Baltimore Belle: A once-popular variety with small, blush, very double blooms in clusters; vigorous.

Doubloons: Large, golden-yellow double blooms on long stems; climber.

Mabelle Stearns: A shrub-like "dooryard" rose with strong, spreading branches bearing very double, fragrant, shell-pink blooms in clusters throughout the season. Buds sometimes ball in June but perfect flowers are produced later in the season; 2 feet with a spread of 6 to 8 feet; hardy.

Meda: Large, double shrimp-pink blooms with long stems.

Polaris: Small, white, very double blooms in large clusters on long, arching green canes. Said to be short-lived but has flourished on our garden walls for fifteen years with little care; occasionally reblooms; to 15 feet.

Queen of the Prairies: Large, double, globular; fragrant, bright pink, sometimes striped white; in clusters; large foliage; vigorous climber.

ROSA SPINOSISSIMA SCOTCH OR BURNETT ROSE

ORIGIN: Asia; Europe.

FLOWER: White, blush or yellowish single, to 2 inches, with reddish buds. Very fragrant. Hips dark brown, small and round.

FOLIAGE: 7 to 9 leaflets; fern-like; disease-resistant. Stems densely spiny.

HEIGHT: To 4 feet.

HABIT: Densely branched. Arching in good soil.

REMARKS: This species and its hybrids prefer a light soil.

SOME VARIETIES AND HYBRIDS:

R. s. altaica: Larger flower; taller, more vigorous than the species.

Harison's Yellow: Double yellow, small; early; 6 to 8 feet, persistent.

Lady Hamilton: Semi-double cream white, flushed pink; 4 feet.

Sonnenlicht: Canary-yellow semi-double; early and very fragrant.

Spring Gold (Frühlingsgold): Golden yellow Shrub Rose; strong, graceful branches packed with bloom; fragrant; disease resistant; 3 to 5 feet.

Stanwell Perpetual: Flesh-pink double; blooms during the entire season; 6 feet; a hedge rose.

ROSA VIRGINIANA *(lucida)* AMERICAN WILD ROSE

ORIGIN: Grows wild from Newfoundland to Georgia and west to Missouri.

FLOWERS: Single, to 2½ inches, pale or rose-pink, usually solitary; bright and sparkling single with golden center. Hips small, round, red, persistent.

FOLIAGE: 7 leaflets, to 2½ inches, of medium green, shining above; erect, brownish, prickly stems.

HEIGHT: To 6 feet.

HABIT: Erect and shrubby. Spreads by underground stems to form persistent, dense thickets.

REMARKS: Grows under adverse conditions as at the seashore. Can be used for high, dense hedges, the red hips making them decorative in autumn.

ROSA WICHURAIANA MEMORIAL ROSE

ORIGIN: Japan; China. Brought to Europe 1859.

FLOWERS: Small, white, fragrant, to 2 inches, in phlox-like clusters.

FOLIAGE: 7 to 9 leaflets to 1 inch long, shining above; stems green, smooth.

HEIGHT: Low.

HABIT: Prostrate or trailing.

REMARKS: Very hardy; understock used for many modern varieties and species; in the breeding of many climbers and trailers, and in a large number of the Brownell Roses.

Some Varieties and Hybrids:

Dorothy Perkins: Small-flowered bright pink double Rambler; very floriferous; long popular in home gardens; still widely grown in seashore locations where it does not mildew as it often does inland.

Ellen Poulsen: Light cherry-pink double in large clusters; glossy leaves; a Polyantha which, of course, reblooms.

Brownell Roses: See pages 272–73.

New Dawn: The remontant form of Dr. W. Van Fleet. Beautifully formed double shell-pink buds and medium-sized Hybrid Tea-like blooms on long stems, singly or in small clusters; very fragrant; hardy and vigorous; to 15 feet.

SHRUB ROSES

The term Shrub Rose is a loose one which is hard to define correctly. It has been used over the years to designate Species and Species Hybrid Roses which are large and luxuriant enough to be grown as specimen plants. (See page 8).

In addition to these, however, there is another group which has come to be known as Shrub Roses. These are of mixed ancestry but of such habit of growth that they may be used as shrubs. They have also been called Dooryard Roses. Here they are:

Autumn Bouquet: Carmine pink blooms borne singly and in clusters on long stems; constant succession of bloom; 4 feet.

Dr. Eckener: Fragrant, semi-double flowers of copper-rose and gold; remontant; 6 feet.

F. J. Grootendorst: Small bright red flowers with fringed edges like carnations; large clusters throughout the season.

Fragrant Beauty: Of the same blood and produced by the same breeder (M. R. Jacobus) as Autumn Bouquet, this is a 5-foot Shrub Rose of great hardiness producing carmine-red Hybrid Tea-like blooms all summer.

Hon. Lady Lindsay: A spreading plant 3 feet wide and 3 feet tall which produces a continuous succession of handsome pointed buff-yellow buds and gold-suffused pink flowers.

Mabelle Stearns: A spreading plant little more than 2 feet tall but spreading to at least 4 feet, this bushy variety produces constantly, well-shaped, peach-blossom pink double flowers with recurved petals. Sometimes "balls" in June but produces handsome, perfect flowers all through July and August when the Hybrid Teas are sulking.

Morning Stars: Clusters of 3-inch, gardenia-like white roses on bushes 4 feet in height.

Pink Grootendorst: Pink form of F. J. Grootendorst.

The Fairy: Long-stemmed clusters of bright, clear pink, 1-inch, double, ruffled blooms are produced in almost constant succession on broad, spreading, 3-foot plants, with small, glossy, trouble-resistant foliage. Resents spraying, but doesn't need it. In our garden The Fairy consistently remains in bloom later than any other rose.

ABBREVIATIONS FOR ROSE CLASSES

(from *Modern Roses IV,* American Rose Society)

Alp	Alpina
Arv	Arvensis
B	Bourbon
C	China
CB	Climbing Bourbon
CC	Climbing China
Cent	Centifolia
CHP	Climbing Hybrid Perpetual
CHT	Climbing Hybrid Tea
CT	Climbing Tea
D	Damask
Evbl.Semi-Cl.	Everblooming Semi-Climber
G	Gallica
HAlba	Hybrid Alba
H.Arv.Cl.	Hybrid Arvensis Climber
HB	Hybrid Bourbon
HBc	Hybrid Bracteata
HBlanda	Hybrid Blanda
HC	Hybrid China
HCanina	Hybrid Canina
H. chinensis minima	Hybrid chinensis minima
HD	Hybrid Damask
HFt	Hybrid Foetida
HG	Hybrid Gigantea
Hug	Hybrid Hugonis
HM	Hybrid Moss
HMacrantha	Hybrid Macrantha
HMs	Hybrid Moschata
HN	Hybrid Noisette
HNut	Hybrid Nutkana
HP	Hybrid Perpetual
HPol	Hybrid Polyantha
HRubiginosa	Hybrid Rubiginosa
HRug	Hybrid Rugosa
HSb	Hybrid Sweetbrier
HSet	Hybrid Setigera
HSp	Hybrid Species
HT	Hybrid Tea
Lamb	Lambertiana
LC	Large-flowered Climber
M	Moss
Mlt	Multiflora
N	Noisette
Pol	Polyantha
R	Rambler
Rug	Rugosa
Rug-Pol	Rugosa-Polyantha
Semi-Cl	Semi-Climber
Semi-Cl.Pol.	Semi-Climbing Polyantha
Semp	Sempervirens
Sp	Species
Spn	Spinosissima
T	Tea
Wich.Pol.	Wichuraiana-Polyantha

RECENT CLASSES (not from *Modern Roses*)

CF	Climbing Floribunda
DFl	Dwarf Floribunda
Fl	Floribunda
Gr	Grandiflora
Mn	Miniature
P	Pillar

PLATE 29

Typical of the striking new colors being developed in roses is Sterling Silver, considered by many the best of the "lavender" roses to date, and always a center of attention in any arrangement class.

PLATE 30

Folks who have a nostalgia for the oldtime favorite rose American Beauty will like its modern counterpart, President Eisenhower, velvety deep, rich red— and fragrant. A vigorous grower, it makes a good show flower.

PLATE 31

Single Roses are not given a conspicuous display in most catalogs. For many, however, their very simplicity of form and perfection of color possess a unique appeal. Dainty Bess (at right), is the favorite variety. For indoor use, cut while still in bud.

PLATE 32

During the past decade or so the Floribundas have gained rapidly in popularity. In shows they are usually exhibited as clusters, preferably with the first flowers still in good condition. Here is Red Pinocchio.

PLATE 33

Form is an important factor in flowers selected for rose show competition. It is well exemplified in these blooms of Rubaiyat. BELOW: *In many garden designs Tree Roses are especially effective. In severe climates Sub-zero varieties—such as Orange Ruffles, always a favorite of visitors to our garden—are the least subject to injury.*

PLATE 34

Two very similar excellent new "quarter-double" roses are Corcorico (at left in photograph) and Wildfire, both with very high A.R.S. ratings. They are ideal as shrubs or for low hedges.

PLATE 36

Orange Everglow, beautiful in both bud and full bloom; really fragrant; extremely vigorous and hardy; and one of our most admired Climbers.

Hybrid Teas, Floribundas, Grandifloras, Polyanthas, Hybrid Perpetuals

> *Suffice it to say, that where Roses were grown twenty years ago by the dozen they are grown by the thousand; and where by the thousand now by the acre. [Date: 1880!]*

The roses most widely grown today belong to several botanical groups, but have in common a number of characteristics which make them especially desirable for use in beds and borders. For this reason they are designated Garden Roses. (See pages 5–6.)

HYBRID TEA ROSES

The Hybrid Tea is by far the most popular rose type today, giving as it does, beautiful form, a great color range, very often fine fragrance, moderate growth, monthly bloom through the growing season, and a fair degree of hardiness.

La France, the first Hybrid Tea, was created in 1867 from a cross between a tender Tea Rose and a Hybrid Perpetual. Since then thousands of varieties have been introduced, good, bad, and indifferent, various blood lines being added over the years. A study of any *Rose Annual* of the American Rose Society will give an idea of the number of new Hybrid Teas appearing each year.

In order to give the cream of the crop, only those with very high rating in the popularity list of the American Rose Society have been chosen, with the exception of a few very promising varieties so new that they have not yet been entered in the Society's lists.

269

HYBRID TEA ROSES
HIGHLY RATED BY THE AMERICAN ROSE SOCIETY
AND NEW VARIETIES

NAME	COLOR	FRAGRANCE	HEIGHT
Reds			
Americana	medium red	yes	med.
Audie Murphy	medium red		tall
Avon	dark red		med.
Christian Dior	medium red	yes	med.
Christopher Stone	medium red	yes	med.
Chrysler Imperial*	oxblood red	yes	med.
Crimson Duke	crimson	slight	med.
Crimson Glory	dark red	yes	med.
Etoile d'Hollande	medium red	yes	med.
Grande Duchesse Charlotte	medium red		tall
Grand Slam	medium red	yes	med.
Mirandy*	dark red	intense	med.
Mr. Lincoln*	bright red	spicy	med.
New Yorker	medium red	yes	med.
Nocturne*	dark red	yes	med.
Rubaiyat*	rose-red	yes	tall
World's Fair Salute	bright red	yes	med.
Pinks			
Blithe Spirit	bright pink		med.
Eiffel Tower	medium light	yes	tall
First Love	light pink	slight	med.
Katherine T. Marshall*	medium pink	fruity	med.
Pink Favorite	medium pink		med.
Pink Masterpiece	light pink	yes	med.
Pink Peace	medium pink	yes	med.
Pink Princess	light pink	yes	tall
Royal Highness*	pale pink	yes	med.
Sweet Afton	pale pink	yes	med.
Pink Blends			
Charlotte Armstrong	light pink; red	fruity	med.
Confidence	light pink; yellow	yes	med.
Granada*	nasturtium; yellow	yes	med.
Mission Bells	pink; yellow	yes	med.
My Choice	salmon pink; yellow	yes	med.

* AARS Winner

NAME	COLOR	FRAGRANCE	HEIGHT
Pink Duchess	pink; yellow	yes	med.
Pink Radiance	light red; pink	yes	tall
Tally Ho	red; pink	yes	med.
*Tiffany**	deep pink; yellow	yes	med.

Yellows

Amarillo	dark yellow	yes	med.
Eclipse	light yellow	yes	med.
Golden Masterpiece	clear golden		med.
Golden Scepter	dark yellow	yes	med.
Golden Sunshine	medium yellow	yes	med.
Gold Glow	dark yellow	yes	med.
*King's Ransom**	chrome yellow	very	med.
Lowell Thomas	dark yellow	yes	med.
Summer Sunshine	bright yellow	very	med.
Town Crier	medium yellow	yes	med.

Yellow Blends

Bronze Masterpiece	golden bronze	yes	med.
*Diamond Jubilee**	ripe wheat	yes	tall
*Garden Party**	pale yellow; rose	yes	tall
*Mojave**	yellow; orange; red	yes	med.
*Peace**	yellow; rose	yes	tall
*Sutter's Gold**	yellow; red	yes	med.

Bicolors

Candy Stripe	rose-white	yes	med.
Chicago Peace	copper; pink; yellow		med.
*Forty-niner**	scarlet; yellow	yes	med.
*Gail Borden**	pink; yellow	yes	med.
Gaujard	cherry; white	yes	med.
Good News	copper; apricot	yes	med.
Kordes Perfecta	rose; cream	yes	med.
Love Song	yellow; melon		med.
Suspense	red; yellow reverse		tall
Tally Ho	light red; dark pink	yes	med.
Tip Toes	red; orange; light pink	yes	med.
Traviata	red; cream base		med.

* AARS Winner

NAME	COLOR	FRAGRANCE	HEIGHT
	Lavenders		
Lavender Charm	lavender	yes	med.
Orchid Masterpiece	orchid	yes	med.
Song of Paris	silvery lavender	yes	med.
Sterling Silver	mauve	yes	med.
	Coral to Orange-Red		
Aztec	scarlet-orange		med.
Hawaii	coral	yes	med.
Orange Flame	smoky orange-red	yes	med.
Polynesian Sunset	coral-orange	yes	med.
South Seas	coral to orange	yes	med.
*Tropicana**	orange-red	yes	tall
	Whites		
John F. Kennedy	white	yes	tall
Matterhorn	white	yes	med.
Pedràlbes	white	yes	med.
*White Knight**	white	yes	med.
White Queen	white	yes	med.

* AARS Winner

SUB-ZERO HYBRID TEA ROSES

The Sub-zero Hybrid Teas, prime favorites with some growers, and unpopular with others, were all created by Dr. Walter Brownell of Little Compton, Rhode Island, a lawyer turned first rose lover, then rose breeder. His long list of iron-hardy rose varieties, produced over a long lifetime of devoted service to *Rosa,* have helped to beautify our rose gardens for many years, and will do so for a long time to come.

Seeking for hardier Hybrid Teas, Dr. Brownell used *R. wichuraiana* as well as other hardy species in his hybridizing and produced many notable varieties.

In twenty years, we have never lost one Brownell rose from our garden, despite low temperatures, frozen snow and ice persisting for weeks at a time, and even hurricanes. A variety like Pink Princess (which blooms continually, is absolutely immune to black spot, and is as hardy as a Rugosa) is hard to beat, even if the Princess is a bit more plump and rounded than some of the more svelte Hybrid Teas.

Many extra-hardy Climbers have also been bred by Dr. Brownell.

Break o' Day: Very double; color of peach ice cream.
Curly Pink: Two-toned, very double pink; 50 recurved petals; constant bloom.
Delightful: Yellow touched with rose.
Handsom Red: Brilliant, light red.
Helen Hayes: Fragrant, yellow touched with rose or pink; semi-double.
Lily Pons: Creamy white; old but reliable.
Pink Princess: A beautiful pink, double; iron-hardy.
Queen o' the Lakes: Deep crimson 5 to 6 inches in diameter; very tall.
Red Duchess: A handsome, deep red.
Tip Toes: Red, orange, and pink blend; fragrant.

SUB-ZERO FLORIBUNDAS

Anne Vanderbilt: Rose-red and copper semi-double; fragrant.
Dolly Darling: Silvery pink double.
Flirt: Salmon-pink and yellow blend.
King Boreas: Clear yellow.
Lady Lou: Rose and red blend; large, double, high-centered blooms.

SINGLE HYBRID TEAS

The Single Hybrid Tea Roses constitute a small but choice group of varieties which are true Hybrid Teas but produce single or quarter-double blooms, many of them with prominent, showy stamens, as in the famous variety Dainty Bess, the stamens of which are deep garnet.

Remarkably hardy and long-lived, the Singles have a delicate charm all their own. Every rose lover who has a feeling for the unusual and for unassuming but rare beauty should have a collection of them. In our former garden at West Nyack, New York we had quite a complete collection which grew, flourished, and bloomed for over fifteen years without the loss of one plant. During a few bitter winters when temperatures went well below zero and stayed there for days on end, the plants were killed back almost to the ground, but May found them producing plenty of new wood and by June they were in full bloom. We cannot recommend them too highly.

B. W. Price: Long, pointed bud; flower deep cerise-pink; 6 to 8 petals; soft foliage; monthly bloom.
Cecil: Golden-yellow; 5 petals; 4 inches; recurrent bloom.

Dainty Bess: Soft shell-pink; 6 petals; 3½ to 5 inches; in clusters; maroon stamens; petals broad, with fluted edges. Tall, vigorous plant with heavy foliage; monthly bloom; generally considered the best of the Singles; scentless.

Golden Wings: Large yellow, amber anthers.

Innocence: White with golden stamens; 10 petals; to 5 inches, in clusters; dark, handsome foliage; recurrent bloom; scentless.

Irish Fireflame: Long, spiral bud; flower orange and gold, veined crimson; 5 petals; to 5½ inches; anthers fawn color; dark, glossy foliage; monthly bloom; very fragrant.

Isobel: Pointed bud; flower light rose-pink, shaded to apricot; 5 petals; to 5 inches; handsome foliage; slight fragrance.

Lulu: Exquisite pointed, orange bud; flower salmon-rose; 8 petals; to 4 inches; rich, dark foliage, disease-resistant; monthly bloom; slight fragrance.

Velvetier: Pointed bud; flower dark, velvety crimson; 8 petals; to 5 inches, in clusters; glossy foliage; recurrent bloom; fragrant.

Vesuvius: Long, pointed bud; flower dark, velvety crimson; 6 petals; light, leathery foliage; recurrent bloom; moderate fragrance.

White Wings: Long, pointed bud; flower white, to 5 inches; leathery, vigorous foliage; fragrant.

Innocence: a ten-petaled Single (or quarter-double) Hybrid Tea; one of the loveliest roses of all time.

FLORIBUNDA ROSES

In 1924 a cross between a Hybrid Tea Rose and a Polyantha produced the first Hybrid Polyantha, or Floribunda. This notable achievement in rose breeding has brought us a long, handsome, and hardy line of large-flowered, brilliantly colored, cluster-flowered varieties which are almost constantly in bloom from June to frost.

They vary greatly in appearance, from the tall, vigorous single Betty Prior to varieties like Independence, Betsy McCall, and Lilibet, the flowers of which are as beautifully formed as those of Hybrid Teas, though here produced in clusters.

Much hardier than most of the Hybrid Teas, the Floribundas are a godsend to those who live in the colder portions of Zone 5 and the warmer sections of Zone 4. But they are not confined to these areas. Their popularity is rapidly increasing and they are seen in every rose garden, and in increasing numbers.

As with the Hybrid Teas, we list here only those varieties which have the highest ratings in the American Rose Society's popularity list.

Floribundas are usually shown as "sprays"—single cut stems with as many blooms as possible "at their most perfect phase." This varies with different varieties.

Semi-doubles with few petals—10 to 20—are likely to be at their most attractive stage of development when sufficiently open to show the contrasting "heart" of the flowers; but the outer petals should be in perfect condition. Sometimes a single flower, if exceptionally fine, will score above a spray, unless the schedule distinctly calls for the latter.

FLORIBUNDA ROSES
HIGHLY RATED BY THE AMERICAN ROSE SOCIETY
AND NEW VARIETIES

NAME	COLOR	FRAGRANCE	HEIGHT
Reds			
Alain	medium red		med.
Carrousel	dark red	yes	med.
Donald Prior	medium red	yes	med.
Eutin	dark red		med.
Frensham	dark red		tall
Permanent Wave	medium red		med.
Red Glory	medium red		tall
Red Pinocchio	dark red	yes	med.
World's Fair	dark red	yes	med.
Orange-Reds			
Anna Wheatcroft	orange		med.
Corcorico	orange-red		tall
Floradora	orange		tall
Fusilier	orange-red		med.
Ginger	orange	yes	med.
Orange Triumph	red and orange		med.
Sarabande	orange-red		med.
Spartan.	orange-red	yes	med.
Pinks and Pink Blends			
Betty Prior	medium pink	yes	tall
Else Poulsen	medium pink		med.
*Fashion**	salmon	yes	med.
Fashionette	pink blend	yes	med.
Frolic	medium pink		med.
Lady Ann Kidwell	light red; dark pink		med.
Ma Perkins	pink blend		med.
Mrs. R. M. Finch	medium pink	yes	med.
Pink Bountiful	medium pink	yes	med.
Rita Simmons	medium pink	yes	low
Rosenelfe	LaFrance pink	yes	low
Salmon Spray	salmon-pink	yes	med.
Sweet and Low	pink blend		low
*Vogue**	deep pink blend		med.

* AARS Winner

NAME	COLOR	FRAGRANCE	HEIGHT
Yellows and Yellow Blends			
Allgold	medium yellow	yes	med.
Circus Parade	yellow blend	yes	med.
*Gold Cup**	clear golden	very	med.
*Golden Slippers**	yellow; orange	yes	low
Little Darling	yellow blend		tall
Masquerade	red; yellow; rose	yes	med.
Starlet	medium yellow		med.
Woburn Abbey	orange; red; yellow		low
Whites			
Dagmar Späth	white	yes	low
Dairy Maid	cream single		med.
Ivory Fashion	cream	yes	med.
*Saratoga**	white	yes	med.
Lavenders			
Lavender Girl	lavender	yes	low
Lavender Princess	lavender	yes	med.
Lilac Charm	lilac single		low

* AARS Winner

GRANDIFLORA ROSES

As Floribunda Roses grew larger and larger, with newer introductions producing beautifully formed, Hybrid Tea-like blooms in
clusters, the problem of how to classify them became acute. A few
years ago a number of large-flowered varieties which naturally

bloomed in clusters were classified as Hybrid Teas, but as more of these were produced, confusion increased. Now the new class Grandiflora has been created to cover very large-flowered cluster varieties of fine form. To date only a few are listed.

NAME	COLOR	FRAGRANCE	HEIGHT
*Camelot**	coral-pink	yes	med.
Carrousel	dark red	yes	med.
*John S. Armstrong**	rich red	slight	med.
Montezuma	coral-red	rich	med.
Mount Shasta	white	yes	tall
*Queen Elizabeth**	salmon-pink	yes	tall

* AARS Winner

POLYANTHA ROSES

The dwarf, small-flowered Polyanthas were the forerunners of the popular large-flowered Floribundas of today but they still have their place for edgings and foreground plantings.

Their ancestry (see chart page 4) includes crosses of *R. multiflora, R. wichuraiana* and a Bengal hybrid, *R. indica major,* a climber. Pierre Guillot introduced the first variety, La Paquerette, in 1875.

Polyanthas are best shown while the first flowers in the cluster to open are still in good condition.

SOME POPULAR POLYANTHAS

(Average height of plants eighteen inches)

Cameo: Salmon to shell-pink.
Carroll Ann: Ranunculus-flowered orange.
Cécile Brunner: Famous pink Sweetheart Rose.
Charlie McCarthy: Very dwarf, floriferous white.
Margo Koster: Orange, flushed pink.
Marie Pavic: Double, open white, center flesh.
Mignonette: Very small, flesh-pink, changing to white.
Orange Triumph: Scarlet-orange in large clusters.
Pinkie: Porcelain pink.
Pink Rosette: Camellia-shaped, soft pink.
Snow White: Ranunculus-flowered white.
Yvonne Rabier: White, sulphur center, in clusters.

HYBRID PERPETUALS

The Hybrid Perpetuals, the immediate forerunners of the Hybrid Teas, were of supreme importance a hundred years ago because they were the first group of really hardy, remontant varieties. With the advent of the Hybrid Teas with their monthly bloom and fine form (though these are less hardy as a class) the Hybrid Perpetuals gradually lost popularity. Today they are grown only in the gardens of collectors and in areas where extremely low winter temperatures make difficult or impossible the culture of Hybrid Teas. There are notable exceptions to this general rule. The magnificent white Hybrid Perpetual Frau Karl Druschki is still one of the best of garden roses.

The ancestry of the Hybrid Perpetuals, like that of many another distinguished family, is somewhat cloudy in certain respects. We know that they are the offspring of *Rosa chinensis, Rosa gallica,* and *Rosa centifolia,* with later infusions of *R. c. odorata* (the Tea Rose) and the Hybrid Chinas (crosses between *R. chinensis* and *R. centifolia*). Later varieties were of more complicated blood lines than the early introductions.

As a class these roses are remontant (blooming in spring and again in autumn) rather than everblooming. The colors range from white to dark, rich red, but there are no yellows except in such varieties as Soleil d'Or, the first Pernetiana, which was really a Hybrid Perpetual. The Hybrid Teas, created by crossing Tea Roses with Hybrid Perpetuals, are of course close relatives of the members of this older class.

SOME HYBRID PERPETUALS

American Beauty (Ledechaux, 1875): Globular buds; flowers very large, cupped crimson-carmine. Fragrant.

Baroness Rothschild (Pernet père, 1868): Light to pale rose with 40 petals; stiff, erect plant.

Black Prince (Paul, 1866): Large, round, cupped; fragrant crimson-maroon.

Captain Hayward (Bennett, 1893): Scarlet-crimson; fragrant; with 30 petals.

Charles Lefebvre (Lacharme, 1861): Large, very double crimson blooms of 70 petals; very fragrant, tall, vigorous.

Clio (Paul, 1894): Very double; globular; satiny flesh, pink in clusters; rampant.

Everest (Easlea, 1927): Very large cream-white with lemon-green center; broad, long, firm petals; fragrant, high-centered blooms.

Ferdinand Pichard (Tanne, 1921): Petals streaked pink and scarlet; recurrent bloom; vigorous grower.

Frau Karl Druschki (Lambert, 1901): Large, chaste, snow-white blossoms of 36 petals; buds blush. No fragrance.

General Jacqueminot (Roussel, 1853): Very fragrant, clear red with golden stamens; bush, to 6 feet.

George Arends (Hinner, 1910): Large, very double, delightfully fragrant; delicate pink; very vigorous growth.

Henry Nevard (Cant, 1924): Scarlet-crimson; fragrant; very large, very double blooms; 3 feet.

Louis van Houtte (Lacharme, 1869): Dark maroon shading to blackish crimson; velvety, 40 petals.

Mrs. John Laing (Bennett, 1887): Pointed buds, flowers soft pink, very large, double, and fragrant; 3 feet.

Paul Neyron (Levet, 1869): Very large, double, fragrant lavender-pink; 4 feet; vigorous.

Ulrich Brunner (Levet, 1882): Large, cupped, cherry-red blooms of 30 petals; tall, upright plant.

CHAPTER *20.* *Climbers and Creepers*

MODERN LARGE-FLOWERED CLIMBERS

For years the rose breeders have been working to create Large-flowered Climbers of fine flower form that will bloom as freely and continuously as the Floribundas and be as reliably hardy.

Very gradually this dream is being realized. Each year brings one or two new varieties in the hardy, everblooming group.

Here are some of the most reliable.

Blaze (Improved): Improved strain of this famous red Climber which is almost continuously in bloom; 8 feet.

Blossomtime: A fragrant, cameo-pink Climber, which is extra hardy and everblooming; 6 to 8 feet.

Coral Dawn: Coral-pink with pointed buds; 4½-inch flowers freely produced in clusters; 6 to 8 feet.

Don Juan: Deep, velvety red, fragrant flowers 5 inches in diameter are produced from pointed buds; fragrant; 8 to 10 feet.

Dortmund: New medium red Climber of great promise.

Gladiator: Huge, high-centered, rose-red blooms continuously produced; 10 feet.

Golden Showers: Daffodil yellow; fragrant, 4½- to 5-inch flowers from pointed buds; long cutting stems, almost thornless; 6 to 8 feet.

High Noon: Bright yellow Pillar of moderate growth in the North. Beautifully shaped blooms on good cutting stems produced each month in season.

Joseph's Coat: A yellow, orange, and red multi-color Climber reaching 6 feet. Can also be grown as a shrub.

282

Dream Girl, a Pillar Rose that blooms almost constantly throughout the season.

Mona Lisa: High-centered, warm pink, fragrant flowers on 10-foot plants.
Morning Dawn: Silvery pink 5-inch blooms, flushed salmon; Old Rose fragrance; hollylike foliage; 6 to 8 feet.
New Dawn: Shell-pink, fragrant, double flowers fading to blush. Everblooming form of Dr. W. Van Fleet.
Royal Gold: Golden yellow; 4-inch blooms in clusters; 5 to 7 feet.
White Dawn: A fragrant white member of the Dawn family, this rose blooms almost constantly and is vigorous and very hardy.

CLIMBING HYBRID TEAS

With the exception of a very few extra-hardy varieties, the Climbing Hybrid Teas are not reliably hardy north of Washington, D.C. For mild climates they make ideal Large-flowered Climbers producing monthly bloom. Each year new varieties appear. Here are some of the best.

Climbing Christopher Stone: Medium red.
Climbing Crimson Glory: Rich red, one of the best and hardiest; hardy North.
Climbing Dainty Bess: Climbing form of the famous Single.
Climbing Etoile de Holland: Scarlet.
Climbing Mme. Henri Guillot: A red blend.
Climbing Mrs. Sam McGredy: Orange blend.
Climbing Peace: The great yellow blooms, touched with rose, are as handsome as the bush form. Hardy on Cape Cod.
Climbing Picture: Light pink.
Climbing Red Radiance: Light red and deep pink.
Climbing Shot Silk: A striking pink blend.

CLIMBING FLORIBUNDAS

The Climbing Floribundas, like thè Climbing Hybrid Teas, are climbing sports of bush varieties but, as a class, much hardier. We have found them perfectly hardy north of New York City. They should do well in Zones 5 and 6. Bloom is almost continuous.

Climbing Cécile Brunner: Light pink.
Climbing Goldilocks: Light, clear yellow; fragrant.
Climbing Pinkie: Medium pink; large clusters of small flowers.
Climbing Spartan: Vibrant orange-red, like its bush form.
Climbing Summer Snow: White; floriferous; fragrant.

TRAILING ROSES

Fortunately for the rose grower, there are a number of varieties of "climbing" roses which much prefer trailing on the ground or over a wall to actual climbing. After all, roses do not "climb," but those with an erect habit, which produce long canes, can be trained and fastened to pillars, arbors, or trellises.

The trailing group is of very real value for covering bare banks and slopes; for training over large rocks or stone walls; and for purposes of a similar nature.

Some varieties which are ideal for covering a fence—like Dorothy Perkins or the lovely yellow single, Mermaid—are equally at home on the ground. In the great rose garden at Hershey, Pennsylvania, Mermaid for many years covered the sloping banks of the large pool, which is a feature of the garden. Few more beautiful sights can be imagined than this rose in full bloom, its exquisite blossoms reflected in the water.

Apricot Glow: Double, 3-inch blush, pink, and copper clusters.
Carpet of Gold: Yellow; fragrant; semi-double, 2 inches in diameter. Very early.
Frederick S. Peck: Clusters of 2-inch, semi-double pink blooms with yellow centers.
Little Compton Creeper: Large, single, wild-rose-pink blooms in clusters; large hips in fall.
Magic Carpet: Double, orange and yellow blooms in clusters.
Max Graf: Pink single; very hardy; handsome, glossy foliage.
Red Creeping Everbloom: Dark red; semi-double, fragrant flowers all summer.
R. rugosa repens alba: Large, single white flowers in clusters; vigorous; fragrant.
R. Wichuraiana (The Memorial Rose): Single, white fragrant flowers in pyramidal corymbs. Almost evergreen; everblooming.
Yellow Creeping Everbloom: Yellow form of Creeping Everbloom.

NOTE: Above varieties bloom only in spring, except as noted.

OLDER REMONTANT CLIMBERS AND PILLARS

Lovers of Old Roses, and collectors of the unusual and traditional, may wish to have in their rose gardens a few of the following old and older climbers, all of which have the desirable characteristic of rebloom. Some are tender.

Clytemnestra (Pemberton Pillar) 1915: Copper buds and fragrant, buff-salmon flowers in clusters; dark, leathery foliage and flexible canes.

Cornelia (Pemberton Pillar) 1925: Double, pale pink, fragrant blossoms orange at base; to 3 inches, in flat sprays.

Maréchal Niel (Noisette) 1864: Pointed buds and huge, fragrant, golden yellow flowers continuously produced; vigorous, bushy but *very tender;* a famous variety.

Mermaid (Hybrid bracteata) 1918: Very large, single, fragrant pale yellow flowers with dark stamens; dark, glossy, disease-resistant foliage on heavy canes to 20 feet. Needs winter protection north of Philadelphia.

Mrs. Alfred Carrière (Noisette) 1879: Large, double, globular, blush-white, very fragrant flowers continuously in bloom on vigorous plant; hardier than most Noisettes.

Mrs. Arthur Curtiss James (Large-fl. Climber) 1933: Fragrant, large yellow flowers on long stems. Very hardy.

Penelope (Pemberton Pillar) 1924: Shell-pink, medium-sized semi-double blooms with a musk fragrance, in clusters.

Prosperity (Pemberton Pillar) 1919: Large, pink-flushed, white gardenialike blooms on long stems, in clusters; vigorous.

Souvenir de la Malmaison (Climber Bourbon) 1893: Very large, double, intensely fragrant, creamy flesh-pink with rosy center. Free but erratic bloom; a very famous variety.

OLDER CLIMBERS FOR JUNE BLOOM

A few of the once popular Large-flowered Climbers which bloom but once during the season are still worth growing. They are of varied ancestry, some sparsely recurrent.

Baltimore Belle (Hybrid *setigera*) 1843: Clusters of very double fragrant, blush-pink blossoms, profusely produced; very hardy and vigorous.

Belle of Portugal (Hybrid *gigantea*) 1903: Pointed 4-inch buds and 4- to 6-inch blooms, semi-double, flesh-pink; blooms over a long period; *tender North;* naturalized in California.

City of York (Large-fl. Climber) 1945: White, open, double, fragrant blooms with prominent golden stamens, literally cover the vigorous 15-foot plants.

Copper Glow: (Large-fl. Climber) 1949: Large, double, high-centered, very fragrant blooms on good cutting stems; glossy foliage; very hardy. Similar to Orange Everglow, now no longer listed.

Dr. W. Van Fleet (Hybrid *Wichuraiana*) 1910: The forerunner of many modern varieties but now superseded by its remontant form New Dawn (see page 283); well shaped, fragrant, shell-pink buds and open, double, fragrant flowers in profusion.

Glenn Dale (Hybrid *Wichuraiana*) 1927: Lemon-white, fragrant, in large clusters; to 10 feet.

Kitty Kininmonth (Hybrid *gigantea*) 1922: Large, semi-double, cupped, fragrant, fadeless, deep pink flowers.

Mary Wallace (Large-fl. Climber) 1924: Exquisite, large, cupped, semi-double rose-pink, fragrant blooms on 12-foot plants.

Paul's Lemon Pillar: (Hybrid Climber) 1915: Very large pale yellow buds open to large, smooth, fragrant, lemon-white double blooms on long stems; vigorous.

Paul's Scarlet Climber: (Large-fl. Climber) 1916: Semi-double, scarlet to crimson blooms in large clusters; vigorous.

Purity (Large-fl. Climber) 1917: Large, semi-double, open, fragrant, pure white blooms on strong stems; thorny; vigorous.

Silver Moon (Hybrid *Wichuraiana*) 1910: Pointed yellow buds open to 4½-inch cream-white, open, semi-double blooms with slight fragrance in clusters on long, sturdy stems; rampant to 20 feet.

Thor (Large-fl. Climber): Bud long-pointed; flower large, double, very fragrant crimson on long stem. Foliage leathery.

RAMBLER ROSES

These old Climbers, with large clusters of small single or double flowers, bloom but once, in May, June, or July. The first of them was Crimson Rambler, introduced in 1890. Today most of the Ramblers which survive are *Wichuraiana* crosses. Even these (with the exception of Chevy Chase) are desirable only near the seashore or in very severe climates where the Large-flowered Climbers are not hardy.

American Pillar (1902): 3-inch, single, rose-pink blooms with white eyes, in huge clusters, on long stems; to 20 feet.

Chevy Chase (1939): A recent Rambler; (R. *Soulieana* x Eblouissant); small, double rose-red blooms in large clusters on short stems; to 15 feet.

Chevy Chase, a new deep rose-red Rambler that is not subject to mildew.

Dorothy Perkins (1901): Masses of bright, light pink, fragrant blooms in July; subject to mildew.

Evangeline (1906): Open, single, fragrant, cameo-pink and white, in clusters on long stems; to 15 feet.

Excelsa (1909): Clusters of light crimson double blooms; sometimes called Red Dorothy Perkins; to 18 feet.

Gardenia (1899): Yellow buds and creamy white double blooms with yellow centers in small sprays on short stems; to 15 feet.

Roserie (1917): Tyrian pink, white base, semi-double; glossy foliage; vigorous.

Violette (1921): Non-fading, pure deep violet blooms in clusters; 10 feet.

CHAPTER *21.* *Miniature Roses*

Frankly, we just love the Miniatures—those hardy, tough Fairy Roses of many uses, the original varieties of which were known and grown in the East more than two centuries ago. Brought to England from China or Japan in 1815, they were again "lost" for almost a century until, in the early 1900s, they were rediscovered on the window sill of a cottage in Switzerland. Introduced by the plantsman, M. Henri Correvon, they were named Rouletti, in honor of Dr. Roulet, their discoverer. Considered a curiosity, *R. Rouletti* was known to comparatively few rose lovers for another half century or so until the late Robert Pyle, then president of the Conard-Pyle Rose Company and a prime mover in the American Rose Society, on a visit to Holland in 1933, found John de Vink breeding miniature varieties, purely as a recreation. Immediately Mr. Pyle visualized their commercial possibilities, and hit upon the idea of selling them in full bloom, in small pots, at the International and other big spring flower shows. Despite predictions to the contrary by many rosarians they have proved to be quite satisfactory as house plants—when treated with some realization of the fact that they *are* roses and not African-violets; and they are also beginning to gain their rightful place in outdoor gardening.

And they are toughies! As yet much less far removed from their original progenitors than are the Hybrid Teas, Floribundas, and other garden roses of today, the Miniatures seem able to withstand more neglect in the way of spraying, feeding, and winter protection (when grown outdoors). A small group which we had for many years in a corner of the rock garden never received the regular spraying or dusting given the Bush Roses; they received practically no fertilizer except a sprinkling of bone meal on the rare occasions when we happened to remember to give it to them; no regular

289

watering; no winter protection; and but one pruning a year in the spring—and yet they flowered happily season after season. Too much fertilizer, incidentally, is not for the Miniatures if they are to keep their midget stature. In Portland, Oregon, we once saw an Oakington Ruby planted in rich soil, which resembled a small shrub rather than a Fairy Rose.

The Miniatures are all that the name implies: replicas of our garden roses in every respect except size. The blossoms vary in different varieties, from a scant half inch to an inch and a half or so, and from perfect little Hybrid Tea-shaped buds and blooms, as in Gold Star, to open, semi-double flowers in clusters. The "bushes" vary in height from six to twelve inches, one or two growing rather thin and tall but most of them low and spreading.

Basing our opinion upon our own experience with them, and that of a number of our acquaintances, we predict for them, as a class, a very bright future. They open up a new world of pleasure to those who love roses—especially to those who have very limited space.

Already a number of hybridizers are busily at work breeding new varieties and extending the color range. Quite likely, as this work progresses, many of the new sorts will fail to possess the hardiness and self-sufficiency the group now boasts—but such is the price of progress. (See list on page 292.) At any rate, we plan to continue adding to our collection of them, and to give them an important place in our new rose garden.

Miniatures in the Garden

In the open garden Miniatures are especially suitable for:

1. Edgings. We have a friend whose yellow rose garden is bordered with bright little plants of Gold Star.

2. Rock Gardens. Sunny beds, more or less level, in the foreground of the rock garden make excellent year-round homes for groups of Miniatures. Even in quite cold climates you will find they "can take it."

3. Children's Gardens. Children love to have gardens of their very own, but most of them prefer these on a small scale. What could be more appealing than the dooryard of an outdoor dolls' house with a tiny formal garden bordered by very small rooted box cuttings enclosing beds of Miniature Roses?

Miniature Roses, now available in many colors, are practical for really miniature gardens as well as for small rock gardens and for growing in pots.

For Winter Bloom Indoors

In three-inch pots, Miniatures give normal periods of bloom indoors if kept in a sunny window in a not-too-hot temperature; or in a cool sunporch. Not only will they make a conversation piece when the Garden Club meets at your home, but they will provide boutonnieres for the man of the house for weeks on end, occasional small shoulder bouquets for the ladies, material for miniature arrangements for home or show, and a colorful display which is not unwieldly to move or handle.

When a burst of bloom is over, prune back to outfacing buds, remove all dead wood, reduce water somewhat until fresh new growth appears. When that happens, you may look for a new crop of buds! If pests or disease rear their ugly heads, apply an all-purpose house plant spray from a pressure can available at any seed or housewares shop. When spring comes, repot if necessary and sink the plants to the rims of the pots in the front of a sunny garden bed outdoors, where they can have a summer vacation of fresh air, sunshine, and rain. Water in dry periods.

MINIATURE, BABY OR FAIRY ROSES

Baby Gold Star: Well-formed, golden, 2-inch blooms. Erect plant.
Baby Masquerade: Miniature form of multicolor Floribunda of same name.
Bit o' Sunshine: Bright yellow; free bloomer.
Bo-Peep: Deep rose-pink.
Cinderella: White.
Cutie: Pink, semi-double; fragrant.
Dwarfking: Red; fragrant.
Midget: Rose-red; very small.
Oakington Ruby: Double crimson, to 1½ inches.
Pink Joy: Double pink, touched with salmon; fragrant.
Pixie: White, flushed pink; very double.
Red Elf: Red, well-formed flowers.
Red Imp: Crimson, very double; opens flat.
Rouletti: Original variety; red; plant 6 inches tall.
Sweet Fairy: Lavender-pink; fragrant.
Thumbelina: Red semi-double.
Tinker Bell: Bright pink.
Tom Thumb: Red with white eye.
Twinkles: White double; fragrant.
Wayside's Garnet: Double, garnet-red flowers on compact plant.
White Pet: White double.

Note: All give continuous bloom when in active growth.

A prize-winning arrangement of roses in which buds and foliage, as well as open blooms, have been employed to advantage. (By Mrs. C. Wyatt Bragg, Quincy, Mass.)

CHAPTER 22. *Roses for Arrangement and Arranging Roses*

Just as roses are the garden flower supreme because of their beauty, variety, fragrance, and long season of bloom, so are they unexcelled as material for arrangement.

WHAT TO GROW

In selecting varieties for indoor decoration, try to secure those which last well, opening their buds slowly, retaining their depth of color and beauty of form to the end, and charming with their fragrance as well as their eye appeal. As a rule the less double Hybrid Teas of twenty to thirty petals (such as Helen Traubel and Sutter's Gold, both exquisite roses) have superb buds, but they open very quickly and quite flat so that an arrangement in which they are included will probably need remaking daily. Very doubles, on the other hand, tend to open slowly. For maximum effect however, select varieties with elegant, pointed buds and with distinct fragrance. Crimson Glory, Confidence, and the new White Knight are examples. (For others see list pages 297–99.)

Many of the Floribundas and a few of the Large-flowered Climbers are equally satisfactory as cut flowers. Among these, long-lasting Floribundas like Pinocchio, Red Pinocchio, and Amy Vanderbilt, and single types like Betty Prior, Corcorico, and Hillbilly, are excellent.

Climbing Pinocchio, salmon; Climbing Break o' Day, peach; Inspiration, pink; Mermaid, rich pale yellow single; and Orange Everglow, with pointed buds and exquisite fragrance, make good cut flowers.

The delicate Single Hybrid Teas, with their lovely, slim pointed buds—much deeper in color than the fully opened flowers—are fleeting in bouquets but so beautiful that I, for one, can never resist using them in bud when they are available. Next day I have an en-

294

tirely different arrangement of fully opened flowers. It is rather like arranging Bearded Iris. The question is, Just which blooms will fade and which buds will open during the night? Deep orange-salmon Lulu, despite its unromantic name, has the most beautiful bud imaginable. Dainty Bess, chamois-pink; wild-rose pink Isobel, very large, and the new Golden Wings are also unusually spectacular indoors.

While many Shrub Roses are not long-lasting when cut, the possibilities of their large persistent hips should not be neglected. A few however, like pink Lady Lindsay, Mabelle Stearns and Rosenelfe, are eminently satisfactory as cut flowers. The small, double, bright pink Shrub Rose, The Fairy, is especially long-lasting indoors, as are many of the small-flowered Polyanthas.

For miniature arrangements, Baby Roses are unexcelled, while the new dwarf edging roses like Pygmy Gold and Pygmy Red, with their well-formed buds and blooms, and the Polyanthas (see page 280) are naturals for small bouquets for the breakfast tray, dressing table, or coffee table and for old-fashioned formal bouquets.

HOW TO USE THEM

There are almost as many ways to arrange cut roses as there are varieties to choose from.

Though nowadays the "arrangers" frown upon arrangements of one species of flower only, if an exception is to be made of any, surely it should be roses.

All sorts of triangles, crescents, S or Hogarth curves, circles, semicircles, etc., may be formed of roses. Several varieties may be used to give a contrast in form and color. Accessory foliage with roses, or roses combined with other garden or florists' flowers and/or foliage offer endless possibilities.

Here are a few suggestions, just to set your own imagination working:

Copper vase or dish:
  Triangular design of—
    Light, pure blue delphiniums
    Buds of yellow Eclipse
    Partly opened and full-blown flowers of Mojave or buds of Golden
      Slippers or Woburn Abbey
    Bronzy large-leaved begonia foliage in a near complementary harmony

Victorian or Georgian vase or urn:
    Mass-line analogous arrangement of—
        Morden's Pink Physostegia
        Lavender-pink Michaelmas-daisies
        Chrysanthemum Chippewa
        Lilac Charm Floribunda Rose

Oblong Oriental dish:
    Right or left right-angle triangular design of—
        Juniper, yew or Red Barberry, in fruit
        Central motif of Rubaiyat, Spartan, or Tally Ho Rose in a complementary harmony

Tall, narrow Oriental vase:
    Vertical, analogous arrangement of—
        Caribbean Gladiolus (pale lavender, crimson blotch)
        Nocturne, Mirandy, or Avon (dark crimson roses)
        Dracaena or canna foliage

Pewter bowl:
    Full- or half-circle design of—
        Eucalyptus sprays, dried wisteria tendrils, or sand-blasted driftwood for main, curving lines
        Central interest and following lines of Fashion, Ma Perkins, or Salmon Spray with forget-me-not, cynoglossum, or blue hardy asters, in a split complementary harmony

Silver vase, dish, or bowl:
    S-curve design of—
        Sterling Silver and Lavender Charm Roses
        White and purple Japanese Anemones
        Pale lavender larkspur
        Artemisia Silver King
        Variegated hosta or cornus foliage in a monochromatic harmony

Alabaster urn:
    Mass arrangement, symmetrical triangle of—
        Pink gladiolus
        Pink and yellow snapdragons
        Pink larkspur, lythrum, stocks, or veronica
        Pale yellow, pink, and rose-pink roses
        Heliotrope, mignonette, violas
        Clematis, variegated ivy, or other vines
        Hosta foliage

Swedish glass vase:
Tall, slim, vertical triangular design of—
Hybrid Tea or Grandiflora buds, full-blown flowers and self foliage.
(Suggested varieties: Mojave, Queen Elizabeth, Eiffel Tower, Charlotte Armstrong, Golden Masterpiece, or Camelot.)

China or pottery dish:
Crescent design or semicircle of—
Golden Arbovitae or potentilla with thermopsis or lupine
Golden Sceptre, Gold Cup, Arlene Francis, Lowell Thomas, or a combination of any available yellow roses, accented with lavender, China-asters or stokesia in a near complementary harmony

Block-shaped vase of pottery or wooden mortar:
S-curve complementary arrangement of—
Canna, aspidistra, Winged Euonymus, or other shrub foliage
Central interest and following lines of buds and flowers of Mr. Lincoln, New Yorker, or Crimson Glory
Dark crimson scabiosas, snapdragons, Red Velvet Chrysanthemums

(For cutting and care after cutting see pages 225–28.)

ROSES FOR ARRANGEMENT

HYBRID TEAS

REDS AND ORANGES

Aztec: Orange-scarlet
Crimson Glory: Crimson
Grande Duchesse Charlotte: Medium red
Mirandy: Dark red
Mr. Lincoln: Bright red
New Yorker: Medium red
Orange Flame: Smoky orange
Polynesian Sunset: Orange
Tropicana: Orange-coral

WHITES

John F. Kennedy: Beautifully formed fragrant white
Mount Shasta: White Grandiflora
White Knight: Fragrant white
White Queen: Fragrant white

PINKS

Confidence: Peach-pink, yellow base
Eiffel Tower: Clear pink
First Love: Soft, delicate pink
Good News: Pink to apricot
Love Song: Salmon-pink, yellow base
Pink Parfait: clear pink
Royal Highness: Pale pink
Sweet Afton: Blush-pink

YELLOWS

Eclipse: Pointed buds, soft yellow
Golden Scepter: dark yellow
Garden Party: Pale yellow, touched with rose
Mojave: Yellow, orange, red
Peace: Yellow, edged rose
Sutter's Gold: Yellow, red

BICOLORS AND BLENDS

Chicago Peace: Copper, pink, yellow
Gail Borden: Pink, yellow
Gaujard: Cherry, white
Good News: Copper, apricot
Mojave: Yellow, red, orange
Suspense: Red; yellow reverse
Tally Ho: Light red and dark pink
Tip Toes: Red, orange, and pink

LAVENDER

Lavender Charm: Lavender
Orchid Masterpiece: Orchid
Sterling Silver: Silvery mauve

FLORIBUNDAS

REDS

Carrousel: Dark red
Corcorico: Geranium red
Frensham: Bright red
Red Pinocchio: Dark, red, long-lasting
Sarabande: Orange-red
Spartan: Coral-red

PINKS

Betsy McCall: Coral-pink
Betty Prior: Single pink
Lilibet: Soft shades of pink
Malibu: Coral-rose
Rosenelfe: Soft pink
Vogue: Deep pinks

WHITES

Ivory Fashion: Cream
Saratoga: White
White Bouquet: White

YELLOWS AND BLENDS

Allgold: Medium yellow
Gold Cup: Unfading, fragrant bright yellow
Golden Slippers: Yellow and red
Woburn Abbey: Yellow and red

LAVENDERS

Lavender Girl: Lavender
Lilac Charm: Single lilac

GRANDIFLORAS

Camelot: Salmon-pink
El Capitan: Bright red
Golden Girl: Yellow
Montezuma: Deep grenadine-rose

Queen Elizabeth: Salmon-pink
Roundelay: Fiery red
Saratoga: White

HYBRID PERPETUALS

Frau Karl Druschki: White   *Mrs. John Laing:* Soft pink

SINGLES

Dainty Bess: Chamois-pink   *Lilac Charm:* Lilac
Golden Wings: Yellow   *White Wings:* White

CLIMBERS

Blaze: Red   *Joseph's Coat:* red, yellow
Blossomtime: Pink   *Morning Dawn:* Silvery pink
Copper Glow: Copper   *New Dawn:* Blush pink
Coral Dawn: Coral-rose   *Silver Moon:* White
Golden Showers: Yellow   *White Dawn:* White

FLOWERS AND FOLIAGE
THAT GO ESPECIALLY WELL WITH ROSES FOR DECORATION INDOORS

Annuals	*Perennials*	*Foliage*
Bachelor's-Buttons	Astilbe	Arborvitae
China-asters	Buddleia	Artemisia
Cobaea scandens	Chrysanthemums	Aspidistra
Cynoglossum	Clematis	Barberry
Heliotrope	Delphinium	Begonias, large-leaved
Mignonette	Dianthus	Calla
Pansies	Forget-me-not	Dracaena
Salpiglossis	Gypsophila	Eucalyptus
Snapdragons	Hardy asters	Gardenia
Stocks	Iris, Dutch and Japanese	Ivy
	Lupine	Juniper
Bulbs	Lythrum	Kalmia
	Poppies	Magnolia
Amaryllis	Stokesia	Pieris japonica
Anemones	Thermopsis	Purple Beech
Gladiolus	Veronica	Statice
Lilies	Viola	Yew
Muscari		
Ranunculus		
Tulips		

CHAPTER *23. Potpourris, Jams, and Jellies*

The making of potpourri is an ancient art which may well be revived by the rose lover, for it is not difficult to preserve for years the delicious fragrance of the June rose garden.

Those who would make potpourri should grow many very fragrant roses (see pages 310–11), for these are the nucleus of the most delightful potpourris.

Dry Method. If you are pressed for time you may use the dry method which is much the simpler, though the product is not quite so delightfully fragrant.

Pick your most fragrant roses before they begin to fade and dry the petals on screens in an airy, dry room or shed. Each day, run your hands through the petals until you find the entire trayful so dry that the petals are brittle. Place a layer of petals in a rose jar and sprinkle with a mixture of cinnamon, ground cloves, a little allspice and mace and sandalwood powder. Repeat the process until the jar is full, and on top sprinkle a few drops of rose or lavender scent. Close tightly and store until fragrances have blended. Dried mint, lemon-verbena, rosemary, and scented geranium leaves may be added to the rose petals if desired.

Wet Method. Gather rose petals and other desired fragrant flowers or leaves before they fade and dry them partially in an airy place, on screens. After three days, pack them in rose jars between layers of salt, adding to each layer sprinklings of orrisroot, spices, herb seeds like caraway, cardamom, etc.; herb leaves, such as thyme, sweet marjoram, sage, mint, and rosemary; and vanilla beans broken in small pieces. When the jar is full, sprinkle with scent, cologne, or even vinegar.

Buccaneer, one of the new Grandiflora group, showing right stages of development for a "three-of-a-kind" exhibit. BELOW: *Chevy Chase, a modern, mildew-proof Rambler that has won great popularity.*

PLATE 39

In arrangements of roses for the house, as well as for shows, the most pleasing effects are attained when flowers of various stages of development are used—as in the vase of Vogue here shown. BELOW: *The thimble-size Miniature Roses, now available in many colors, are becoming more and more popular both indoors and in gardens.*

PLATE 40

The Climbing Polyanthas, with dense clusters of small flowers and bright, lacy foliage, are effective and long-lasting indoors as well as out. This is Climbing Nassau. BELOW: One of the several new repeat-blooming Sub-zero Pillar Roses, Number 84, which, like the Hybrid Teas, flower freely the first season. Some varieties of these are self-supporting; others tend to trail.

PLATE 43

Enjoy your roses indoors as well as out! No need to make a flower-show type of arrangement; just keep a few simple bowl-shaped containers handy, and when cutting, take some buds along with open flowers. ABOVE: *Mme. Henri Bonnet in a glass vase.* BELOW: *Pinocchio in a blue container.*

PLATE 44

Rose Scent. You can make your own rose scent by placing the petals of extremely fragrant roses in a bottle of wine or spirits. Cork it tightly and when you open it after three months you will find that you have a very delightful rose tincture which is just the thing for moistening your wet potpourris.

Fixatives. However you make your potpourris, fixative must be used to absorb the fragrant oils and preserve the fragrance. Orris-root is the one most commonly used, but others are powdered benzoin or storax, and calamus powder. A quarter pound of any one of these is enough for a one-quart rose jar.

For a more lasting but more expensive wet potpourri, oil of roses, jasmine, bergamot, lavender, violet, etc. may be added to the dried rose petals. In short, there is almost no fragrant oil, powder, leaf, or blossom which may not be added to advantage.

Warning. Moldy rose petals are anything but fragrant! If you use the dry method, be sure they are *totally dry*. In the wet method, use enough salt to preserve them and prevent mold.

ROSE DELICACIES

If you enjoy the flavor of roses, you may make rose jelly, rose jam, and crystallized or candied rose petals.

In these days of effective but poisonous insecticides and fungicides, however, the safest method is to use the petals and hips from a special planting of very fragrant Old Roses (see page 310) which are disease-resistant enough to produce bloom and fruit without spraying.

Rose Petal Jam

    2 lbs. well-washed fragrant rose petals
    4 lbs. sugar
    3 lemons (juice)
    1 quart water

Crush the petals in half the sugar, using a wooden masher or pestle. Add one quart of water. Place in a preserving kettle with the rest of the sugar and boil down rapidly until your jelly thermometer reaches 221°. Remove from heat, add the juice of three lemons, and pour into sterilized jars. Cover with paraffine.

Rose Petal Jelly

    4 quarts well-washed, fragrant rose petals
    2 quarts water
  Boil down to 1 quart, in covered pot. Strain.
    3 cups above infusion
    7 cups sugar
    1 bottle Certo
    4 tablespoons lemon juice

Place infusion in preserving kettle. Add water and sugar and bring quickly to a boil. Add lemon juice and Certo and bring to a full, rolling boil for one minute, stirring constantly. Remove from heat, add a few drops of red coloring, remove scum, and pour into sterilized glasses. Cover with paraffine.

Rose Hip Jam

    1 quart Rugosa Rose hips, touched by frost
    1 quart water
    1 pound sugar for each pound strained pulp

Wash hips and remove calyxes. Place in kettle with water and boil until tender, mashing with a wooden spoon. Force pulp through food mill to remove seeds. Boil sugar and pulp together until jelly thermometer registers 221°. Place in sterilized jars and cover with paraffine. Rose hip jam tastes of roses and is full of vitamins!

Crystallized Rose Petals

    red rose petals
    white of egg
    granulated sugar

Select perfect petals of fresh, fragrant red roses. Remove the white base of each petal. Dip the petals into or paint them on both sides with white of egg. Spread dipped petals out on trays covered with waxed paper and sprinkle freely with sugar. Turn petals and add sugar if necessary. Dry thoroughly in warm, dry place. Store in tight tin boxes when completely dry.

Rose Finder

What can I offer besides the hand of friendship and the praise of an old Rosarian to these brave brethren of the Rose? I subjoin for them a list of those varieties which are, in my opinion, most likely to repay their anxious care. Let them be planted in the best place, and in the best soil available, avoiding drip and roots. . . .

ROSES FOR ARBORS AND TRELLISES
(All are everblooming or remontant)

Aloha: Rose-pink buds, silvery pink flowers to 5 inches.
Blaze (New Strain): Clear red; 8 feet.
Dr. J. H. Nicolas: Large double, pink; constant bloom; 10 feet.
Dream Girl: Salmon-pink; 8 feet.
Gladiator: Rose-red, 5-inch blooms; 8 to 10 feet.
Gold Rush: Deep, tawny gold blooms on new wood; very hardy.
Golden Showers: Recent A.R.S. winner; large yellow blooms produced continuously; 6 to 8 feet.
High Noon: Unfading yellow blooms on 8- to 10-foot plant; somewhat tender North.
THE DAWN FAMILY. (Descendants of New Dawn, the remontant form of Dr. Van Fleet):
    Coral Dawn: Coral-pink, 4½-inch blooms; 4 to 8 feet.
    Morning Dawn: Silvery-pink to rose-salmon 5-inch blooms; 6 to 8 feet.
    New Dawn: Appleblossom pink, delightfully fragrant; to 15 feet.
    White Dawn: Snow white gardenia-like blooms all summer.
Royal Gold: Golden-yellow blooms on 6- to 8-foot thornless plants.
CLIMBING FLORIBUNDAS:
    Climbing Goldilocks: Yellow; floriferous; 10 feet.
    Climbing Pinocchio: Salmon-pink, floriferous; 10 feet.
    Climbing Summer Snow: Pure white; floriferous; 10 feet.

ROSES FOR ARRANGEMENTS (See pages 297–99.)

ROSES FOR BEDDING

Roses for bedding need not necessarily be low-growing but should be more or less uniform in height, producing masses of flower clusters to give a solid mass effect. Continuous bloom is also a requirement if the beds are to be colorful throughout the season. Floribundas and Grandifloras best fill this niche, but there are also others suitable for this purpose.

Amy Vanderbilt: Very double, lavender-rose; 2 to 2½ feet.
Anne Vanderbilt: Coppery-orange semi-double; 3 feet.
Baby Blaze: Bush form of Blaze. Medium red; 2 to 3 feet.
Betsy McCall: Pink, overlaid with gold; 2 to 3 feet.
Betty Prior: Pink, single, fragrant; 3 to 4 feet.
Circus: Multicolor; 2 to 2½ feet.
Dagmar Späth: White; 1½ to 2 feet.
Donald Prior: Red, single, fragrant; 3 to 4 feet.
Fashion: Salmon; 2½ feet.
Floradora: Brick red; 3 feet.
Frolic: Light pink, open double; very profuse; 2½ feet.
Fusilier: Scarlet-orange; 3 feet.
Glacier: Pure white; 2 to 2½ feet.
Gold Cup: Yellow, fragrant; glossy foliage; 2½ to 3 feet.
Gruss an Aachen: Yellow buds, blush flowers; 3 feet.
Irene of Denmark: White; 2 to 3 feet.
Jiminy Cricket: Coral-orange to pink-coral; 3 to 4 feet.
Independence: Irridescent orange-scarlet; 2½ to 3 feet.
Lavender Pinocchio: Lavender; 2 to 2½ feet.
Lilibet: Pink tones; 2 to 3 feet.
New World: Dark red, fragrant; 2½ feet.
Pink Bountiful: Soft silver pink, double, open flowers; 2 feet.
Poulsen's Bedder: Pink; 3 feet.
Rochester: Cream to apricot; 2½ feet.
Siren: Bright red; 2 feet.
Spartan: Orange-red; 3 feet.
Sumatra: Orange-red; 2½ to 3 feet.
Summer Snow: White, very profuse; 2 to 3 feet.
Queen Elizabeth: Pink flowers to 4 inches; 3 feet.
Vogue: Rose-red, coral tints; 3 feet.
Wildfire: Scarlet semi-double; 2 to 3 feet.
White Bouquet: White to cream; 2½ to 3 feet.
World's Fair: Dark red, single, fragrant; 2 to 3 feet.

ROSES FOR CONSTANT BLOOM

FLORIBUNDAS: See pages 275–78.

GRANDIFLORAS: See page 279.

HYBRID PERPETUAL:

   Mrs. John Laing, clear pink.

HYBRID TEAS: Produce blooms each month but most of them are not in constant bloom. See pages 270–74.

SHRUB:

   Autumn Bouquet: Pink.

   Belinda: Soft pink, fragrant, in large clusters; 6 to 8 feet.

   F. J. Grootendorst: Red.

   Hon. Lady Lindsay: Pink.

   Mabelle Stearns: Pink.

   Pink Grootendorst: Pink.

   Prosperity: White rosette-like blooms in large clusters.

   Will Scarlet: Red.

SUB-ZERO HYBRID TEAS: See pages 272–73.

LARGE-FLOWERED CLIMBERS:

   Climbing Floribundas: See page 284.

   Coral Dawn: Coral-pink.

   Dream Girl: Salmon-pink.

   Dr. J. H. Nicolas: Pink.

   Golden Showers: Yellow.

   High Noon: Yellow (tender).

   Inspiration: Pink.

   Mermaid: Single yellow (tender).

   Parade: Rose-red.

   Pink Cloud: Pink.

   Royal Gold: Yellow.

   Temptation: Red.

ROSES FOR CORSAGES

Roses most in demand for corsage material are of moderate size, glowing and long-lasting color, fine form, preferably with long, pointed buds. If they have the added virtue of fragrance, so much the better. Unfortunately, however, many of the Floribundas lack fragrance, and it is in this group that we find most of our corsage material.

There are marked exceptions to this rule, like new Gold Cup

with its delightful Tea fragrance; Vogue, which has a carnation scent; Ma Perkins, and others.

A single large cluster of one of the better Floribundas will yield flowers and buds for several small corsages. If the variety lacks fragrance, a spray of rosemary, scented-leaf geranium, lemon-verbena, or mignonette more than compensates, in addition to adding variety to the corsage.

FLORIBUNDAS AND POLYANTHAS

Betsy McCall: Coral, 3-inch blooms.

Carol Ann: Large clusters of small, ranunculus-like orange blooms.

Cécile Brunner (Sweetheart): Small, bright pink, long pointed buds and well-formed, fragrant flowers.

Crimson Rosette: Clusters of small, camellia-like, crimson blooms.

Garnette: Clusters of small, long-lasting dark red, perfectly formed roses.

Gold Cup: Unfading yellow, small Hybrid Tea-like buds and blooms; fragrant; glossy foliage.

Golden Fleece: Tawny gold, long-lasting, large blooms.

Lilibet: Beautiful sprays of small, well-formed, silvery pink flowers.

Marionette: Medium-sized, cream-colored blooms, in clusters; a sport of Pinocchio.

Margo Koster: A salmon-pink and orange, similar to Carol Ann.

Pink Rosette: Pink form of Crimson Rosette.

Pinocchio: Exquisite salmon-pink in clusters; ideal for corsages.

Rochester: Medium-sized yellow, flushed carmine, in clusters.

Rosenelfe: Beautiful medium-sized pink Hybrid Tea-like blooms in clusters.

Siren: Flaming red, double blooms all season.

Spartan: Orange-red, large, in clusters.

MINIATURE

Gold Star.

SHRUB

The Fairy.

SINGLE HYBRID TEAS

(Use in quite close bud only.)

ROSES, EARLY AND LATE

FOR VERY EARLY BLOOM

Enchantment (HT): Rose-apricot, suffused with gold to 6 inches in diameter.

Mme. Grégoire Staechelin (CHP): Long, pointed bud and very large, fragrant, soft pink blooms marked with red in reverse; 14 feet.

Orange Everglow (LC): Beautifully formed orange buds and very fragrant, orange-gold blooms on long stems; 12 feet.

ROSA HUGONIS: Single, solitary, light yellow flowers on drooping, slender branches; 6 feet.

ROSA RUGOSA AND HYBRIDS (See pages 264–65.)

FOR VERY LATE BLOOM

Betty Prior (Fl): Large, single pink.

Blaze (LC): Bright scarlet, cupped double in clusters; 8 to 10 feet.

Crimson Glory (HT): Crimson; fragrant.

Dickson's Red (HT): Scarlet-crimson; fragrant.

Frau Karl Druschki (HP): Large, pure white; to 8 feet.

Gruss an Teplitz (HT): Rather small, double, open velvety scarlet; very fragrant; 6 feet.

Kirsten Poulsen (HPol): Single, scarlet flowers in clusters.

Mary Margaret McBride (HT): Pink.

Mojave (HT): Deep orange-copper.

Mrs. E. P. Thom (HT): Yellow.

Permanent Wave (Fl): Cerise-red, ruffled, semi-double flowers in clusters.

Pinocchio (Fl): Salmon-pink, deeper edges.

Red Ripples (Fl): Small, semi-double, open, dark red.

Rosenelfe (Fl): Beautifully formed, soft pink blooms in clusters.

Soeur Thérèse (HT): Red and gold.

ROSES FOR EDGING

Each year now new dwarf rose varieties are being introduced which, together with the older, small-flowered Polyanthas, give the gardener quite a wide range of choice if he wishes to edge his rose beds or borders or other plantings with low-growing roses.

Baby Chateau (HPol): Dark red in large clusters; fragrant; continuous bloom.

Cameo (Pol): Salmon to shell-pink; continuous bloom.

Carol Ann (Pol): Ranunculus-flowered, orange; 18 inches.

Charlie McCarthy (Pol): Profuse white bloom, globular plants, continuous bloom.

Chatter (Fl): 3-inch crimson, long-lasting bloom; 18 inches; continuous bloom.

China Doll (Pol): Bright pink, yellow base; 18 inches; continuous bloom; fragrant.

Crimson Rosette (Pol): Crimson, camellia-shaped bloom; 18 inches.

Dagmar Späth (Fl): Large, semi-double, cupped white, flushed pink at edges, in large clusters; 2 feet; fragrant.

Garnette (Fl): Ruby-red blooms in large clusters; 18 inches.

Lafayette (HPol): Semi-double, crimson, in large clusters; 18 inches; fragrant.

Margo Koster (Pol): Orange, flushed pink; 18 inches.

Orange Triumph (Pol): Scarlet-orange in large clusters; 18 inches.

Pigmy Gold (DFl): 1-inch, golden yellow double flowers; 12 inches.

Pigmy Red (DFl): Dark red, open double flowers; 12 inches; continuous bloom.

Pinkie (Pol): Porcelain-pink, 2-inch flowers; 18 inches; continuous bloom; fragrant.

Pink Rosette (Pol): Camellia-shaped soft pink blooms; 18 inches.

Siren (Fl): Large, flaming red double flowers; 2 feet; continuous bloom.

Starlet (Fl): Buttercup yellow, 2½-inch very double flowers on low, rounded bush; continuous bloom.

Valentine (Fl): Brilliant red double blooms in large clusters; 18 inches; continuous bloom.

ROSES FOR EXHIBITION

The rose lover whose ambition is to win blue ribbons in Rose Shows or Garden Shows naturally selects varieties of proven excellence. Characteristics which win points are long straight stems, handsome, healthy foliage, pointed buds, and high-centered, perfect blooms of good color.

Very often, therefore, the most desirable garden roses (those which produce masses of bloom throughout the growing season) are not always the best varieties to select for competition. This is particularly true of Hybrid Teas, but it also applies to other classes. Some Hybrid Teas which have been consistent prize winners are given below.

HYBRID TEAS

Aztec: Orange-scarlet to 6 inches.

Blanche Mallerin: White, fragrant.

Charlotte Armstrong: Carmine-red to 5 inches.

Confidence: Peach-pink, to 6 inches.

Chrysler Imperial: Rich red, fragrant, to 6 inches. Strong stems.

Comtesse Vandal: Copper, bronze, and pink.

Contentment: Pink suffused with yellow, fragrant, to 6 inches.

Crimson Glory: Crimson.

Enchantment: Peach-pink, to 6 inches. Early.

Gail Borden: Pink to apricot, 5½ to 6 inches; glossy foliage.

Golden Masterpiece: The largest yellow rose, 6½ to 7½ inches; fragrant; fine foliage.

Linda Porter: Unfading pink of good texture and fine form; fragrant.

Helen Traubel: Lovely apricot-pink; fragrant.

Isobel Harkness: Delicately colored yellow, 5 inches.

Katherine T. Marshall: Glowing pink, on long, strong stems; fragrant.

Konrad Adenauer: Fine red; strong stems.

Mojave: Rich, coppery orange, on stout stems.

Peace: Huge, fine yellow, buds and opening flowers edged pink; strong foliage and stout stems.

Peaceful: A coral-rose descendant of Peace.

Suzon Lotthé: Pearly, shell pink, very double, fragrant.

Tiffany: Deep pink with golden base.

White Knight: New, free-blooming white.

ROSES FOR FENCES

Almost any climbing roses, except the few Pillars which insist on growing erect, are suitable for training on fences. Most Climbers produce more bloom when the canes are trained horizontally so that the blooming stems are encouraged to shoot upward. (See page 157.) Many of the newer Large-flowered Climbers give a satisfactory succession of monthly bloom; the older Rambler types produce one great burst of color only.

LARGE-FLOWERED CLIMBERS

New Blaze: A strain which gives almost continuous bloom.

Dream Girl: Salmon-pink; to 8 feet.

Gladiator: Rose-red; 8 to 10 feet.

Cl. Goldilocks: Yellow; 6 to 10 feet.

Inspiration: Pink; 8 feet.

Morning Dawn: Silver-pink; 6 to 8 feet.

Parade: Rose-red; 8 to 10 feet.

Pink Cloud: Deep pink; 6 to 8 feet.

Prosperity: White; constant bloom.

Cl. Summer Snow: White; free blooming.

Temptation: Rose-red; 8 feet.

RAMBLERS

American Pillar: Single, carmine-pink with white center; 20 feet.

Chevy Chase: Rose-red; 15 feet.

Dorothy Perkins: Pink double; showy; subject to mildew.

OTHERS

Frau Karl Druschki: Magnificent white Hybrid Perpetual; can be trained to rail fence.

ROSA HUGONIS: Single, pale yellow species; very early; can be trained to fence.

ROSES FOR FRAGRANCE

Many of the Old Roses have such delightful fragrance that only by visiting a collection of these in full bloom does one realize how much many of the large, showy modern varieties have lost of this charming characteristic. Breeders and hybridizers are now conscious of this lack and are working to correct it.

SPECIES AND SPECIES HYBRIDS

ROSA CENTIFOLIA—Cabbage or Provence Rose
  Königin von Dänemark: Flesh pink.
  Red Provence: Rose-pink, deeper center.
  Vierge de Cléry: White.
ROSA CENTIFOLIA MUSCOSA—Moss Rose
  La Neige: Pure white.
  Mme. Louis Lévêque: Bright salmon-pink.
ROSA CHINENSIS—China Rose
  Maréchal Niel: Yellow double; tender.
ROSA DAMASCENA—Damask Rose
  Maiden's Blush: Rosy white to salmon pink, semi-double.
  Marie Louise: Deep pink double.
  Mme. Hardy: White.
  Professeur Emile Perrot: Delicate pink.
ROSA EGLANTERIA—Sweetbriar
  Green Mantle: Fragrant foliage.
ROSA GALLICA CONDITORUM—Large, single tawny pink; very hardy.
ROSA MOSCHATA—(Musk) and hybrids.
ROSA RUGOSA—and hybrids.
ROSA SPINOSSISSIMA—Scotch Rose.

HYBRID TEAS

Aida: Red.
Anne Vanderbilt: Red, gold.
Arlene Francis: Yellow.
Charles Mallerin: Dark red.
Charlotte Armstrong: Rose-red.

Chrysler Imperial: Dark red.
Confidence: Golden pink.
Crimson Glory: Dark red.
Dainty Bess: Single; buff-pink.
Etoile de Hollande: Red.

Fort Vancouver: Medium pink.
Golden Dawn: Yellow.
Good News: Pink, gold.
Hector Deane: Red, gold.
Kaiserin Auguste Viktoria: White.
Konrad Adenauer: Red.
La France: Pink.
Marcia Stanhope: White.
McGredy's Sunset: Orange to scarlet.
Mirandy: Dark red.
Mme. Butterfly: Yellow.
Mme. Cochet-Cochet: Copper to orange.
Mrs. Chas. Bell: Light Pink.
Neige Parfum: White.
Nocturne: Dark red.
Numa Fay: Coral-pink.
Pink Princess: Light pink.

Pennsylvanian: Orange-apricot.
President Herbert Hoover: Maroon and orange.
Radiance: Pink.
Red Radiance: Light red.
Rhapsody: Orange blend.
Rose of Freedom: Rose-red.
Rubaiyat: Rose-red.
Sutter's Gold: Gold-touched orange-red.
Suzon Lotthé: Pearly shell-pink.
Sweet Sixteen: Pink blend.
Tallyho: Rose-red.
Tawny Gold: Old gold.
Tiffany: Rose-pink.
The Doctor: Pink.
Yours Truly: Medium pink.

FLORIBUNDAS

Gold Cup: Yellow.
Chatter: Red.
Fashion: Salmon.
Geranium Red.
Golden Fleece: Yellow.
Holiday: Orange-red.
Jiminy Cricket: Orange-salmon.
Lilibet: Pink.

Ma Perkins: Coral-pink.
Poulsen's Yellow.
Red Sweetheart.
Rosenelfe: Pink.
Spartan: Orange red.
World's Fair: Dark red.
Vogue: Rose-pink.

POLYANTHAS

Charlie McCarthy.
Denise.
Fair Marjorie.
Golden Perfection.

Margy.
Paulette.
Titania.

CLIMBERS

Baltimore Belle: Blush to white.
Blossomtime: Light pink.
Cl. American Beauty: Rose-red.
Cl. Crimson Glory: Crimson.
Cl. Etoile de Hollande: Medium red.
Cl. Heart's Desire: Dark red.
Cl. Sutter's Gold: Yellow, tipped red.
Countess of Stradbroke: Dark red.

Dream Girl: Salmon-pink.
Inspiration: Pink.
Morning Dawn: Silvery pink flushed salmon.
New Dawn: Blush pink.
Orange Everglow: Orange-gold.
Paul's Lemon Pillar: Yellow.

ROSES FOR HEDGES

For a rose hedge, strong, vigorous growing plants are needed which will form a barrier and give privacy, which can be kept at the desired height, and which will provide the maximum in colorful bloom. Varieties of different heights are given in the list below.

FLORIBUNDAS

Baby Blaze: Red, 3 feet.

Belinda (Hybrid Musk): Continuous phlox-like pink clusters of bloom; 4 to 6 feet.

Betty Prior: Pink single; 4 feet.

Fashion: Salmon; 3 feet.

Frensham: Brilliant, rich red; 4 to 5 feet.

Frolic: Pink, very floriferous; 2½ feet.

Gay Heart: Rose-pink; 4 feet.

Grootendorst, F. J.: Red; 4 feet.

Lipstick: Cerise, semi-double; continuous bloom; 5 to 6 feet.

Mandarin: Dark red; 4 feet.

Masquerade: Multicolor; 3 feet.

Pink Grootendorst: Pink; 4 feet.

Summer Snow: White; very floriferous; 2 feet.

SHRUBS AND SPECIES

ROSA HUGONIS: Yellow single; early; 6 feet.

ROSA RUGOSA: Purplish red; 4 feet; dense.

ROSA RUGOSA *alba*: White; 4 feet; dense.

ROSA RUGOSA hybrids: 4 feet; dense.

ROSA SPINOSISSIMA: White, very fragrant; 3 feet.

Sara Van Fleet: Bright rose-pink; remontant; 7 to 8 feet.

Sir Thomas Lipton: White; continuous; 6 to 8 feet.

The Fairy: Big clusters of small, clear pink double blooms all summer long on 3 foot, bushy plants.

FOR PERGOLAS

For training on pergolas, the more robust climbers should be selected. Here the 6- to 8-foot Pillars are inadequate. There is a chance, instead, to use the really tall-growing varieties.

Climbing Break o' Day: Peach-pink; hardy; 12 feet.

Climbing Crimson Glory: Climbing form of famous Hybrid Tea. Unusually hardy for a Cl.H.T.; 12 feet.

Climbing Peace: Yellow; 12 to 15 feet.
(Other Climbing Hybrid Teas are suitable for pergolas in mild climates.)
Gladiator: Rose-red, 5-inch blooms; 10 feet.
New Dawn: Blush-pink; 15 feet.
Spectacular: Orange-red; 10 feet.
Thor: Dark red, 4-inch blooms; 15 feet.
White Dawn: Pure white; 15 feet.

FOR SEVERE CLIMATES

American Pillar: Red, white center; 20 feet.
Baltimore Belle: Blush pink.
Climbing American Beauty: Rose-pink.
Queen of the Prairies: Double, globular, fragrant bright pink; 20 feet.
Seven Sisters: Pale rose to crimson.

ROSES IN POTS FOR PATIO AND TERRACE

FLORIBUNDAS

Garnette: Dark red.
Pinocchio: Salmon-pink.
Siren: Red.
Spartan: Orange-red.
Summer Snow: White.
Vogue: Coral-rose.

POLYANTHAS

All. See page 280.

ROSES FOR SCREENS

For screens, dense growth is needed from 6 to 12 feet in height. Climbers or vigorous Shrub Roses can be used for this purpose.

Blaze: Red climber; 8 to 10 feet.
City of York: White, double; 10 feet; climber.
Frau Karl Druschki: Hybrid Perpetual, white; to 8 feet.
Frensham: Vigorous red Floribunda of dense growth; 6 to 8 feet.
New Dawn: Blush pink, fragrant climber; to 15 feet.
Oratam: Hybrid Damask with copper blooms; 8 to 10 feet.
Sarah Van Fleet: Pink; 8 feet.
Silver Moon: Vigorous climber; white; 12 feet.
Sir Thomas Lipton: White; 8 feet.
Vanguard: Large orange-salmon; 8 feet.

ROSES FOR SLOPES AND BANKS

There are a few varieties of climbing roses which creep as readily as they climb—some more readily. These are ideal for use on slopes and banks. In addition to the old Ramblers, the following are recommended:

Carpet of Gold: Yellow.
Clytemnestra: Coppery buds, buff-pink flowers.
Coral Creeper: Red buds; apricot blooms.
Creeping Everbloom: A red, double, fragrant, remontant creeper.
Little Compton Creeper: Single, deep rose pink.
Max Graf: Pink single; hardy.
Magic Carpet: Semi-double yellow touched with orange, scarlet, and rose.
Mermaid: Exquisite large, single, lemon yellow flowers on very strong, sturdy plant; everblooming; somewhat tender.
R. RUGOSA REPENS ALBA: Large white, single flowers in clusters.
R. WICHURAIANA: Single, white, fragrant 1½ to 2-inch; blooms all summer; very hardy.

ROSES FOR UNDER GLASS

Cécile Brunner: Long, pointed bud; bright pink flowers in clusters; dwarf; fragrant.
Garnette: Small, double dark red fragrant flowers; bushy growth.
Gold Cup: Bright, unfading yellow pointed buds and well-formed, very fragrant blooms; holly-like foliage; 2 feet.
Lilibet: Tones of pink; small, well-formed buds and flowers; fragrant; 2 feet.
Miniatures: All; see page 289.
Pink Rosette: Soft pink, gardenia-like blooms; 18 inches.
Pinocchio: Salmon-pink and gold; well-formed blooms and buds in large clusters.
Red Sweetheart: Red form of Cécile Brunner.
Red Rosette: Dark red, similar to Pink Rosette.
Siren: Scarlet.
Spartan: Orange-red.
Vogue: Coral-rose.

TEA ROSES FOR THE SOUTH

Duchesse de Brabant (*Guava Rose* in Key West): Large, double, well-formed soft rose-pink to bright rose, fragrant flowers; blooms freely.

Etoile de Lyon: Fragrant, double, golden yellow. Stems weak; low growing.

Lady Hillingdon: Long, pointed, fragrant, deep apricot yellow buds and semi-double flowers; bronzy foliage; unusually hardy for a Tea.

Lady Roberts: Reddish apricot double with coppery red base; edges orange; fragrant.

Maman Cochet: Very double, high-centered, pale pink, fragrant flower with pale yellow base and deeper center; vigorous; persistent.

Minnie Francis: Deep pink, open flowers; popular in Florida.

Mrs. Campbell Hall: Very large creamy buff edged with carmine; center cerise-coral-fawn; very fragrant; vigorous.

Mrs. Dudley Cross: Chamois-yellow, touched red in autumn; light fragrance.

Pillar of Gold (E. Veyrat Hermanos): Double apricot-yellow and soft pink; very fragrant; climber.

Rosette Delizy: Large, well-formed yellow, apricot reverse; outer petals carmine.

ROSES FOR ALKALINE SOIL—SOUTHWEST

(Reduce *p*H in rose beds, page 12.)

HYBRID TEAS

Dainty Bess	*Golden Scepter*	*Santa Anita*
Best Regards	*Grande Duchess Charlotte*	*Show Girl*
Bravo	*Helen Traubel*	*Sutter's Gold*
Butterscotch	*Lowell Thomas*	*Sweet Sixteen*
Capistrano	*McGredy's Sunset*	*Taffeta*
Condesa de Sástago	*Mme. Chiang Kai-shek*	*Talisman*
Crimson Glory	*Mrs. E. P. Thom*	*Tawny Gold*
Etoile de Hollande	*Mrs. Sam McGredy*	*Tallyho*
First Love	*Nocturne*	*The Chief*
Good News	*Peace*	*The Doctor*
Golden Harvest	*Rubaiyat*	*White Swan*
Golden Masterpiece		

FLORIBUNDAS AND GRANDIFLORAS

All varieties—see pages 275–79.

HYBRID PERPETUALS

American Beauty	*General Jacqueminot*
Frau Karl Druschki	*Ulrich Brunner*

CLIMBERS

Blaze: 8 feet.

Carpet of Gold: 8 feet.

Climbing Hybrid Teas: Select climbing forms of Hybrid Teas listed above.

Dream Girl: 8 feet.

Mermaid: To 12 feet; trailing or climbing.

Max Graf: Trailing.

Paul's Scarlet: 10 feet.

VERY TOUGH SHRUB ROSES

Harison's Yellow

Persian Yellow

ROSA SPINOSISSIMA and hybrids

ROSA WICHURAIANA and hybrids

HARDY ROSES FOR HIGH ALTITUDES (4,000 to 7,000 feet)
WEST AND SOUTHWEST

HYBRID TEAS

  Condesa de Sástago

  Charlotte Armstrong

  Crimson Glory

  Dainty Bess (single)

  Eclipse

  Etoile de Hollande

  Golden Dawn

  Good News

  Horace McFarland

  Mary Margaret McBride

  Mme. Jules Bouché

  Mrs. Sam McGredy

  Nocturne

  Peace

  Poinsettia

  Tallyho

HYBRID PERPETUALS

  American Beauty

  Frau Karl Druschki

  General Jacqueminot

  Mrs. John Laing

  Paul Neyron

FLORIBUNDAS

  Betty Prior

  Donald Prior

  Else Poulsen

  Goldilocks

  Ideal

  Pinocchio

  Rosenelfe

  World's Fair

SHRUBS

  Harison's Yellow

  Harison's Hardy

ROSA RUGOSA AND HYBRIDS

  (see pages 264–65)

Other hardy Shrubs (pages 267–68)

  The Fairy

CLIMBERS

  American Pillar

  Brownell Climbers

  Coralie

  Doubloons

  Dr. Huey

  Dr. J. H. Nicolas

  Elegance

  Inspiration

  Mary Wallace

  Mrs. Whitman Cross

  New Dawn

  Nubian

  Silver Moon

  Thor

ROSES FOR THE SEASHORE

HYBRID TEAS
Brownell's Sub-zero Hybrid Teas.
Others can be grown with special
care.

FLORIBUNDAS AND GRANDIFLORAS
All (see pages 275–79) with special
care.

CLIMBERS
Brownell's Climbers and Creepers.
Ramblers (all varieties). See pages
287–88.
Max Graf.

Mermaid (needs winter protection
North).
Large-flowered   Climbers,   with
special care.

SHRUB ROSES
Hon. Lady Lindsay.
Lady Penzance.
Mabelle Stearns.
The Fairy.
ROSA RUGOSA and hybrids. See pages
264–65.

HARDY ROSES* FOR ZONES 3 and 4
MIDWEST AND GREAT PLAINS

(Areas of high light intensity, rapid and wide fluctuations in temperature, low humidity, deficient rainfall, winter cold, and hot, drying summer winds.)

HYBRID ALBA
Mme. Plantier: Large, double fragrant, cream-white blooms in clusters on long stems; small foliage; plant vigorous, spreading, hardy, persistent.

HYBRID BLANDA
Betty Bland: 3-inch, double blooms of rose-pink; gray-green foliage; disease-resistant; plant erect, vigorous; winter color of canes dark red; 5 feet.
Little Betty: Dwarf form of above; 3½ feet.
Lillian Gibson: 3-inch, double pink, fragrant blooms; pillar to 5 feet.
Zitkala: Velvety red; almost thornless, with red canes.

ROSA CINNAMOMEA PLENA: 2 to 2½-inch double, rose-pink, blooms very early in spring; foliage dark, hairy beneath; plant slender; 6 feet.
ROSA DAMASCENA TRIGINTIPETALA: 4-inch, double, bright rose-pink blooms profusely borne; very fragrant; 5 feet.

HYBRID FOETIDA
Harison's Hardy: Like *Harison's Yellow,* but well-formed plant; 5 feet.
Harison's Yellow: Small, semi-double, open, fragrant, bright yellow blooms covering plant in June; foliage small, rich green; plant vigorous, enduring; 6 feet.

*Need no winter protection.

Persian Yellow: Small, semi-double, bright yellow blossoms along canes; foliage small; plant vigorous, shrub-like.

ROSA GALLICA GRANDIFLORA (Alika): 4-inch, semi-double, fragrant bright red, with prominent stamens; profuse June bloom; foliage leathery; 4 feet.

ROSA HUGONIS: 2½-inch, light yellow, single flowers on slender pedicels; very early; arching canes.

ROSA RUGOSA and hybrids. See pages 264 and 319.

HYBRID SETIGERA

Prairie Youth: Large, double, rose-pink blooms, opening flat; sparingly remontant.

Queen of the Prairies: Large, double, globular, fragrant, bright pink, in clusters; climber.

HYBRID SPINOSSISSIMA ALTAICA: Large, white blooms; 3 to 4 feet.

Stanwell Perpetual: Pale pink to white, double, 4-inch flowers borne freely in June; remontant; blue-green, persistant foliage; low, arching, mound-like habit.

Frühlingsanfang: 4-inch, single, pale yellow blooms in clusters; vigorous, bushy; 8 feet.

Frühlingsgold: As above, but semi-double, fragrant.

Frühlingsmorgen: As above, but ivory-white and red.

Frühlingszauber: As above, but with 5-inch, single or semi-double, rose-red blooms with white centers.

CLIMBERS AND TRAILERS
HARDY WHEN GROWN ON THE GROUND

American Pillar: Carmine-pink, white eye.

Baltimore Belle: Blush-white.

Climbing American Beauty: Large, double rose-pink on long stems.

Lady Duncan: Single, 3-inch rich pink with prominent stamens; glossy foliage; 6 feet.

Max Graf: 3-inch, pink, single blooms in June; glossy foliage; trailer.

ROSA RUGOSA REPENS ALBA: Double rose-pink trailer.

Queen of the Prairies: See under Hybrid *setigeras.*

Seven Sisters (R. MULTIFLORA PLATYPHYLLA): Large, rose to crimson in clusters.

ROSA WICHURAIANA: White, 2-inch, single, fragrant clusters from June to September.

CREATIONS OF DR. N. E. HANSEN, BROOKINGS, S. D.
(Hardy Hybrid species, bred for Northwest prairie country.)

Amdo (1927): Pink, semi-double of sixteen petals, in clusters; blooms heavily through July and August.

Ekta (1927): Pink single, blooming June and early July; tall, upright habit.

Kitana (1927): Semi-double lavender-pink to 3 inches with intense fragrance; blooms June and July.

Koza (1927): Semi-double, rose-pink; blooms July and early August; 7 feet.

Lillian Gibson (1938): Double, fragrant rose-pink; blooms late June.

Minisa (1927): Semi-double, richly fragrant deep crimson; free bloomer.

Mrs. Mina Lindell (1927): Light pink, semi-double wild rose found in South Dakota; dwarf.

Okaga (1927): Semi-double, deep pink blooming June and early July; low-growing.

Sioux Beauty (1927): Very double (100 petals), fragrant bright rose-pink turning dark crimson at center; blooms July and early August.

Tegala (1926): Deep pink semi-double; blooms in June; low-growing.

Teton Beauty (1927): Bright crimson, cup-shaped very double, intensely fragrant; blooms through July and August.

Tetonkaha (1912): The first cross in this series; rich pink, semi-double, very fragrant; June bloom; dwarf upright habit.

Yanka (1927): Semi-double pink in clusters; blooms July and early August.

Yatkan (1927): Semi-double 2½-inch clear pink; blooms through July.

Yuhla (1927): Semi-double crimson; blooms through July and August.

Zani (1927): Semi-double dark crimson with a white streak; blooms June and early July; 8 feet.

Zika (1927): Semi-double, shell-pink, fragrant.

Zitkala (1942): Rich, velvety red, almost thornless; canes red.

BACKGROUND SHRUBS—FOR ROSE GARDENS

EVERGREEN

Abelia grandiflora

Azalea *indica alba*

Buxus (Boxwood)

Cotoneasters

Cytisus (Broom)

Euonymus japonica

Ilex (Hollies), in variety

Kalmia latifolia (Mountain Laurel)

Leucothoe Catesbaei

Mahonia (Holly-grape)

Pieris japonica and P. *floribunda* (Andromeda)

Pittosporums (tender)

Taxus, dwarfs (Yew)

DECIDUOUS

Azaleas:

  Mollis

  mucronulatum

  Schlippanbachi

Callicarpa japonica (Beauty Berry)

Caryopteris (half-hardy)

Cotinus (Smoke Tree)

Deutzias

Euonymus patens

Hydrangea Macrocephala

Kolwitzia (Beauty Bush)
Philadelphus (Mock-orange)
Spireas
Tamarix odessana

Viburnums:
carlcephalum
opulus
setigerum
tomentosum

COMPANION PLANTS FOR ROSES

EDGINGS

Ageratum
  Blue Bedder: 4 inches.
  King of Blues: 6 inches.
  Midget Blue: 3 inches
Alyssum, Sweet
  Carpet of Snow: 4 inches.
  Little Gem: 4 inches.
  Royal Carpet (purple): 4 inches.
Anagallis: 6 inches.
Browallia: 12 inches
Dianthus, dwarf.

Lobelia
  Blue Gown: 4 inches.
  Crystal Palace: 4 inches.
Mignonette, dwarf: 6 inches.
Nierembergia: 8 to 12 inches.
Pansy.
Phlox drummondi, dwarf: 6 inches.
Torenia: 9 to 12 inches.
Verbena, dwarf: 8 to 12 inches.
Vinca rosea: 12 inches.
Viola cornuta.

TALLER PLANTS

Baby's Breath (Gypsophila)
Cynoglossum
Delphinium
Dianthus
Germander (Teucrium)
Heliotrope
Lavender
Lilies

Lupine
Petunias
Rosemary
Salvia farinacea
Sideritis
Stocks
Thermopsis

Addenda

ROSE DISPLAY GARDENS

ALABAMA	Birmingham	Avondale Rose Gardens
CALIFORNIA	Berkeley	Berkeley Rose Garden
	Los Angeles	Exposition Park
	Oakland	Oakland Municipal Rose Garden
	Ontario	Charlotte Armstrong Memorial Rose Garden
	Sacramento	Municipal Rose Garden
	San Jose	San Jose Municipal Rose Garden
	San Marino	Huntington Library and Botanic Garden
	Santa Barbara	Santa Barbara Memorial Rose Garden
COLORADO	Denver	Denver Arboretum and Rose Garden
	Pueblo	Mineral Palace Park
CONNECTICUT	Hartford	Elizabeth Park
	Norwich	Norwich Memorial Rose Garden
DELAWARE	Wilmington	Jasper Crane Rose Garden
IDAHO	Boise	Municipal Rose Garden
	Caldwell	Caldwell Memorial Rose Garden
	Nampa	Nampa Lakeview Park
	North Lewiston	Lewiston Memorial Park Rose Garden
ILLINOIS	Pocatello	Rotary Rose Garden
	Chicago	Washington Park Rose Garden
	Highland Park	Highland Park Memorial Rose Garden
INDIANA	Fort Wayne	Lakeside Rose Garden
IOWA	Davenport	Municipal Rose Garden
	Des Moines	Greenwood Park Rose Garden
KANSAS	Topeka	Reinisch Rose Garden
MICHIGAN	East Lansing	Michigan State College
	Lansing	Cooley Gardens
MINNESOTA	Minneapolis	Minneapolis Municipal Rose Garden

MISSOURI	Independence	Glendale Rose Garden
	Kansas City	Rose Garden
	St. Louis	Jewel Box Rose Garden
MONTANA	Missoula	Missoula Memorial Rose Garden
NEBRASKA	Lincoln	City of Lincoln Municipal Rose Garden
NEW YORK	Bronx Park, N.Y.C.	New York Botanical Garden
	Brooklyn	Brooklyn Botanic Garden
	Buffalo	Niagara Frontier Trail Rose Garden
	Farmingdale	L.I. Agricultural and Technical Institute
	Flushing	Queens Botanical Gardens
	Ithaca	Cornell University Test Garden
	Middletown	State Hospital Rose Garden
	Newark	Jackson & Perkins Company Rose Garden
	Rochester	Municipal Rose Garden
	Syracuse	Dr. E. M. Mitts Rose Garden
NORTH CAROLINA	Charlotte	Sunnyside Rose Garden
OHIO	Barberton	J. E. White Nursery
	Bay Village	City of Bay Village Rose Garden
	Columbus	Columbus Park of Roses
	Mentor	Paul R. Bosley Nursery
	Mentor	Joseph J. Kern Rose Nursery
OKLAHOMA	Oklahoma City	Municipal Rose Garden, Will Rogers Park
	Woodward	Woodward Rose Garden
OREGON	Portland	International Rose Test Gardens
PENNSYLVANIA	Harrisburg	Breeze Hill Gardens
	Harrisburg	Municipal Rose Garden
	Hershey	Hershey Rose Gardens
	Kennett Square	Longwood Gardens
	Philadelphia	Mellon Park Rose Gardens
	Pottstown	Pottstown Municipal Rose Garden
	Reading	Municipal Rose Garden, City Park
	State College	University Park
RHODE ISLAND	Little Compton	Brownell Rose Research Gardens
SOUTH CAROLINA	Orangeburg	Edisto Gardens
TEXAS	Amarillo	Memorial Park Rose Garden
	Fort Worth	Rotary Park Botanic Gardens

	Tyler	Tyler Rose Park, Municipal Rose Garden
UTAH	Provo	Provo Memorial Rose Garden
	Tooele	Tooele City Municipal Rose Garden
VIRGINIA	Norfolk	Lafayette Park Municipal Rose Garden
WASHINGTON	Aberdeen	E. C. Miller Memorial Rose Garden
	Tacoma	Tacoma Municipal Rose Garden
WEST VIRGINIA	Huntington	Ritter Park Rose Garden
WISCONSIN	Hales Corners	Whitnall Park Botanical Gardens

AGRICULTURAL EXPERIMENT STATIONS

ALABAMA	Alabama Polytechnic Institute, Auburn, Ala.
ALASKA	University of Alaska, Palmer, Alaska.
ARIZONA	University of Arizona, Tucson, Ariz.
ARKANSAS	University of Arkansas, Fayetteville, Ark.
CALIFORNIA	University of California, Los Angeles, Cal.
COLORADO	Colorado Agricultural College, Fort Collins, Colo.
CONNECTICUT	University of Connecticut, Storrs, Conn.
DELAWARE	University of Delaware, Newark, Del.
FLORIDA	University of Florida, Gainesville, Fla.
GEORGIA	University of Georgia, Athens, Ga.
IDAHO	University of Idaho, Moscow, Idaho.
ILLINOIS	University of Illinois, Urbana, Ill.
INDIANA	Purdue University, Lafayette, Ind.
IOWA	Iowa State College of Agriculture, Ames, Iowa.
KANSAS	Kansas State College, Manhattan, Kans.
KENTUCKY	University of Kentucky, Lexington, Ky.
LOUISIANA	Louisiana State University, Baton Rouge, La.
MAINE	University of Maine, Orono, Maine
MARYLAND	University of Maryland, College Park, Md.
MASSACHUSETTS	University of Massachusetts, Amherst, Mass.
MICHIGAN	Michigan State College, East Lansing, Mich.
MINNESOTA	University of Minnesota, St. Paul, Minn.
MISSISSIPPI	Mississippi State College, State College, Miss.
MISSOURI	University of Missouri, Columbia, Mo.
MONTANA	Montana State College, Bozeman, Mont.
NEBRASKA	University of Nebraska, Lincoln, Neb.
NEVADA	University of Nevada, Reno, Nev.
NEW HAMPSHIRE	University of New Hampshire, Durham, N.H.

NEW JERSEY	Rutgers University, New Brunswick, N.J.
NEW MEXICO	New Mexico College of Agriculture, Mesilla Park, N.M.
NEW YORK	Cornell University, Ithaca, N.Y. and Geneva, N.Y.
NORTH CAROLINA	University of North Carolina, State College Station, N.C.
NORTH DAKOTA	North Dakota Agricultural College, Fargo, N.D.
OHIO	Ohio State University, Columbus, O. and Wooster, O.
OKLAHOMA	Oklahoma Agricultural College, Stillwater, Okla.
OREGON	Oregon State College, Corvallis, Ore.
PENNSYLVANIA	Pennsylvania State University, State College, Pa.
RHODE ISLAND	University of Rhode Island, Kingston, R.I.
SOUTH CAROLINA	Clemson Agricultural College, Clemson, S.C.
SOUTH DAKOTA	South Dakota State College, College Station, S.D.
TENNESSEE	University of Tennessee, Knoxville, Tenn.
TEXAS	Texas Agricultural College, College Station, Tex.
UTAH	Utah State Agricultural College, Logan, Utah.
VERMONT	University of Vermont, Burlington, Vt.
VIRGINIA	Virginia Agricultural Experimental Station, Blacksburg, Va.
WASHINGTON	State College of Washington, Pullman, Wash.
WEST VIRGINIA	West Virginia University, Morgantown, W.Va.
WISCONSIN	University of Wisconsin, Madison, Wis.
WYOMING	University of Wyoming, Laramie, Wyo.

ROSE BOOKS OF SPECIAL INTEREST

A Book About Roses, S. Reynolds Hole, 1880 (7th edition). Out of print.
American Rose Society Annuals, from 1916. American Rose Society, 4048 Roselea Place, Columbus 14, Ohio.
Anyone Can Grow Roses, Cynthia Westcott. Van Nostrand, 1954.
Climbing Roses, Helen Van Pelt Wilson. Barrows,.1955.
History of the Rose, Roy E. Shepherd. Macmillan, 1954.
Modern Roses I, II, III, IV, J. Horace McFarland Co. and American Rose Society.
Old Garden Roses, Edward A. Bunyard. Scribner, 1937.
Old Roses, E. E. Keays. Macmillan, 1936. Out of print.
Roses for Every Garden, R. C. Allen. Barrows, 1948.
Roses of the World In Color, J. Horace McFarland. Houghton Mifflin, 1936.
The Guide to Roses, Bertram Park. Van Nostrand, 1956.

TOOLS AND EQUIPMENT

A. M. Leonard & Son, Inc., Piqua, Ohio. (See photographs, pages 128, 215.)

SOME LEADING ROSE FIRMS

Armstrong Nurseries
408 No. Euclid Ave.
Ontario, Cal.
Bobbink & Atkins (Old Roses)*
East Rutherford, N.J.
The Bosley Nursery (Old Roses)*
Mentor, Ohio.
Buntings' Nurseries, Inc.
Selbyville, Del.
Carroll Gardens
Westminster, Md.
The Conard-Pyle Co.
West Grove, Pa.
Farmer Seed & Nursery Co.
Faribault, Minn.
Germain's
Terminal St.
Los Angeles 21, Cal.
Roy Hennessey (Old Roses)*
Scappoose, Ore.
Paul J. Howard's
11700 National Blvd.
Los Angeles 64, Cal.
Howard & Smith
1200 Beverly Blvd.
Montebello, Cal.
Inter-State Nurseries
Hamburg, Iowa.
Jackson & Perkins Co.
Newark, New York.
R. M. Kellogg Co.
Three Rivers, Mich.
Kelly Bros. Nurseries, Inc.
Dansville, N.Y.
Jos. J. Kern Rose Nursery
Box 33
Mentor, Ohio.

The Krider Nurseries, Inc.
Middlebury, Ind.
Maloney Bros. Nursery Co., Inc.
Dansville, N.Y.
Peterson & Dering
Scappoose, Ore.
Portland Rose Nursery
7240 S. E. Division St.
Portland 6, Ore.
Putney Nursery, Inc.
Putney, Vt.
Rosedale Nurseries, Inc.
Eastview, N.Y.
Rosemont Nurseries
P.O. Box 839
Tyler, Tex.
Somerset Rose Nursery, Inc.
New Brunswick, N.J.
Stark Bros. Nurseries
Louisiana, Mo.
Will Tillotson's Roses
Brown Valley Rd.
Watsonville, Cal.
Van Barneveld California Roses
(Old Roses)*
P.O. Box L
Puente, Cal.
Vaughan's Seed Co.
601 W. Jackson Blvd.
Chicago 6, Ill.
The Wayside Gardens Co.
(Old Roses)*
Mentor, Ohio.
Melvin E. Wyant (Old Roses)*
Route 84
Mentor, Ohio.

*NOTE: The firms above marked (Old Roses) make a specialty of these, but also carry the modern varieties.

Index

Acidity, 12, 47–48, 85
Acti-dione PM, 185
Agricultural experiment stations, 322–24
Agri-mycin, 88–92
Air circulation, 100, 111
Air drainage, 9, 29, 32–33
Air layering, 201–3, 201 *ill.*
Alkaline soil: diseases of, 180–81; roses for, 315–16
Alkalinity, 12, 85, 180–81, 184
Altitude dominance, 107, 156, 157 *ill.*, 158, 222
American Rose Annuals, viii, 91, 93, 132, 182, 222, 269
American Rose Society, vii, viii, 7, 93, 131, 268, 269, 289; information on, 241; point scoring, 7, 218; rose ratings: Floribundas, 277–78, Grandifloras, 279, Hybrid Teas, 270–72; show rules, 233–34
Ammonium sulfate, 46, 180–81, 220
Anthers, 57, 211, 214
Antibiotics, 89–92
Apical dominance, 107, 156, 158, 222
Arbors, 152, 285, 303
Arches, 151–52, 151 *ill.*
Arrangements: *plate 10, between* 44–45; *plate 29, between* 268–69; *plates 39, 40, 43, 44, between* 300–1; design suggestions, 295–97; roses for, 294–99; suitable flowers and foliage, 299; *see also* Decorations

Baby Roses; *see* Miniatures
Bagasse, 100, 123
Beauharnais, Josephine de, 4, 255

Beds, 6 *ill.,* 22, 269; borders for, 22–23, 51, 320; plan for, 21, 34–36; preparations, 45–51; roses for, 304; soil analysis, 44
Bengal Roses, 4, 255, 259–60; Ragged Robin, 63
Birch chip mulch, 102
Black spot, 13, 14, 58, 94, 99, 177–78, 177 *ill., plate 22, between* 76–77; control of, 99; transmission of, 209; *see also* Diseases
Blooms: continuous, 15, 282, 305; early, 306; late, 307; from seedlings, 216
Bluing, 34, 58; protecting from, 223–25
Boerner, Gene, viii, *plate 23, between* 76–77
Bone meal, 48, 50–51, 74, 80
Borders, 13, 22–23, 51, 269; other plants, 22–23; roses, 13, 290, 307–8, 312
Boron deficiency, 182
Bourbon Roses, 5, 258
Brownell, Dr. Walter D., 206, 209, 272, *plate 24, between* 76–77
Brownell Hardy Climbers, 7, 15; Sub-zeros, 6, 14, 272–73, *plate 12, between* 44–45, *plate 34, between* 268–69
Buccaneer Rose, 5, *plate 37, between* 300–1; *see also* Grandifloras
Buck, Griffith, 5, 132, 134
Buckwheat hull mulch, 101–2
Budding, 203–7, 204 *ill.,* aftercare, 207; understock, 203
Buds, 61, 110–12, 203, 206–7; cutting, 206; pruning, 108; shield, 206; sticks, 203–7, 205 *ill.;* timing, 225–27; *see also* Eyes
Burnett Rose, 266

326

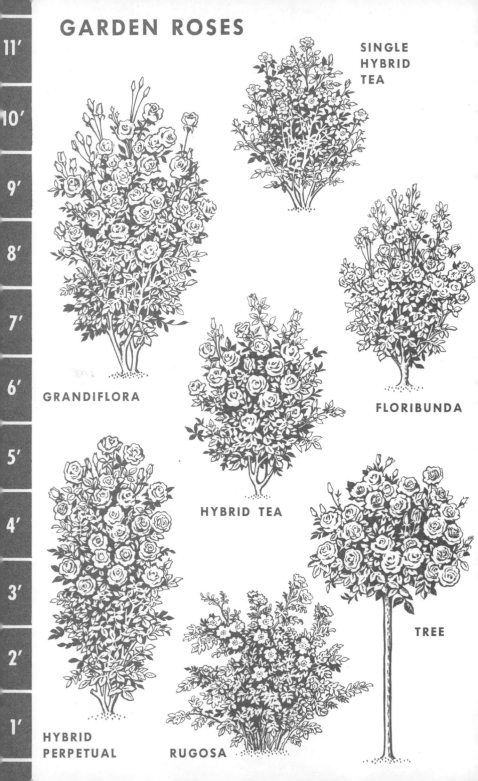

GARDEN ROSES

11'
10'
9'
8'
7'
6'
5'
4'
3'
2'
1'

SINGLE
HYBRID
TEA

GRANDIFLORA

FLORIBUNDA

HYBRID TEA

HYBRID
PERPETUAL

RUGOSA

TREE